CORRECT

ENGLISH

Brian Phythian is 1　　　　　　　　ungiey Park Boys'
School, Beckenham, ..ent, and was previously Senior
English Master of Manchester Grammar School. He is a
graduate of the Universities of Oxford and Manchester,
and a well-known writer on the teaching of English.

His books include *Teach Yourself English Grammar* and
four Concise Dictionaries: *Correct English*, *English
Slang*, *English Idioms* and *Foreign Expressions*, all published by Hodder and Stoughton. He is also the author of
Help Your Child: Spelling, editor of the Macmillan
Shakespeare *Henry V*, and author and editor of a
number of school textbooks in English language and
literature.

CORRECT ENGLISH

B. A. Phythian M.A., M.Litt.

TEACH YOURSELF BOOKS

Hodder and Stoughton

British Library Cataloguing in Publication Data

Phythian, B. A. (Brian Arthur)
 [Good English]. Correct English.–
 (Teach yourself books).
 1. English language. Usage
 I. [Good English]   II. Title
 428

ISBN 0 340 42996 8

First published 1985 as *Teach Yourself Good English*
Reissued 1988 as *Teach Yourself Correct English*
Impression number 17 16 15 14 13 12 11 10 9 8
Year   1998 1997 1996 1995 1994 1993

Typeset by Rowland Photosetting Ltd, Bury St Edmunds, Suffolk.
Printed in Great Britain for Hodder & Stoughton Educational, a division of
Hodder Headline Plc, Mill Road, Dunton Green, Sevenoaks, Kent TN13 2YA by
Cox & Wyman Ltd., Reading, Berkshire.

Contents

Preface

This book aims to increase the reader's skills in applied English, in four principal areas:

Grammar Chapters 1–4 summarise the main rules of grammar and punctuation, with particular reference to correct sentence construction and to common grammatical errors.

Vocabulary Chapters 5–10 are about the meanings of words, and deal with such issues as verbosity, tautology, cliché and fashion, as well as with correct usage and spelling.

Style Chapters 11–14 analyse how English is used in a wide variety of contexts ranging from the simple transmission of information to the sophisticated deployment of language in creative writing. The featured topics also include the language of persuasion and journalism, and the techniques of narrative, descriptive and discursive writing. There are sections on formal and informal English, colloquialism and slang, paragraphing, tone, rhythm, metaphorical language and many other aspects of prose style, illustrated by over fifty long and short extracts from published writing.

Use of English Chapters 15–19 concentrate on English as most people are likely to need it day by day – letters, reports, summaries and minutes, for example. Exam preparation in the skills of essay and précis writing is incorporated, as is a section on common mispronunciations.

The emphasis throughout is practical, and every attempt has been made to keep in mind the needs of the everyday user of English who seeks to improve his effectiveness in handling the language.

B. A. P.

1

Parts of Speech and Grammatical Terms

1.1 Some words have simple meanings. Many words have several meanings. The word *round*, for example has quite different meanings in

A round shape.
The third round of a boxing match.
Come round for a chat this evening.

The different meanings of *round* stem from the different uses to which the word may be put. In *a round shape*, for example, the word has a describing function; in *the third round* it has an identifying function, naming a feature of a boxing match.

To understand the structure of English, it is necessary to understand the various such functions which words can have. These functions are usually known as 'parts of speech'. Always remember that many words have more than one function.

1.2 A **noun** names a person or thing:

child, rabbit, street, France, wisdom, committee.

The 'thing' may be a place (*field*, *Yorkshire*), quality (*ugliness*, *tranquillity*), state (*illness*, *calm*), action (*intervention*, *work*) or concept (*democracy*, *crime*). It may be tangible or intangible.

Nouns may be **singular** (*forest*, *woman*, *quality*) or **plural** (*forests*, *women*, *qualities*). A few are the same in the singular and plural (*aircraft*, *sheep*), and some have no singular (*scissors*, *pants*).

Nouns which name a group of people or things (*crowd*, *collection*, *herd*) are called **collective nouns** and may be regarded as either singular or plural depending on whether the emphasis is on the singular entity or its plural components. See **4.1** (*e*) on page 36.

Nouns which name special or unique persons or things (*the*

President of the Republic, **Nicholas Nickleby**, *the Museum of Modern Art*) have capital letters and are known as **proper nouns**. See **3.12** on page 32.

Two nouns are sometimes found side by side, one of them identifying or explaining the other:

> *George Thompson, a farmer*, pleaded guilty.
> *The pedestrian, a schoolboy*, was unhurt.

Such nouns are said to be **in apposition**.

1.3   A **pronoun** stands in place of a noun:

she, we, it, everybody.

Pronouns are a handy device for avoiding the repetition of nouns. Instead of writing

> The tree has been felled. The tree had been damaged in a storm.

we are able to write

> The tree has been felled. *It* had been damaged in a storm.

The noun that the pronoun stands in place of is called its **antecedent**. Here, the antecedent of *It* is *tree* in the previous sentence. In

> The players thought *they* had won.
> The actress forgot *her* lines.

the antecedents of *they* and *her* are *players* and *actress* in the same sentence.

Pronouns may be singular (*I, he, she, it*) or plural (*we, they*); the pronoun *you* may be singular or plural depending on whether it refers to one person or to several.

The most important categories of pronoun are:

(*a*)   **personal** e.g. I, me, my, mine; you, your, yours; he, him, his;

(*b*)   **demonstrative** e.g. this, these, that, those (as in *This belonged to my father*);

(*c*)   **interrogative** e.g. who, whose, which, what (as in *Who did that?*);

(*d*)   **indefinite** e.g. anybody, none, no-one, either, each;

(*e*)   **relative** e.g. who, whose, which, what, whom, that.

Relative pronouns are so called because, as well as acting as pronouns, they relate or join groups of words. Instead of writing

> The tree has been felled. The tree (*or* It) had been damaged in a storm.

we may write

The tree, *which* had been damaged in a storm, has been felled.

thus joining two short sentences into one by using a relative pronoun.

Pronouns are more fully discussed in **4.2** on page 40.

1.4 An **adjective** describes a noun or pronoun:

enthusiastic, eighth, tallest, invisible.

Adjectives are normally placed before the nouns they describe (*several large white* whales) but other positions are possible:

The morning was *misty* and *cold*.
The morning, *misty* and *cold*, depressed his spirits.

If adjectives are formed from proper nouns, they too have capital letters (the *American* way of life, the *Christian* religion).

It is a particular flexibility of English that words which are used as nouns may be used as adjectives (*country* customs, *office* manager, *beauty* treatment).

1.5 A **verb** expresses an action or state of being:

walked, think, fought, arm.

Verbs may consist of several words:

They *should have known* that he *was working*.

Verbs have different forms to indicate the times when actions take place. These forms are called **tenses**:

Present tense: I *agree*
Past tense: I *agreed*, I *had agreed*
Future tense: I *shall agree*

There are many varieties of tense, such as the **continuous tense** (I *am agreeing*, I *was agreeing*). The main problems are dealt with in later chapters.

The **subject** of a verb is the word or group of words that performs the action of that verb:

He fell over. *To delay too long* would be risky.

The **object** of a verb is the word or group of words that receives the action of that verb:

I stubbed *my toe*. Do you like *the colour*? Try *jogging*.

It is not necessary for a verb to have an object:

She was sleeping. They are trying very hard.

Some pronouns have different forms depending on whether they are subject or object of a verb:

I saw *him* but *he* did not see *me*.

The words *I* and *me* refer to the same person, as do *him* and *he*, but *I* and *he* are subject-forms, and *me* and *him* are object-forms.

Some verbs, notably the verb *to be* (*am*, *are*, *is* and their past and future tenses) cannot have an object because they do not express an action which can affect or transmit to an object. They express a state:

> I *am* a neighbour of his. He *is* helpful.

The words following these verbs are called **complements**. Verbs which take complements are sometimes called **linking verbs** (or copulas) because their function is to link subject and complement, as distinct from expressing an action performed by a subject upon an object. They are more fully described at **2.5** (*d*) on page 12.

A verb that has a subject is called a **finite verb**. Sometimes, mainly when a command is expressed, the subject is omitted but clearly implied: for example, in *Keep Off the Grass*, the subject of *Keep* is 'understood' to be *you*, and the verb is finite even though no subject is stated.

A verb that does not have a subject is called a **non-finite verb**. Examples of non-finite forms of verbs were seen in

> *To delay* too long would be risky. Try *jogging*.

which are verb forms without subjects. Non-finite verbs may be used as nouns

> *Shopping* is easiest on Mondays.

or as adjectives

> The *shopping* bag is full of *squashed* tomatoes.

A verb is said to be **transitive** when it has an object, and **intransitive** when it does not. Many verbs function both transitively and intransitively, with a difference in meaning:

> The neighbours *were burning* garden rubbish. (*transitive*)
> The lamps *were burning* brightly. (*intransitive*)

Some verbs, however, are always intransitive (e.g. *rise*, *pause*, *shudder*) and others always transitive.

A verb is **active** when the subject performs the action

> I misled you.

and **passive** when the subject suffers it

> I was misled by you.

The form of some verbs is affected by whether the subject is singular or plural:

> The roof *leaks*. The pipes *leak*.

This **agreement** of subject and verb is an important feature of English. See **4.1** on page 35.

1.6 An **adverb** describes a verb, adjective or other adverb:

He called *loudly*. There was a *very* faint reply. He called *more* loudly.

When an adverb describes a verb, it usually indicates how, when, where or why the action of the verb takes place.

Most adverbs are formed by adding *-ly* to adjectives (*casual*, *casually*), though this is not always so. Some adverbs have the same form as adjectives:

They deliver *weekly*. (adverb) There is a *weekly* delivery. (adjective)

Occasionally, an adverb may describe a preposition or conjunction (see below).

Some adverbs affect the sense of a whole sentence rather than just one of its components (e.g. the verb). The word *then* is used as a straightforward adverb of time in

The book *then* goes on to describe the cause of this revolution.

(indicating the time when the action of the verb occurs), but in

The book, then, makes an important contribution to our understanding of modern South America.

then (meaning *in this way*) has a dual purpose: it enlarges the meaning of the verb *makes*, and also – more importantly – expresses a relationship between the whole sentence and what has gone before. The preceding sentences have, presumably, been about *the book*, and the writer wishes to draw a conclusion from them; *then* indicates that the conclusion expressed in the sentence follows logically from what he has previously written.

A different sort of relationship – not a logical conclusion but a contrast – is found in

Food is expensive. Wine, *however*, is cheap.

Adverbs used in this way are known as **sentence adverbs** (because they affect a whole sentence) or **conjuncts** or **conjunctive adverbs** (because of their linking function). They normally occur at or near the beginning of sentences, and often need to be marked off by commas. See also **3.9** on page 28.

Adverbs which are found as conjuncts include *incidentally*, *instead*, *namely*, *so*, *likewise*, *indeed*, *moreover*, *therefore*, *still*, *consequently*, *nevertheless*, *yet*, *then*, *otherwise*, *for*, *thus*, *besides*, *accordingly*, *again*, *furthermore*, *hence*.

1.7   A **preposition** expresses a relationship between a noun or pronoun and some other part of the sentence:

> He disappeared *into* the crowd. She took it *from* me.

A preposition usually precedes ('governs') a noun or pronoun, or a group of words having the same grammatical function as a noun, and expresses its relationship to some other word (normally a verb, noun or adjective) in another part of the same sentence. This other part is usually earlier in the same sentence. In

> You must walk *round* the wood, not *through* it.

the prepositions indicate different relationships of place between *walk* (verb) and *wood/it*. Prepositions may express relationships of time

> They arrived *during* the afternoon/*before* nightfall/*after* lunch.

or of manner

> Hit it *with* a hammer. It was delivered *by* hand.

Prepositions are sometimes omitted

> They showed (*to*) him the way.

and may occasionally come after the noun/pronoun they govern: instead of

> *With* what did you mend it?

it is more natural to say

> What did you mend it *with*?

It has already been shown that some pronouns (*I*, *he*, *she*, *we*, *they*, *who*) adopt a different form when used as the object of a verb (*me*, *him*, *her*, *us*, *them*, *whom*). These object-forms must also be used when the pronouns are governed by a preposition:

> Share it *between him* and *me*. *For whom* is it intended?

The same word may be a preposition (Wait *outside* the door) or an adverb (Wait *outside*) depending on its function in a sentence.

1.8   A **conjunction** joins two words or groups of words:

> blue *and* white stripes; take it *or* leave it; I went early *because* I was tired.

The conjunction need not always be placed between the words being linked:

> Because I was tired, I went early.
> Although he was injured, he went on playing.

It is possible for a word to be a conjunction in one sentence and a different part of speech in another:

Look *before* you leap. (conjunction)
It has happened *before*. (adverb)
We left *before* the end. (preposition)

Conjunctions are dealt with more fully at **4.6** on page 64.

Grammatical function

1.9   Several examples have been provided to show how a word may act as several different parts of speech, depending on its function in a particular sentence.

Put it *down*. (adverb)
Let's walk *down* the hill. (preposition)
These pillows are filled with *down*. (noun)
Is there any *down* payment? (adjective)
They decided to *down* tools. (verb)

It is important to think of parts of speech as categories of work, and to bear in mind that many English words belong to more than one category. Most dictionaries indicate what these categories are.

1.10   A group of words may act as a part of speech. The next chapter shows how parts of speech, whether as single words or groups, are built into sentences.

2

Phrases, Clauses and Sentences

In order to understand sentence-structure, it is helpful to know the difference between *phrases* and *clauses*.

Phrases

2.1   A phrase is a group of words having the same function as a noun/pronoun, adjective or adverb. Phrases may be regarded as 'equivalents' of these parts of speech.

(*a*)   Phrases as noun/pronoun equivalents:

> *His former friends* helped him. (noun phrase as subject)
> Do you know *his probable time of arrival*? (noun phrase as object)
> She is *a friend of the family*. (noun phrase as complement)

Pronoun phrases function in similar ways:

> *None of the students* failed. (pronoun phrase as subject)

Two noun phrases (or a noun and a noun phrase) may be in apposition:

> The local newspaper, *now a fortnightly publication*, will soon appear weekly. (subject)
> He opened *the morning post, the usual collection of bills and circulars*. (object)
> The man responsible was *the Commander-in-chief, a controversial figure*. (complement)

Like a noun/pronoun, a noun/pronoun phrase may act as a subject, object or complement of a verb, or as object of a preposition.

(*b*)   Phrases as adjective equivalents:

> The candidate, *confident as ever*, emerged from his car. (adjectival phrase describing noun)

He was *pale with fatigue*. (adjectival phrase as complement)

(c) Phrases as adverb equivalents:

Ring me *before the end of the day*. (adverbial phrase of time)
It is stored *in the basement of the building*. (adverbial phrase of place)
He sat *with his feet on a stool*. (adverbial phrase of manner)

2.2 A phrase may include a **non-finite verb** (a verb without a subject). There are three categories of non-finite verb:

(a) The infinitive. This is easily recognised when it is preceded by *to*:

They decided *to walk*. It is difficult *to understand*.

It is also found, without *to*, after a number of verbs including *can, could, should, would, may, must, might, shall, will*:

We must *replace* it. I couldn't *see*.

In phrases, the infinitive may be used to form a noun/pronoun equivalent:

To cut it down will be dangerous. (subject of verb *will be*)
He prefers *to do it himself*. (object of verb *prefers*)
His intention is *to succeed at all costs*. (complement)

(b) The participle ending in -*ing* (sometimes misleadingly called the present participle). This participle is a verb-form that may be part of a tense:

People were *running* from the building.

or used as an adjective:

a *walking* stick, at *walking* pace

or used as a noun (sometimes called a verbal noun or gerund):

Walking is excellent exercise. (subject)
I enjoy *walking*. (object).
My favourite pastime is *walking*. (complement)

In phrases, the -*ing* participle may be used in adjective equivalents:

Entering the house hurriedly, he tripped over the mat. (adjectival phrase describing *he*)
I heard his radio *playing music very loudly*. (adjectival phrase describing *radio*)

It may also be used in noun equivalents:

He started *driving like a madman*. (noun phrase, object of *started*)

(c) The participle ending in -*ed* (or -*d*, -*t*, -*en*, -*n*, etc: see list of irregular verbs), sometimes called the past participle. Like the -*ing* participle, the *-ed* participle is a verb-form that may be part of a tense:

> He has *complained*. I had not *kept* it. Have you *chosen*?
> The performance has *begun*.

or used as an adjective:

> *bruised* feelings, *sworn* enemies, *spoken* words, *burnt* pan.

It cannot act as a noun or be in a noun phrase, but it occurs in adjectival phrases:

> He woke up *refreshed by his long sleep*. (phrase describing subject *He*)
> She found the book *hidden under a pile of newspapers*. (phrase describing object *book*)

Clauses

2.3   Like a phrase, a clause may act in place of a single noun/pronoun, adjective or adverb. The difference is that a phrase is a group of words that may contain a non-finite verb, but a clause is a group of words that *must* contain a finite verb (a verb with a subject).

2.4   If a group of words containing a finite verb (i.e. a clause) makes complete sense, it is known as a sentence (see 2.5 on page 12):

> He *slammed* the door angrily.

If the adverb *angrily* is replaced by a clause

> He slammed the door *because he was angry*.

there are now two finite verbs (*slammed*, *was*) in the sentence, and therefore two clauses. *He slammed the door* still makes complete sense, and is therefore called the **main clause**. However, *because he was angry* does not make complete sense; it cannot stand on its own, and cannot be fully understood unless it is attached to the main clause *He slammed the door*. In other words, it *depends* on the main clause to make it fully understood. It is therefore called a **dependent** or **subordinate clause**.

A subordinate clause is a group of words containing a finite verb but not making complete sense. Just as there are three sorts of phrase (noun, adjective and adverb equivalents), there are three sorts of subordinate clause: the noun clause, the adjectival clause and the adverbial clause.

(*a*)   A **subordinate noun clause** does the same work in a sentence as a noun:

What he said surprised everyone. (noun clause subject of *surprised*)

He regretted *that he had lost his temper*. (noun clause object of *regretted*)

Forgetting *that his keys were inside*, he shut the door. (object of *-ing* participle in adjectival phrase describing the subject *he*)

They walked from *where they had parked the car*. (noun clause governed by preposition *from*)

The truth is *that they were unprepared*. (noun clause complement)

It is unfortunate *that it happened*. (noun clause in apposition to *It*. The clause explains or identifies the subject *It'*; it does not complete the sense of the verb as a complement. The complement is *unfortunate*.)

(*b*) A **subordinate adjectival clause** does the same work in a sentence as an adjective:

The clock-tower, *which was falling down*, has been demolished. (describing subject noun)

The service suits travellers *who are pressed for time*. (describing object noun)

The pronoun introducing such a clause is sometimes omitted:

That isn't a style (*which*, *that*) I like.

(c) A **subordinate adverbial clause** does the same work as an adverb, usually adding to the sense of a verb:

The ship docked *when the storm subsided*. (says *when* the action of the verb *docked* took place)

He put it back *where he found it*. (says *where* the action of the verb *put* took place)

but Here's the place *where he found it*. (adjectival clause describing noun *place*)

They played *as they had never played before*. (adverbial clause of manner)

Because supplies were held up, prices soared. (adverbial clause of reason)

He ran *so that he wouldn't be late*. (adverbial clause of purpose)

He ran so fast *that his spectacles steamed up*. (adverbial clause of result)

If it gets hot, switch it off. (adverbial clause saying under what conditions the action of the verb *switch* should happen)

Sentences

We have now looked at some of the ways in which groups of words – phrases and clauses – may do the same work as some of the parts of speech examined in Chapter 1. We may now see how these elements fit into the structure of the English sentence.

2.5   A sentence contains a maximum of five elements:
   subject
   verb
   object(s)
   complement
   adverbial

(*a*)   The **subject** is the word or group of words a sentence is about. Usually, but not necessarily, it comes first in a sentence. It may be a single noun/pronoun:

> *I* agree.

or an equivalent phrase:

> *Several interested onlookers, including some children*, gathered round.

or an equivalent subordinate clause:

> *Whoever said that* was mistaken.

(*b*)   The **verb** is the essential element. Because it has a subject, it is a finite verb. The subject may, however, be 'understood' rather than stated in the case of verbs expressing commands, requests or advice:

> Stop it! Do sit down. Don't forget to check it regularly.
> Help yourself.

(*c*)   There are two kinds of **object**:

Direct object   This is the word, phrase or clause affected by the action of the verb:

> They welcomed *him*.
> We decided *to hold regular meetings*. (noun phrase with infinitive verb)
> He knew *that it would happen*. (noun clause object)

The direct object is located by asking 'who or what receives the action of the verb?' In these examples, who or what was welcomed, decided and known?

Indirect object   This is the word or words *to* or *for* which the action of the verb is performed (though the words *to* and *for* are omitted):

> The shop sold *him* a faulty camera.
> They sent *all their customers* an offer of a refund.

The indirect object is located by asking 'to or for whom or what is the action of the verb performed?'

   An indirect object is found only in a sentence that also contains a direct object. The indirect object precedes the direct object.

(*d*)   The **complement** is the word, phrase or clause that is needed to complete the sense of the verb in the main clause by reference to its subject or direct object.

Subject complement Some verbs (e.g. *to be*, *become*, *taste*, *seem*, *appear*) express a state of being rather than an action, and do not have a direct object because there is no action for such an object to 'receive' (i.e. they are intransitive):

> The cat looked *ill*.
> The atmosphere remains *tense*.
> He'll become *a good player*.
> It seems *to have broken down*.

The italicised words, completing the sense of the verbs *looked*, *remains*, *become* and *seems*, refer to the subjects of these verbs, and are subject complements.

A clause may act as a subject complement:

> That is *what I have heard*.
> The difficulty was *that the lock had jammed*.

Note the difference between

> He made *an excellent chairman*. (subject complement)

and

> He made *a rice pudding*. (direct object)
> He grew *older*. (subject complement)

and

> He grew *vegetables*. (direct object)

Object complement This is a word or group of words that completes the meaning of a verb by referring to its direct object:

> They kept it. (subject + verb + direct object)
> They kept it *secret*. (subject + verb + direct object + *object complement* referring to the direct object *it*).
> I think (*that*) *it's a pity*. (subject + verb + noun clause object)
> I think it *unlikely*. (subject + verb + direct object + *object complement*)

The object complement follows the direct object, and may be an adjective or noun or an equivalent.

(*e*) The **adverbial** is any adverb, adverbial phrase or adverbial clause. There may be more than one adverbial in a sentence.

2.6 A sentence cannot contain more than the above five elements.

They	–	subject
appointed	–	verb
him	–	(direct) object
manager	–	(object) complement
yesterday	–	adverbial

The elements need not appear in that order, though there are certain rules which have already been mentioned above such as the one about the relative positions of direct object and complement, for example. The adverbial is especially movable. The elements, of course, may consist of more than one word:

subject – { *The directors of the club,* (noun phrase)
who had previously been in disagreement, (adjectival clause)

adverbial – *finally* (adverb)
verb – *decided*
(direct) object – { *to appoint* (infinitive)
him (object of infinitive) } (noun phrase)
(object) complement – *manager of the club* (noun phrase)
adverbial – *when they met yesterday.* (adverbial clause of time)

2.7 The smallest number of elements a sentence may have is two – subject and (intransitive) verb – though one-word sentences are possible when the subject is understood (*Help! Run!*). A sentence must also make complete sense. Examples of sentences in this most basic form, subject and verb, are

I agree. Night is falling. The work was delayed.

Such a sentence, with one finite verb, is called a **simple sentence**. Even if this basic pattern is elaborated by adding the other three elements, it remains a simple sentence as long as there is only *one* finite verb, i.e. as long as subject, object, complement and adverbial consists of single words or phrases and do not include any subordinate clauses, which by definition contain finite verbs.

2.8 Two simple sentences, such as

They knocked. Nobody answered.

may be linked by a conjunction to form one long sentence

They knocked but nobody answered.

Such a sentence, sometimes called a double sentence, has two main clauses, both of equal weight and importance, and no subordinate clauses. In a more elaborate version, such a sentence may have three, four or five of the sentence-elements in each of the two main clauses:

Soaked to the skin, they knocked on the huge door repeatedly, but nobody answered from within the house.

Having two finite verbs, and two clauses linked by a conjunction, the sentence remains a double sentence.

2.9 This sort of construction may be extended to embrace three or more main clauses. While it is correct to write

> The judge entered. He bowed to the court. He blew his nose. He then sat down.

– and there may be occasions when such a series of simple sentences is desirable, perhaps to create suspense or to be emphatic – it would be more normal to run these four simple sentences into one, to avoid jerkiness and the tedious repetition of the same subject, which may be omitted as 'understood':

> The judge entered, bowed to the court, blew his nose, and then sat down.

Here, commas are used to link the first three main clauses; conjunctions could have been used, but the resultant *and . . . and . . . and* would have been clumsy. Such use of commas is correct as long as a conjunction occurs at the end of the list to signal the final item. The comma before this final conjunction is optional. This sort of sentence is called a multiple sentence.

2.10 Any sentence which contains a subordinate clause, or more than one, is called a **complex sentence**, whether it has one main clause or several. Like a main clause, a subordinate clause may have a minimum of two elements (subject and verb)

> The man *who died* had been a passenger in the car.

and a maximum of five

> The funeral, *which they kept very private*, was held last week.

In this example, the five elements in the subordinate adjectival clause are subject (*they*), verb (*kept*), direct object (*which*, relative pronoun with joining function), object complement (*private*), adverbial (*very*). The main clause consists of subject (*The funeral*), verb (*was held*) and adverbial (*last week*).

The following examples show subordinate clauses acting as sentence-elements:

as subject	*What he said* surprised everyone. (noun clause)
as indirect object	His strong voice gave *what he said* an air of conviction. (noun clause)
as direct object	Everyone believed *what he said*. (noun clause)
as complement	That is *what he said*. (noun clause, subject complement)
as adverbial	*If it gets hot*, switch it off. (adverbial clause)

2.11   The following five permutations are possible in both subordinate and main clauses:

subject + intransitive verb

subject + transitive verb + direct object

subject + transitive verb + indirect object + direct object

subject + linking verb (see 1.5) + subject complement

subject + transitive verb + direct object + object complement

} All these may add adverbials

2.12   To summarise, a sentence may range from two words – subject + intransitive verb – to a complex structure with several main and subordinate clauses, all of them containing between two and five elements. Apart from the verb, which may be one word or several, the elements themselves may be single words, phrases or clauses.

In simpler language, a sentence consists of a subject, stating what the sentence is about, and a predicate (the rest of the sentence). The latter says something about the subject, and consists of a finite verb together with any extension of the verb's meaning.

There are peculiarities in sentences beginning with *It* and *There* because these subjects do not mean anything:

It's snowing. There's no hope.

Even so the total sentence makes sense and is correctly constructed.

2.13   The only exceptions to this pattern are found in speech and informal writing when verbs or parts of them are sometimes omitted, as they are in newspaper headlines, telegrams and announcements:

Any news from home yet?
Four cups of coffee, please.
Six Killed in Motorway Fog.
No Parking.

Exclamations may be regarded as sentence equivalents even though they may have no verbs:

Good Heavens!   Nonsense!   Oh bother!   What a surprise!

3

Punctuation

The purpose of punctuation is to show the reader how a writer has grouped his words. The best practice is to use punctuation only when it is necessary for this purpose.

3.1   The full stop is used

(*a*)   at the end of a sentence;

(*b*)   when a word is abbreviated:

  J. C. Robinson, Jan. 21, Esq., i.e., Rev., e.g.

though it has long been common to omit the full stop if the last letter of a common abbreviation is the same as in the unabbreviated word:

  Dr, Mr, Mrs, St, 4th, Rd

A study of newspapers and magazines will show that the dropping of full stops after most if not all abbreviations is now widespread, presumably on the grounds that abbreviations are readily recognisable and understood without the need for punctuation. The ordinary user of English may not wish to go as far as that, but he would certainly not be criticised for dropping full stops in common abbreviations (which are often better known than the words they stand for) such as BBC, RSVP, TV, BA, MP, USA, plc, BC, AD, NB, PS, mpg, EEC.

  Acronyms (made up of initials but pronounced as words) do not have full stops. Examples of these are NATO, UNESCO and VAT.

  Three full stops (. . .) are used to indicate the omission of words in a passage that is being quoted. Novelists use the same device to express hesitation, tailing-off, or interruption in quoted speech.

3.2   The **question mark** is needed

(*a*)   at the end of a sentence that poses a question:

> Who was that on the telephone?

even though a question may be worded as a statement:

> You don't really believe that?

(*b*)   at the end of a quoted question:

> 'Who was that on the telephone?' she asked.

At the end of a sentence, the question mark has the force of a full stop and is followed by a capital letter. Do not use a question mark *and* a full stop.

A question mark is not used

(*a*)   at the end of a reported or implied (as distinct from a direct) question:

> She asked who was on the telephone.
> I'd like to know whether or not you'll be coming.

(*b*)   when a question is really a statement, instruction or request, even though it is phrased as a question out of politeness:

> Could you please let me have an early reply.
> Would it be possible to send me a catalogue.

3.3   The **exclamation mark** is used

(*a*)   instead of a full stop at the end of a sentence expressing strong feeling, such as surprise or anger:

> I most certainly will not!

It allows the writer to choose between a mild expression of feeling

> I never dreamt he would be so stupid. Please listen.

and a stronger one:

> I never dreamt he would be so stupid! Please listen!

(*b*)   after single words or phrases (greetings, expletives, toasts, warnings, commands, cries for help, insults, etc.) which have an exclamatory nature, and when a loud or sharp tone of voice needs to be represented:

> Ow! Good heavens! You idiot! Hello there! Look out! What a pity!

It is not a rule that such expressions have to be followed by an exclamation mark; the writer must decide whether the context calls for special strength. Note the difference between

> Hello there! Can you hear me?
> Good heavens! That's incredible!

and

> Hello, how are you?
> Good heavens, that was ages ago.

Note too the use of capital letters after exclamation marks in these examples, and of commas after exclamations that are not strong enough to deserve exclamation marks.

The over-use of exclamation marks may become monotonous and thus have the opposite effect to that intended. They should be used sparingly.

(*c*) to express irony or sarcasm, or to indicate a joking tone of voice:

> That was clever! What a life!

It is never necessary to use two (or more) exclamation marks after an expression.

3.4 The **comma** separates words, phrases or clauses when the sense demands a slight pause. There are few rules for the comma: its use is often a matter of taste or emphasis. The most common error, apart from using a comma when a full stop is essential, is over-use of the comma in a way that interrupts the flow of a sentence by introducing unnecessary and distracting slight breaks.

Commas help to clarify, occasionally to avoid ambiguity, and to provide the reader with little breathers or pointers in the middle of long constructions. They often work in pairs, bracketing an expression to mark it off from surrounding expressions.

The best policy is to use a comma only when it contributes something to the sense. Such occasions are most likely to occur:

(*a*) in a list of nouns, adjectives, verbs or adverbs:

> Butter, milk, eggs and cheese are in short supply.
> The play was long, boring, tasteless, and badly acted.
> The children laughed, cheered and shouted.
> It should be sung softly, gently and lightly.

A comma before *and* introducing the final item in a list is optional but normally unnecessary. It may add a little emphasis to the final item, as it does in the second of the above examples.

There is no need for commas when a list of adjectives precedes a noun in a flowing way:

> A big old orange estate car drew up alongside.

but commas help emphasis if adjectives jar with each other:

> An angular, twitching, untidy-looking young man.

(*b*) in a list of phrases or clauses (main or subordinate):

> His favourite relaxations are listening to music, cultivating rasp-
> berries, and sailing his boat at weekends. (*phrases*)
>
> We went to a restaurant, spent a long time over our meal, and talked of
> old times. (*main clauses*)
>
> He said that he had bought the house as a ruin, renovated it at
> considerable expense, and then sold it. (*subordinate clauses*)

In such longer constructions, a comma before *and* introducing the
final item is a helpful signpost, but it is not obligatory, and some
people would argue that it is superfluous and fussy.

(*c*) in marking off adjectival and adverbial clauses and phrases
when the sense demands a slight pause. This usually happens in
sentences with lengthy components:

> When the battle ceased after four long months, and after the gains and
> losses had been painfully reckoned, the bitter truth at last became
> apparent.
>
> The animal, which until then had been sleeping, suddenly leapt to its
> feet.
>
> Having managed to climb the ladder, though it had creaked ominously
> from time to time, he began to feel less apprehensive.

The comma is not always needed to mark off a clause or phrase; its
assistance is seldom required in a simple construction:

> When you come back it will be finished.
> In all the excitement he had not noticed the time.

Even so, the lack of a comma in even a short sentence may cause
momentary ambiguity or untidiness. In

> From the hill beyond the village looks smaller.

the reader gets as far as *looks* before realising that *village* is the
subject of the verb, not the object of *beyond*. A comma after *beyond*
makes the structure clear.

(*d*) in long double sentences, to mark off main clauses linked by a
conjunction, especially when the clauses have different subjects:

> To the north, where the land rises gently, an old farmhouse stands on
> the site of an ancient castle, *but* no other trace now remains of the
> village that formerly stood there.

(*e*) in marking off words in apposition:

> The writer, a man deeply interested in the sense of community,
> described the suburbs as being peopled by rootless beings, nomads
> who have no tribe.

(*f*) in marking off words which are not part of the central structure of a sentence but inserted by way of parenthesis. These include interjected expressions such as *I think*, *in conclusion*, *of course*, *yes*, *no*, *isn't it*, *please*, *thank you*; the names of persons being addressed; exclamations which are part of a sentence, not separate expressions beginning with a capital letter and ending with an exclamation mark (see **3.3** on page 18); and linking adverbs (e.g. *however*, *moreover*, *therefore*, *perhaps*, *nevertheless*) and corresponding phrases (e.g. *on the other hand*, *on the whole*, *even so*) which relate a sentence to a preceding one. In all cases, commas should be used only when the sense of parenthesis is present:

> The book, *I believe*, is out of print.
but I believe the book is out of print.
> He is thinking of changing his job. His wife, *however*, is worried about this.
but *However* hard he tried, he could not give up smoking.
> The whole wall, *of course*, had to be rebuilt.
but Of course he can come.
> That's very kind, *thank you*.
but Thank you for waiting.
> *Good gracious*, that is surprising, isn't it? *No*, I don't think so.
> *John*, would you please open the window?
> Can you tell me, *please*, where it is?

Note that when such expressions occur in the middle of sentences, commas are placed before and after, but obviously only a single comma is necessary (or possible) before or after an interjectory expression occurring at the beginning or end of a sentence.

Commas should not be used
  (i) between subject and verb
 (ii) with restrictive clauses (see **4.2** (*m*))
(iii) to link two sentences, however short:

> Please come soon, I miss you.
> A meeting has been arranged, this will be held next week.

In the first of these a dash should replace the comma, because the second statement explains the first (see **3.6**(*f*) on page 23). In the second a semicolon would be best, to indicate a relationship between the two statements. Alternatively, a full stop followed by a capital letter would be possible in both examples. But a comma can never link complete sentences unless it is followed by a conjunction:

> A meeting will be arranged, and this will be held next week.

As several of the above explanations show, commas are often used in pairs to mark off parts of sentences. A common mistake is to forget the second comma:

> Famine, as has often been noticed is prevalent in . . .
> Drama classes, despite their popularity with younger members have had to be withdrawn.

Punctuation is needed after *noticed* and *members* to complete the parenthesis.

3.5   Brackets are used to insert a word, phrase or clause into a sentence inconspicuously, by way of comment under the breath, as it were, or as a brief note of explanation, afterthought, illustration or additional fact. Brackets often carry the meaning 'that is to say'.

> All the patients who had consulted him during the previous five years (several thousand in all) were questioned by the police.

The writer sometimes has the choice between brackets and commas, as he does in

> The town-crier of Mayfair (hired for the occasion by a Japanese film crew) was also present.

Brackets indicate that the words in parenthesis are a shade less important, more detached from the main content of the sentence, than they would have been if contained between commas.

A bracketed expression is independent of the grammar of the sentence that includes it: the sentence would still be complete without it. No punctuation is required before or after the brackets except that which would be needed to construct the same sentence without brackets:

> Wholemeal (or wholewheat) flour contains nothing but wheat (the entire grain is milled), but granary flour contains malt as well.

Note that the second brackets in this example contain a complete sentence, but without a full stop or initial capital letter. The only punctuation needed inside brackets is whatever the sense demands:

> Awkward customers complained (they would, wouldn't they?) that the explosion, which killed two cooks in the kitchen, had interrupted their lunch.

If a whole sentence is put in brackets between two other whole sentences, or as the final sentence in a paragraph, it should begin with a capital letter and end with a full stop within the brackets. Note the position of the final full stop in

> The President may even cancel the visit. (This is thought to be unlikely.)

The President may even cancel the visit (though this is thought to be unlikely).

Brackets are used only in pairs, and their contents should be kept as brief as possible so as not to interrupt the flow of a sentence. Too much dependence on brackets makes writing disjointed, and can become an irritating habit.

3.6 The **dash** may be used in pairs with exactly the same function as brackets. The physical appearance of the double dash – more open than that of brackets – makes parentheses between dashes slightly more prominent, less enclosed and subsidiary, than parentheses in brackets.

The single dash is used at the end of a sentence

(*a*) to add special emphasis:

These are the facts – facts that are incontrovertible.

(*b*) to introduce an afterthought, parenthesis, or sudden change of direction:

That was the end of the matter – or so he thought.

(*c*) to indicate an anticipatory pause before a surprise:

You'll never guess what came into our garden last night – a white badger.

(*d*) to sum up:

Courtesy, helpfulness, sympathy, good humour – these are among the most admired of attributes.

(*e*) to indicate, in reported speech, that it is unfinished because of interruption:

'I didn't expect –.'

(*f*) to introduce an explanation or illustration:

A newspaper has several aims – to inform, to comment, to entertain and to provoke.

Confusion may be caused if double and single dashes are used within the same sentence.

3.7 Quotation marks (sometimes called **inverted commas** or **speech marks**) denote that a speaker's actual words (i.e. 'direct speech') are being quoted.

Different printers use different conventions, and in particular there is some argument about whether double (". . .") or single

('. . .') quotation marks should be employed. The following examples illustrate the most common practice.

(*a*) When the spoken words come first:

> 'You've put it in upside down,' he retorted.

Although the quotation is a complete sentence, it is followed by a comma. This is placed *inside* the closing quotation mark, the full stop being postponed until the end of the complete sense-unit.

A question mark, exclamation mark or dash (denoting interrupted speech) may be used in place of the comma, as appropriate. No other punctuation is permitted.

(*b*) When the spoken words come last:

> She asked, 'When is the closing date?'

Even though it comes in mid-sentence, the first word of direct speech has a capital letter, and is preceded by a comma before the opening quotation mark.

The punctuation at the end of the quoted words must be a full stop, question mark, exclamation mark or dash, though some writers prefer three dots (. . .) to denote an interruption or trailing-off. Such punctuation also concludes the whole sense unit (subject + verb + quoted speech). No punctuation is placed after the closing quotation mark.

(*c*) When two pieces of direct speech are separated by indirect speech:

> 'Sit down,' he said, 'and tell me all about it.'
> 'Sit down,' he said. 'Tell me all about it.'

It will be seen that these examples generally follow the rules already quoted, but the first example has a comma after *said* because what follows is a continuation of a sentence. The resumption of direct speech after *said* needs no capital letter for the same reason. However, the second example has a full stop and capital letter after *said* because what follows is a new sentence.

(*d*) If direct speech consists of several sentences spoken by the same person it is wrong to close quotation marks at the end of every sentence and immediately reopen them at the beginning of the next one. Closing quotation marks are used only when the speaker has finished.

If direct speech runs into more than one paragraph, it is customary to open quotation marks at the beginning of each paragraph (to remind the reader that speech is continuing), but not to close them at the end of a paragraph if the speech is continuing into the next.

(*e*) Whenever there is a change of speaker, the new speech begins on a fresh line, indented like a paragraph.

(*f*) If a passage of direct speech is followed by the resumption of indirect speech (e.g. normal narrative), many writers and printers mark the change by beginning a new paragraph. A new paragraph is often used when direct speech first opens. Neither device is necessary if direct speech is only briefly introduced in the middle of a paragraph.

(*g*) On the rare occasions when it is necessary to quote within a quotation, double inverted commas may be used for the inner quotation (or single ones if doubles are used for normal quotation):

> The Prime Minister replied, 'I never said "There is no alternative".'

Because inner quotations are invariably short, there is no need for more punctuation than this.

> The Prime Minister replied, 'I never said, "There is no alternative.".'

is over-elaborate.

(*h*) Quotation marks are also used when quoting words, such as those which someone else has spoken or written, for example in a book, speech or letter:

> Churchill is often said to have invented the term 'iron curtain' in 1945, but he did not.

No other punctuation is required to open or close such a quotation. If the sentence had ended at *curtain*, the full stop would have been placed after the quotation mark.

A lengthy quotation, such as a passage from a book, is normally introduced by a colon and begins without quotation marks, on a new line which is indented. All subsequent lines are similarly indented, until the quotation ends. The main text resumes on a fresh line against the normal margin (unless a new paragraph is to begin). In this way, a long quotation is clearly distinguished from the main body of the text by having its own margin, and the use of quotation marks is avoided.

(*i*) They are used when quoting the title of a book, play, film etc. Alternatively, titles may be underlined, as they usually are in typescript. See **3.13** on page 33.

(*j*) When using a piece of slang, or a foreign expression that has not become part of the English language they can be used:

> To enter a restaurant at 9 p.m. and to be told 'We're closed' is to encounter the 'vice anglais'.

Some writers put inverted commas round words intended to be sardonic or ironic.

3.8 The **colon** is a sharp punctuation, second only to the full stop in weight. It often carries the general sense of 'that is to say', and is used:

(*a*) to introduce a list when the sense demands a pause:

> The car has a number of optional extras: sun roof, tinted windows, rear seat-belts, and electrically adjustable wing-mirrors.

A dash would have been possible here: see **3.6**(*f*) on page 23.
No punctuation is required when no pause is needed before a list. It is incorrect to write

> Items of kit which are needed include: waterproofs, map, compass and a torch.

(*b*) to introduce a long quotation. See **3.7**(*h*) on page 25.

(*c*) before a word, phrase or clause which explains, amplifies or exemplifies whatever precedes the colon:

> That is the main problem: to filter the air.
> The school is highly regarded: academic standards are high, the staff are pleasant, and children enjoy going there.

A dash would be acceptable in some such cases (see **3.6**(*f*) on page 23), but is weaker than the colon. The words after the colon in the second example above are important clauses, and deserve the stronger introductory punctuation.

(*d*) before a word or words which have a sense of climax or need emphasis:

> There can be only one reason for this delay: incompetence.
> At last he made up his mind: he would sell it.

Heavier emphasis could be given to *he would sell it* by putting a full stop and capital letter after *mind*. To do the same after *delay* in the first example is allowable, but the resultant one-word 'sentence' *Incompetence* may be over-dramatic.

(*e*) to join two (usually short) sentences which balance each other while presenting contrasting ideas:

> Such cruelty might be forgiven: it could never be forgotten.
> There were times when good sense prevailed: there were others when dissension and strife carried the day.

Full stops would be possible here, but the effect would be more jerky. The colon has the effect of drawing attention to the antithesis. It may occasionally have a similar pointing function when there is no balance or contrast:

> He wasn't himself tonight: he didn't insult anybody.

The colon and dash (:–) is an unnecessary punctuation. The colon on its own is sufficient.

3.9   The **semicolon** is stronger than the comma and weaker than the full stop in the length of pause or degree of separation it imposes.

Just as two complete sentences

> I slipped. I was not hurt.

may be expressed as a single sentence (with two main clauses) by using a conjunction when they are related

> I slipped but I was not hurt.

the semicolon is used to join into a single sentence two (or more) complete statements which could be expressed as separate sentences but which deserve to be linked:

> Kent has the oldest churches in England; no other county has so many with Saxon remains, and some have Roman tiles.

A full stop could have been used here after *England*, but since there is a close relationship between the first statement and the second, a semicolon is preferable; it signals to the reader that what follows is to continue and amplify what has gone before, just as the semicolon in this sentence signals an explanation of why something has been described as *preferable* in the first half of the sentence. In a well constructed paragraph, of course, all sentences are related in that they flow on from each other in a smooth or logical way, but the semicolon adds a nuance by indicating a closer relationship than that implied by the full stop.

A conjunction and sometimes a dash may be substituted for a semicolon but a comma can never be. It is essential that the construction following a semicolon must be capable of standing on its own as a complete sentence (except for one case, described below). In other words, a semicolon must be followed by the equivalent of a sentence – a main clause, with or without subordinate clauses – not by a phrase or phrases, or by subordinate clauses without a main clause to depend on.

Semicolons frequently precede conjuncts (see **1.6** on page 5). Because semicolons have a linking function, and conjuncts too express a link between sentences, it is natural to associate the two:

> It's a pity it's closed; *still*, we can come back tomorrow.

However, it is arguable that the semicolon and conjunct merely duplicate each other, and that the conjunct alone is sufficient to indicate closeness of relationship between two statements:

> It's a pity it's closed. Still, we can come back tomorrow.

The only occasion when the semicolon may be used as a substitute for the comma is when there is the possibility of confusion:

> The Chairman welcomed the Mayor, Councillor Scott Barlow, the President of the Society, Mr Jon Hills, the Secretary, Mr Richard Parkin, the Treasurer, Mrs Barbara Long, and Professor Kevin Moore, who was the guest speaker.

Is Councillor Barlow the Mayor, the President, both or neither? Semicolons after *Barlow*, *Hills*, *Parkin* and *Long* would make all clear. In such circumstances, but in no other, semicolons may be used to separate phrases or subordinate clauses.

Because the semicolon may be used in place of the full stop, some writers use it indiscriminately, tacking on main clause after main clause, almost dispensing with full stops, and ignoring the special shade of expression that the semicolon brings to a sentence through its ability to indicate relationship. Unless the semicolon is used sensitively it loses its point.

3.10   The **hyphen** joins two or three words into a single entity:

> brother-in-law, bullet-proof, hair-raising, so-called, get-together.

It helps to prevent ambiguity or momentary confusion, as may be seen by observing the differences between

a geriatric ward nurse	*and*	a geriatric-ward nurse
a smoking compartment	*and*	a smoking-compartment
extra marital sex	*and*	extra-marital sex
four wheeled vehicles	*and*	four-wheeled vehicles
forty odd customers	*and*	forty-odd customers
a little used car	*and*	a little-used car
main road traffic	*and*	main-road traffic

The writer is at liberty to use hyphens to circumvent difficulties of this kind, and should not hesitate to do so.

To lay down other rules for using hyphens is not easy because many hyphened words (especially those with prefixes such as *post-*, *anti-*, *re-*, *pre-*, *by-*) gradually shed their hyphens as time goes by and begin to appear in dictionaries as single words. In recent years this has happened to *bypass*, *multinational*, *antifreeze* and *prenatal*, for example, though not all dictionaries agree. It does not much matter whether one uses *post-graduate* and *co-operate* or the simpler and increasingly common *postgraduate* and *cooperate*, but if there is any doubt, follow the dictionary's recommendations.

(*a*) Hyphens are used when writing out fractions (*four-fifths*), numbers between twenty-one and ninety-nine, and compound adjectives containing numbers or adjectives formed from numbers:

> four-storey building, eight-month delay, twelve-year-old boy, second-class citizens, three-and-a-half-hour meeting, first-floor bedroom, five-ton lorry

Hyphens are not used in

> a building of four storeys, a delay of eight months, a boy twelve years old, citizens who are second class, a meeting lasting three and a half hours, a bedroom on the first floor, a lorry weighing five tons

where no compound term is used.

(*b*) Many hyphened expressions are compound adjectives consisting of a participle preceded by an adverb, adjective or noun:

> fast-moving, well-known, hard-earned, terror-stricken, medium-sized, blue-eyed, home-made, never-failing, hand-picked, wide-ranging, middle-aged, ill-tempered, best-selling, ready-made, long-winded

Hyphens are a helpful courtesy in such cases. The reader of a sentence about *a hard working man* reaches *man* before finding out that *hard* is an adverb attached to *working*, not an adjective – as it usually is – belonging to an impending noun. There is no such flicker of doubt in a *hard-working man* (or *hard working-conditions*). Anything that causes even momentary doubt in the reader's mind should be avoided.

The hyphen is not used in

> The firm is well known / well equipped / well respected

because *known*, *equipped* and *respected* are part of the main verb, described by the adverb *well*, and not as part of a compound adjective.

No hyphen is needed in the familiar *adverb* + *adjective* combination:

> an unusually fierce storm, a thoroughly mischievous suggestion

(*c*) Hyphens are normally used after such prefixes as *vice-* (*vice-captain*), *ex-* (*ex-serviceman*), *self-* (*self-conscious*) and *non-* (*non-starter*), and are usually needed before *up* (*close-up*), *back* (*come-back*) and *off* (*brush-off*) in the formation of compound words. Thus

> He plans to make a come-back.

but

> Please come back tomorrow.

Hyphens are always needed between a prefix and a proper noun:

> pro-American, un-English, ex-President.

(*d*) Compound adjectives are often made by combining *adjective* + *noun*:

> *middle-class* values, *full-time* job, *west-country* town, *short-term* prospects, *left-wing* views.

The hyphen is not used when such words are used as straightforward adjectives and nouns, not as compounds:

> a town in the west country, the left wing of the party.

In the same way, hyphens found in other compounds (*out-of-date equipment*) should be dropped when the same words are used with their normal grammatical function (*The equipment is out of date*).

(*e*) Hyphens should always be used in words which, unhyphenated, would be ambiguous (*re-form*, *re-sign*, *re-cover*) or ugly (*full-length*, *semi-invalid*).

(*f*) The writer has freedom to use more than one hyphen in the interests of clarity. A *semi-house trained dog* implies that there exists a trained dog capable of being described as *semi-house*. The correct punctuation is *semi-house-trained dog*.

3.11   The **apostrophe** is a raised comma ('). It has two important functions: to indicate possession and to punctuate contractions.

(*a*) **Possession** is denoted by adding an apostrophe followed by *s* to the end of a singular word

> the family's plans, the firm's address, the orchestra's reputation

and an apostrophe without *s* to the end of a plural word ending in -*s*:

> ladies' shoes (i.e. shoes for *ladies*), the brothers' disagreement (i.e. the disagreement of the *brothers*)

This rule does not apply when a plural word does not end in -*s* (e.g.

men, *children*, *women*). In such cases, the apostrophe followed by *s* is needed to denote possession:

men's pyjamas, children's toys, women's magazines

There is some disagreement about singular words ending in -*s*. Both *James' wife* and *James's wife* are acceptable. The former is perfectly clear; the latter reflects normal pronunciation more accurately. The modern preference for simplicity in punctuation favours the former: *Keats' poetry*, *Guy Fawkes' night*. However, *for goodness' sake* is invariable.

An apostrophe is never used with possessive pronouns:

hers, yours, theirs, his, ours, whose, its

(when *its* = belonging to it: see below for *it's*). The possessive *one's* needs an apostrophe; the plural *ones*, of course, does not:

One must do one's best.
Those are the ones I like.

The apostrophe should be used in

a month's holiday, in a week's time, several years' imprisonment, a term's work, four hours' delay

and in

I must go to the butcher's. Their prices were lower than other companies' (short for *the butcher's shop* and *other companies' prices*).

In phrases, the *'s* comes at the end:

the Chancellor of the Exchequer's proposals, somebody else's turn, sister-in-law's illness

The same is true of joint ownership

Colin and Philippa's house

but not of separate possession

Colin's and Philippa's presents.

The apostrophe is often omitted in the names of well-known firms (*Barclays Bank*, *Marks and Spencers*).

It is permissible, and increasingly common, not to use an apostrophe after a plural noun that has an adjectival rather than a possessive sense:

Rates Office, Accounts Section, Students Union, Social Services Department, Girls School

This is no excuse for omitting the apostrophe in a word which ends in *s* specifically to indicate the possessive, not the plural: *mens club*, *Womens Institute*, *childrens home* need apostrophes.

(*b*) **Contractions** are words written with certain letters omitted to reflect the way they are commonly pronounced. The omitted letters are replaced by an apostrophe. The words most frequently affected are

would, had *shortened to* 'd	(I'd, you'd, he'd, they'd, who'd)
has, is *shortened to* 's	(she's, it's, that's, who's, where's)
not *shortened to* n't	(hadn't, don't, couldn't, aren't, isn't. *Note the irregular* can't, won't, shan't)
am *shortened to* 'm	(I'm)
shall, will *shortened to* 'll	(I'll, you'll, he'll, who'll)
have *shortened to* 've	(they've, you've, who've)
are *shortened to* 're	(you're, we're)

Contractions are general in speech and in informal writing. They are seldom used in formal writing.

The apostrophe may indicate dropped letters in dialect or rough speech:

o' (of), 'em (them), 'ope (hope), hangin' (hanging)

In rare cases, the apostrophe is used to form plurals

do's and dont's, if's and but's, the three R's, p's and q's, dot the i's and cross the t's

when the omission of the apostrophe would confuse the reader with unfamiliar and momentarily puzzling word-shapes. In print, the apostrophe denoting the plural is often omitted after numbers and abbreviations, but in writing most people still prefer

the 1980's, Liberal MP's, temperature in the 90's

3.12   Capital letters are needed at the beginning of sentences, and in direct speech (see **3.7**(*b*) and (*c*) on page 24. They are also used for:

(*a*) proper nouns, naming particular people, places (*the Lake District*), rivers, buildings (*Manchester Town Hall*), institutions (*the Anglican Church*), establishments (*Charing Cross Hospital*), firms (*British Leyland*), organisations (*the National Trust*), castles, countries, towns, streets, months of the year, days of the week, festivals (*Whit, Easter*), mountains, pets, house-names, etc. Adjectives formed from proper nouns have capital letters (*French, Shakespearean*).

(*b*) the titles of books, films, plays, television programmes, newspapers, magazines, songs, etc. The first word of a title always has a capital; unimportant words in the title (*of*, *the*, *in*, *and*) are generally spelt without one (*The Importance of Being Ernest*, *Lord of the Flies*).

The titles of people have capital letters (*Lord Clark, former Chancellor of the University of York*).

(*c*) abbreviations of proper nouns (*the UN*, *ICI*, *USSR*).

It is normal practice to use capital letters for the particular, and small letters for the general:

the Queen of England	*but*	the kings and queens of England
the Bishop of Birmingham	*but*	He was made a bishop
South Africa	*but*	We drove south
Edinburgh University	*but*	He had a university education
the present Government	*but*	governments since 1945

In literature, capital letters are given to personifications. See **14.2** on page 185.

3.13 Underlining may be used to emphasise a word or expression but should not be overdone, otherwise it will produce too shrill an effect. It is better to avoid it altogether.

Titles of books (**3.12**(*b*)) may be underlined as an alternative to inverted commas. In writing or typing for publication, underlining words denotes that they are to be italicised in print.

Conclusion

3.14 In music, stillness is often as important as sound. Slight breaks, short silences or longer pauses help to shape musical phrases and ideas, to communicate the composer's intention and to assist the listener in his understanding and enjoyment. These silences may sometimes be obvious; on other occasions a performer may place them so unobtrusively and deliberately that the listener may hardly be aware of them, though their effect may unconsciously shape his appreciation and response. Perhaps it is only when silences are clumsily handled that their importance is fully noticed: too long a pause between musical ideas may destroy the connection they are supposed to have; too short a pause may destroy a sense of separation the composer wanted, and create a jarring feeling of rush because the listener is not given enough time to assimilate one idea before being hurried on to the next.

Punctuation has the same function in writing as silences have in music. A comma represents the shortest pause, then come the semicolon, colon and full stop in that order. Their use must follow certain rules or conventions: bad punctuation may render meaning incomprehensible; idiosyncratic punctuation may baffle or irritate. But in addition to observing rules and conventions the writer has considerable freedom to use punctuation to suit his own purposes, orchestrate his meaning, adjust rhythm and pace, play words and phrases subtly against each other, and create a sense of speaking with his own special voice. So punctuation is not just a matter of rules, though it may be for the workaday writer. It is capable of endless variety, interest and refinement, projecting the personality of the writer and the distinctiveness of his work. Not all writers and even fewer readers are aware of these reserves of punctuation and their role in shaping the music as well as the sense in writing. But a good writer repays careful study. Sensitive readers, or those who wish to develop a good ear, should study his punctuation, using this chapter as guidelines, but asking themselves why a particular piece of punctuation has been chosen and noting how flexibly and individually a writer may interpret the conventions. In this way, the business of reading and understanding, as well as writing, can become a much richer and subtler experience. These ideas will be more fully explored in Chapter 14.

4

Some Grammatical Rules

Subjects and verbs

4:1   If a subject is singular, the verb must be singular. Subject and verb are said to be in agreement:

> Autumn *is* approaching.
> The shop *opens* at nine.
> Behind the house *was* a large field. (The subject is *field*)

If a subject is plural, the verb must be plural:

> The nights *are* becoming shorter.
> The shops *open* late.
> Behind the houses *were* large fields.

This rule is more complicated than it appears because to ascertain whether a subject is singular or plural is not always easy.

(*a*)   Two singular nouns or pronouns or phrases become plural when linked by *and*; they should then be followed by a plural verb:

> My wife and I *are* going.
> The jet *airliner*, en route to Paris, and the *helicopter*, piloted by an instructor, *were* nearly in collision.

A few common expressions (e.g. *bread and butter*, *eggs and bacon*, *salt and vinegar*, *milk and sugar*) are regarded as singular even though they may contain a plural noun:

> Fish and chips *is* a popular dish.
> Where*'s* the salt and pepper?

A plural verb, however, would not be incorrect.

(*b*)   If a subject consists of *singular noun* + *of* + *plural noun* (*a pile of plates*, *a pair of socks*), the subject-word is the first noun (i.e. the singular one) and the verb is singular:

> A pound of potatoes *costs* more this year.
> A selection of goods *was* on display.

The prepositional phrase (*of* + plural noun) functions adjectivally and does not affect the singular nature of the first noun, or of the following verb.

This rule need not apply when the singular noun in such a construction is a collective noun. See **4.1**(*e*) below.

(*c*) If a subject consists of *singular noun* + *with/along with/together with/as well as* + *singular or plural noun*, it is the first noun that acts as subject-word, taking a singular verb:

> The Foreign Secretary, together with several advisers, *is* to make the visit.

Again, the prepositional phrase (*together with* + *plural noun*) is adjectival. The subject-word is *Foreign Secretary*, needing the singular *is*.

If *and* had been used instead of *together with*, the subject would have been plural, requiring the plural verb *are*, in accordance with **4.1**(*a*).

(*d*) With *either . . . or*, *neither . . . nor* and *not only . . . but also . . .* , if both subjects are singular, so is the verb:

> Neither the *policy* nor the *thinking* behind it *carries* much conviction.

If both subjects are plural, the verb must be plural:

> Either credit cards or cheques are accepted.

If one subject is singular and the other plural, the verb should agree with the immediately preceding subject, and it is better if this is the plural one:

> Neither the boy nor his friends *were* to be found.
> Not only the captain but all the team-members *believe* that.

Likewise, where the alternative subjects require different verbs, it is safe to make the verb agree with the immediately preceding subject:

> Either you or I am wrong.

If this sounds awkward – and purists would argue that the subject *you* cannot go with the verb *am* – the sentence should be rephrased so that each subject gets its proper verb:

> Either you are wrong or I am.

(*e*) A collective noun in the singular (e.g. *audience*, *committee*), or any singular noun that can be used to denote plurality (e.g. *government*, *industry*, *the public*), may be used with a singular or plural verb as the sense demands. If the emphasis is on the single unit, a singular verb is appropriate:

> The group *is* too large.

If the emphasis is on the members of the unit, a plural verb is more natural:

> A group of children *were* running around.

In many cases it does not matter, provided that there is consistency within a sentence, i.e. either singular forms or plural forms, not a mixture of the two, should be used throughout:

> The Government prefers to let matters rest, but events may make them change their minds.

Here, the sentence begins in the singular (the verb *prefers* shows that *Government* is regarded as a singular noun) and slips into the plural (*them*, *their*, referring to *Government*). Either *prefers* should be plural (*prefer*) in line with *them* and *their*, or *them/their* should be singular (*make it change its mind*) in accordance with the singular verb *prefers*.

The collective noun *number* is plural in *a number of*

> A large number of trees *were* uprooted.

because *a number of* is clearly plural in sense even though the word *number* is singular. However, in the expression *the number of* the sense is clearly singular:

> The number of smokers *is* declining year by year.

(*f*) A plural noun (especially when used with numbers) may take a singular verb when the noun denotes a singular entity such as a single distance, length, weight or sum:

> Eighty pounds *is* too much to pay.
> Seven weeks *was* a long time to wait.
> The United States *offers* the tourist a wide choice.

(*g*) *There* is often used at the beginning of a sentence to anticipate the subject. For example,

> There is no need to apologise.

means

> No need to apologise is (i.e. exists).

and *There* has little or no meaning. It is an anticipatory or introductory subject. What it anticipates is the singular *need*, so the verb is singular.

It follows that *There is* . . . is required when the following subject is singular, and *There are* . . . when it is plural:

There *are*, despite his optimism, even his conviction that nothing can go wrong, many *reasons* for being cautious.

(*h*) In sentences with complements, the verb always agrees with the subject, even though this may mean that a singular subject and verb are followed by a plural complement, or a plural subject and verb by a singular one:

It is results that matter.
The subject of this chapter is grammatical rules.
Grammatical rules are the subject of this chapter.

(*i*) When linked by *or*, singular subjects take a singular verb, plural subjects a plural one:

Cooking fat or oil *is* needed.
Bushes or shrubs *are* to be planted.
One or the other *is* right.

When one subject is singular and the other plural, the verb agrees with the nearer one:

Gravel or pebbles are suitable.
Pebbles or gravel is suitable.

The former is more natural, and it is therefore best in such circumstances to place the plural subject second.

(*j*) A singular verb is needed after *one of + plural noun* and *more than one of + plural noun*:

One of the divers *is* missing.

A singular verb is likewise needed after *more than one*, even though it may sound plural:

It is now known that more than one diver *is* missing.

With *one of + plural noun + adjectival clause*, note

He is one of those people who *are* hard to please.
Here is one of the files that *were* mislaid.

In the first example, the relative pronoun *who* belongs to the plural word *people* (it is *those people who are hard to please* he is one of). The pronoun therefore has a plural sense and, being the subject of the verb in the adjectival clause *who are hard to please*, it needs the plural verb *are*. The same argument applies to *that* in the second example. But in

He is a man who is hard to please.

the *who* is singular because it refers to *man*; the verb it governs is therefore singular, *is*.

(*k*) In the above examples, the verb in the adjectival clause agrees with the appropriate noun in the main clause through the medium of the joining pronoun. There must be similar agreement when an adjectival clause relates to a pronoun in the main clause:

It is I who *am* responsible.

Here, *who* relates to *I*, and so the verb of which *who* is the subject must be *am*. Likewise *you who are*, *he/she who is*, etc.

(*l*) Despite a common belief that *none* is always singular, it may be singular or plural depending on which sense is needed. It is clearly singular, meaning *no amount*, in

None of the wine was drinkable.

and plural, meaning *no persons*, in

Spectators arrived in huge numbers, but none *were* turned away.

In other cases, a singular or plural verb may be used according to the sense or emphasis desired:

None of the windows *were* clean.

implies that the writer was thinking of several windows, or the condition of all of them, while

None of the windows *was* clean.

has the effect of individualising each window more emphatically, the sense of *none* here being *not one*. In many cases, however, such distinctions are unimportant, and a plural verb is generally found because *none of* + *plural noun/pronoun* has a plural feel.

(*m*) *Each* is a singular when it is the subject of a sentence, acting as a pronoun:

Each *was* allowed to speak for no more than five minutes.

This use of *each* should not be confused with its more familiar use as an addition to a subject which may be plural:

We each *were* allowed to speak.
They were given a present each.

Each of, and *each* as an adjective (*each man*), are singular.

(*n*) A clause may begin with *what*. It is singular when it means *the thing which*:

What they enjoyed most was the fair-ground.
What matters is results.

It is plural when it is intended to mean *the things which*:

He is making what *appear* to be unreasonable demands. (not *appears*) (*o*) Errors tend to occur in long sentences or clauses if subject and verb are well separated. It often happens that a writer begins with a singular subject, and follows it with various phrases and subordinate clauses, some of them dealing with plural matters, so that by the time he arrives at his verb he has forgotten that he needs a singular one. The verb is attracted into the plural, so to speak, by the generally plural feel that the sentence has developed, as in this example:

> Despite the protestations of the country's leaders, their *failure* to foresee the outcome of their policies, especially at a time when many people warned them of worsening economic conditions on the world markets, which have shown no signs of recovery in the months ahead, *deserve* serious rebuke.

The singular *deserves* should have been used to match the singular subject *failure*. Vigilance must be exercised, and errors of this kind are less likely if subject and verb are not too much separated, or if sentences are not allowed to become too long or complex.

Pronouns

4.2 (*a*) The following pronouns, called **indefinite pronouns**, are singular:

anyone	anybody	anything	everyone
someone	somebody	something	everybody

no-one	either	everything
nobody	neither	nothing

When one of these acts as the subject of a sentence or clause, it needs a singular verb:

> Nothing but books *is* sold in the shop.

If an indefinite pronoun acts as antecedent to a subsequent personal pronoun, the personal pronoun must also be singular:

> Has *either* of the girls passed *her* exam?
> Has anyone got room in *his* car?

In this second example *his* does duty, as it traditionally has done, for the more correct but cumbersome *his or her*.

In speech, and increasingly in writing, the plurals *they* and *their* replace the technically correct singulars *he* (or *he or she*) and *his* (or *his or her*):

> Everybody (*singular*) got what they (*plural*) wanted.
> Has anybody got room in their car?

At the moment, this usage, however convenient (and non-sexist), is not sufficiently widely accepted for it to be regarded as correct, whatever may happen in the future. The safe rule is that when the subject of a sentence is an indefinite pronoun, the sentence should continue in the singular with *she* or *he* (also standing for *he or she*) or *her* or *his* (also standing for *his or her*) as appropriate:

> Somebody *has* left *his* car lights on.
> Everybody got what *he* wanted.

(*b*) A collective noun may act as either a singular or a plural antecedent, depending on the required sense:

> The team *is* confident *it* will win. (stresses the unanimity)
> The team *are* disheartened by *their* injuries. (stresses the disarray)

It is often immaterial whether the collective noun is used in the singular or plural, but any pronoun to which it is antecedent should agree:

> The team *is* confident that *they* will win.

is wrong.

(*c*) Pronouns are unusual in having

| a subject-form: | I | he | she | we | they |
| an object-form: | me | him | her | us | them |

(*You* and *it* are the same whether subject or object.)

The object-form is used when a pronoun is used as a direct object (*I overtook him*), indirect object (*He lent her his car*) or as object of a preposition (*Give it to them*).

Errors often occur when two pronouns are used as the object of a verb or preposition, especially when one of the pronouns is *I*; there is a widespread belief that . . . *and I* is always right and . . . *and me* is always wrong. The following are incorrect:

> Between you and I, I think he's worried. (object of preposition; should be . . . *and me*)
> They sent my wife and I an invitation. (indirect object; should be . . . *and me*)

(*d*) Linking verbs (e.g. *is*, *are* and all the other tenses of the verb *to be* – see **1.5** on page 4) are followed by complements, not direct objects. Logically, then, when pronouns form complements they should not be in the object-form:

> Hello, it's *I*. It wasn't *they*. That's *we* in the photograph.

However, the object-form is invariably used in speech

> It's *me*. It wasn't *them*. That's *us* in the photograph.

and if such expressions have to be written down it is sensible to follow this universal spoken practice.

When a pronoun-complement is followed by an adjectival clause, the formally correct subject-form is more often found:

> It was *she/he/I* who first had the idea.
> Was it *they* or *we* who suggested it?

(*e*) The pronouns *myself, yourself, himself, herself, itself, ourselves, yourselves, themselves,* are called **reflexive** when they act as object or complement, because they 'reflect' the subject:

> I hurt myself. He's not himself. She prides herself on her work.

When such pronouns merely add emphasis, they are called **intensive**:

> She said she would do it herself. I saw them myself.

There is no good reason for misusing these pronouns by substituting them for personal pronouns:

> The house belongs to my brother and myself. (should be . . . *and me*)
> Perhaps I and yourself can repair it. (should be *you and I*)

Such misuse is common. No *-self, -selves* pronoun is correctly used if a personal pronoun (see **1.3** on page 2) can replace it.

(*f*) The interrogative pronoun *who?* is unique in having its own object-form (*whom?*) and possessive form (*whose?*).

> Who was that on the phone? (subject)
> Whom did you meet? (object)
> To whom does it belong? (object of preposition)
> Whom does it belong to? (object of preposition)
> Whose are they? (possessive)

Few speakers of English now bother with the *whom* form, so much so that it sounds unnatural in all but the most formal contexts. It remains desirable when coming immediately after a preposition

> *To whom* does it belong? *For whom* is it intended?

but one is more likely to find

> Who does it belong to? Who is it intended for?

which must now be regarded as standard.

(*g*) Pronouns are often used to form clauses. The two sentences

> The builder has just opened another business.
> The builder has a good reputation locally.

may be linked into a single complex sentence

> The builder, who has a good reputation locally, has just opened another business.

The pronoun *who* stands in place of the noun *the builder* in the second of the original sentences, and also links what has now become a subordinate adjectival clause to the main clause. The antecedent of *who* is *builder* in the main clause. Because of its joining or relating function, *who* is here a relative pronoun. Other relative pronouns include *whom, which, what* and *that.*

The object-form *whom* is used as object of a verb

> He's a writer whom few people now read. (object of *read*)

or as object of a preposition

> The man to whom you ought to write is . . . (object of *to*)

even when the preposition is separated from the pronoun it governs:

> She is the candidate whom you ought to vote for. (object of *for*)

Despite the widespread use of *who* in all these circumstances in spoken English, *whom* is still desirable in formal writing.

Whom is incorrect in

> She is the one whom I think saw what happened.
> They appointed someone whom they knew was ambitious.

because the relative pronouns are the subjects of *saw* and *was*, not the objects of *I think* and *they knew*, which are a sort of parenthesis:

> She is the one who (I think) saw what happened.
> They appointed someone who (they knew) was ambitious.

These parenthetic expressions do not affect the grammar of their clauses, which would still be complete grammatically – if not in meaning – if they were omitted. Compare

> They appointed someone whom they knew to be ambitious.

Here *whom* is correct as the object of *they knew*, which is not used as a parenthesis but as the finite verb of the clause (*to be ambitious* is non-finite).

Whom is incorrect in

> There is some doubt about whom should take his place.

where the writer presumably felt that the object-form *whom* was appropriate after the preposition *about*. The rule is that, as relative pronouns, *who* and *whom* act as subject or object of their own clauses. In this case, the subject-form *who* is needed as the subject of *should take.*

Who else is more normal than *whom else* as an object-form (*Who else did you see?*).

(*h*) Generally, *who/whom/whose* are used of people, and *which* of things, though *who* is often used of animals (*the cat who walked alone*) and *whose* of things (*the aircraft whose engines failed*) because of the cumbersome nature of the alternative *of which* (*the aircraft of which the engines failed*). It is incorrect to apply *which* as a relative pronoun to people (*the pupils which I teach* should have *whom*) except with a collective noun (*the crowd which assembled*), though as an interrogative pronoun *which* may be freely applied to people (*Which doctor did you see?*).

(*i*) It is possible for *which* to be used with a particular antecedent

> Catch *the bus which* leaves from the post office.

or a general one

> He said it would take three weeks to repair, which is nonsense.

where *which* refers to the whole idea of 'taking three weeks to repair', not to any specific antecedent noun. Care must be taken to avoid ambiguity:

> Everyone said how much they had enjoyed the wedding, which delighted her parents.

does not make it clear whether it was specifically the wedding which delighted or the more general idea of 'everyone saying how much they had enjoyed the wedding'. The lack of clarity is avoidable:

> Everyone said how much they had enjoyed the wedding, and their remarks delighted her parents.

or

> The wedding delighted her parents, and everyone said how much they had enjoyed it.

There is also ambiguity in

> I will write to you after my return from holiday, which will be in a fortnight.

It is not clear whether *which* has a particular antecedent (*holiday*) or a general one ('my writing to you') i.e. whether a letter may be expected in a fortnight or after a holiday that begins in a fortnight.

This use of *which* with a general antecedent may cause unintended humour:

> The Speaker rose to his feet, which silenced everybody.

(*j*) Other pronouns, notably *this*, *that* and *it*, may be used when their antecendent is a general idea, not a specific noun or pronoun:

> Trains were delayed by weather conditions. This made hundreds of passengers late.

The antecedent of *this* is not a singular noun/pronoun; indeed there is no singular word in the preceding sentence except *weather*, which is adjectival. The antecedent is the general fact of trains being delayed by the weather. Such use of the pronoun is legitimate when the meaning is clear, but in

> They plan to raise prices to cover the increased cost of steel. This may, of course, reduce demand for their products.

the reader reaches the end of the second sentence before realising that *This* does not refer to *steel* or *cost* but to the whole notion of prices being raised. Such looseness is to be avoided.

(*k*) Special problems attach to *it* because of its use not only with a specific or general antecedent but also as an anticipatory subject

> It has taken six months to plan the programme.
> It is often said that . . .

– even as a meaningless subject:

> It's snowing. It's ten o'clock.

The reader may experience confusion if these functions are mixed or unclear:

> The Council has not yet announced its intentions, but there must now be a question-mark over a programme it has taken six months to plan.

While *its* is clearly a reference to the antecedent *Council*, the reader does not know whether *it* is an anticipatory subject, which it sounds like, or a second reference to the Council. Has the Council taken six months, or someone else? A similar looseness is evident in

> They were drinking cold beer because it was warm.

A writer should be mindful of this problem and ensure that *it* is used with precise reference.

> Parents are slow to allow their children independence, and adolescents resent it.

Resent independence? The writer intended *it* to have a general antecedent (parents' slowness to allow independence), but the reader's first assumption is that *it* relates, as it usually does, to a particular antecedent, which can only be *independence*. He should not be put to the trouble, however brief, of working out the meaning for himself or making allowances for the writer's sloppiness:

> Parents are slow to allow their children independence, and adolescents resent this slowness/reluctance etc.

Always pause before writing *it*, and make sure its reference is clear and tidy. Careless use of *it* is one of the main causes of looseness in writing.

(*l*) Similar ambiguity may be caused by the careless use of other pronouns.

> By the time the climber had scrambled down and reached his friend, he was in a state of shock.

The next sentence or two will probably make clear whether it was the climber or his friend who was in a state of shock, but the reader's momentary confusion could and should be avoided:

> The climber was in a state of shock by the time he had scrambled down and reached his friend.

or

> The writer scrambled down and reached his friend, who by then was in a state of shock.

Sometimes the same pronoun is repeated though its antecedents are different:

> If an interior aerial is used, plug *it* into the video recorder and turn *it* on.

The first *it* refers to *aerial*, the second *it* to *recorder*, but one could be forgiven for assuming that the second *it*, like the first, refers to *aerial* and waste much time trying to turn *it* on.

Place a pronoun as close as possible to its antecedent; ensure that there is no doubt about what the antecedent (specific or general) is; if there is any ambiguity or looseness, repeat the antecedent or recast the sentence.

(*m*) Clauses introduced by *who/whom/whose*, *which* and *that* belong to one of two important types, most usually known as the defining (or restrictive) and the non-defining (or non-restrictive). The difference is seen in

> The children who ate too much became ill.
> The children, who ate too much, became ill.

The first sentence means that *some* children (those who ate too much) became ill, and implies that others (who did not eat too much) stayed well. The second sentence means that *all* the children referred to in the sentence became ill, and adds the information that they ate too much. This difference in meaning is transmitted solely by two commas. In the first sentence the adjectival clause is inseparable from the subject; it defines the subject, and restricts it to those who became ill (as distinct from those who did not). In the second sentence the adjectival clause is subsidiary to the main statement *The children . . . became ill*; the placing of the adjectival clause between commas makes it additional or parenthetic; it could be left out without interference with the main statement, and is therefore non-restrictive. In the first sentence the adjectival clause is integral.

> People who live in glass houses should not throw stones. (restrictive)
> People, who generally do not live in glass houses, have often ignored this proverb. (non-restrictive)
> Screws which have left-handed threads are sold in Ireland. (restrictive)
> Screws, which are handy things to have about the house, are much easier to use if they are flat-headed. (non-restrictive)
> The man (that) I was thinking of was quite old. (restrictive)
> The man, who was quite old, showed a remarkable turn of speed. (non-restrictive)

Restrictive clauses must not have commas round (or before) them; non-restrictive clauses do have commas.

A restrictive clause may be introduced by *that* (as an alternative to *who(m)* or *which*); non-restrictive clauses may be introduced only by *who/whom/whose* or *which*. It is therefore wrong to place a comma before a subordinate clause beginning with *that*.

Wrongly placed commas round (or before) a restrictive clause may have a serious effect on the intended sense:

> Men, whose eyes are close together, are not to be trusted.

> Don't use commas, which aren't necessary.

(*n*) Some pronouns are used with the general sense of *people* or *a person*:

> *They* say that troubles never come singly.
> *One* mustn't complain.
> *You* can't tell the difference.

Such constructions should not be mixed, as in

> *One* can get an immediate booking if *you're* lucky.

The over-use of *one* is stuffy:

> One should do one's best to make oneself understood.

is better as *People should do their best . . .* or *You should do your best . . .*

Modifiers: phrases and clauses

4.3 Modifiers are words, phrases or clauses that add to the meaning of other words. Modifiers must have unambiguous relations with other words. A modifier should be placed as closely as possible to the word(s) it relates to.

(*a*) Adverbial and adjectival phrases need careful placing.

> A new washing-powder is now on sale in the shops called 'Shift'.

is correct if there is a chain of shops called 'Shift', but the intended sense is probably

> A new washing-powder called 'Shift' is now on sale in the shops.

Most problems of this kind arise when phrases are tacked on at the end of sentences without sufficient forethought about where they really belong, but phrases sometimes go adrift in the middle of sentences:

> The judge ruled that statements made *about adultery in court* should not be published in the press.

The phrase *in court* is (one assumes) not adjectivally linked to *adultery* but adverbially to *made* (and the phrase *about adultery* belongs to *statements*). The two phrases are correctly positioned in

> The judge ruled that statements about adultery made in court should not . . .

Phrases beginning *as* are often unrelated:

> As a rate-payer, the shortage of text-books in our schools concerns me.

After the adjectival *As a rate-payer* the reader logically expects the noun/pronoun the adjectival phrase refers to:

> As a rate-payer, I am concerned about . . .

(*b*) Phrases containing infinitives need similar care.

> You should stop using the car to lose weight.

The placing of *to lose weight* next to *car* implies that the car is being used by *you* to lose weight. It is more likely that the writer means

> To lose weight, you should stop using the car.

where the phrase is correctly placed alongside the person it applies to. There is no problem with

> You should stop using the car *to carry garden fertilizer*.

because the modifying phrase is put next to the appropriate word.

(c) An adjectival phrase constructed with a participle (see **2.2** on page 9) must have a noun/pronoun to go with.

> Starting from the bus station, the sea can be reached in ten minutes.

begins with a participial phrase, indicating that the writer has in mind a person *starting*; at the end of the phrase the sentence changes course and there is no further reference to such a person. Either the sentence must be revised to include a noun/pronoun for the modifier to attach to

> Starting from the bus station, you/people/visitors can reach the sea in ten minutes.

or the modifier should be revised; if it is turned into a clause, so that the non-finite verb becomes a finite one with its own subject, the problem disappears:

> *If you start from the bus station*, the sea can be reached in ten minutes.

(*d*) A slightly different version of this problem occurs when the noun/pronoun to which the modifier is intended to refer is included but not placed next to the modifier. The rule is that if there is more than one noun/pronoun in a sentence, a modifying participle will attach itself to the nearest one.

> *While walking home*, a storm forced him to take shelter.

Grammatically, the storm is walking home. Either the appropriate word should be placed next to the modifier

> While walking home, *he* was forced to take shelter . . .

or the non-finite participle *walking* should be made finite, so that there is no ambiguity about who is performing its action:

> *While he was walking home*, a storm forced him to take shelter.

The habit of beginning business letters with the participle *Referring* sometimes produces an unrelated modifier.

> Referring to your letter of October 16, the goods have now arrived.

The modifier (*Referring . . . 16*) attaches itself to the nearest noun, *goods*, as if the goods were doing the referring. This may be corrected by changing the non-finite modifier to a finite statement

> I refer/Please refer to your letter of October 16. The goods have now arrived.

or by inserting an appropriate pronoun for the modifier

> *Referring* to your letter of October 16, *I* am glad to say that the goods . . .

(*e*) An anticipatory subject, such as *it* or *there*, may be unrelated to a modifier. The following example begins with a modifier in the form of an adjectival phrase:

> Not knowing the house well, it is difficult for me to explain to you.

The modifier attaches to *it* in a meaningless way. The correct version is either

> Not knowing the house well, I have difficulty in explaining to you.

or

> As you don't know the house well, I have difficulty in explaining.

(*f*) The unrelated participle does not usually lead to serious ambiguity, as the above examples show. Usually it produces a loose effect, a brief hesitation in the reader's mind. Clarity as well as correctness are aided if the writer is alert to the need for precise relations between modifier and what is modified, especially when beginning a sentence with a participle phrase.

This problem should not be confused with other functions of the participle. For example, the initial *-ing* word in

> Marching down the street was a splendidly uniformed brass band.

is simply part of an inversion, for reasons of emphasis, of

> A splendidly uniformed brass band was marching down the street.

where *marching* is part of the main verb, not an adjectival modifier.

(*g*) Some commonly used participles, such as *considering*, have come to be regarded as prepositions, so that there can be no objection to the lack of agreement in

> *Considering* all the circumstances, *he* has kept remarkably cheerful.

even though it is obvious that *he* was not doing the *considering*. The opening phrase is capable of standing on its own as a prepositional phrase (like *In view of all the circumstances* . . .); it is not acting as a modifier, and needs no attachment to a noun. Compare

> After considering his position, he decided to resign.

where *considering* is used adjectivally and obeys the rule that a modifier must relate clearly to a noun/pronoun.

Other -ing words that have attained prepositional status are illustrated in

> *Owing* to heavy seas, the race was cancelled.
> *Talking* of football, what did you think of last night's match?
> *Assuming* (that) all goes well, the car should be repaired tomorrow.

The prepositional phrases are independent, and there is no need to ensure that the following noun in the main clause relates to them, as would be necessary if they were adjectival.

Other words often used in this way include *supposing, concerning, regarding, seeing (that), provided/providing that, failing that/*

this, and a few infinitive phrases (*To cut a long story short*; *to summarise*; *to tell the truth*).

The participle *following* is not regarded as a preposition and should be used as an adjectival modifier, properly related:

> Following their band, the Scouts marched smartly by.

Its loose use may have a comic effect:

> Following a police hunt, a man was arrested.

and *after*, *at the end of*, *as a result of* are safer alternatives (unless, of course, the man *was* arrested while following a police hunt).

(*h*) Subordinate clauses must be clearly related to the words they modify.

> The tanks on the battlefield which had been destroyed by accurate firing impeded the advance of reinforcements.

It is likely that it was *tanks* rather than *battlefield* which had been destroyed, and the subordinate clause should be repositioned accordingly:

> On the battlefield, the tanks which had been destroyed . . .

Note the important difference between

> The field where they used to play has been dug up.
> The field has been dug up where they used to play.

(*i*) Subordinate clauses are sometimes shortened by the omission of their subjects.

> Although often unreliable, the bus service is valued by people in the village.

This is short for

> Although it is often unreliable, the bus service is valued by people in the village.

Such omission is in order when the omitted subject in the subordinate clause corresponds to the stated subject in the main clause. Confusion may be caused if such correspondence is not observed:

> Although often unreliable, people in the village value the bus service.

Modifiers: single words

4.4 (*a*) *Only* should be placed immediately before the word it is intended to modify.

> I only saw her yesterday.

means, strictly speaking, that *I only saw*, i.e. I did not converse or do anything else, whereas the intended meaning is probably

> I saw her only yesterday.

i.e. as recently as yesterday. Often the positioning of *only* makes little or no difference to the sense, but there are times when careless positioning causes ambiguity.

> Her condition can only be helped if she goes into a nursing home.

means that her condition can *only be helped*, not cured.

> Her condition can be helped only if she goes into a nursing home.

means something different: *helped* is not restricted, and the implication is that cure is not ruled out.

> Only he may unlock the safe. (and no-one else)
> He may only unlock the safe. (and do nothing else, such as remove the
>   contents)
> He may unlock only the safe. (and nothing else that needs unlocking)

(*b*) Similar care is required with *even*:

> Even he could not find the hammer. (let alone anyone else)
> He could not even find the hammer. (let alone do anything with it)
> He could not find even the hammer. (let alone any other tool)

The word should be placed in front of the word(s) to be emphasised or contrasted.

(*c*) Other words whose positioning may be crucial include *just, ever, quite, mainly, often, rarely, also, hardly, scarcely, barely, nearly, almost, such as*.

> He almost passed without noticing me. (but he did not pass)
> He passed almost without noticing me. (he did pass)
> Mountaineers who injure themselves often have to pay higher in-
>   surance premiums. (ambiguous)
> Mountaineers who often injure themselves have to pay higher in-
>   surance premiums. (clear)
> Mountaineers who injure themselves have often to pay higher in-
>   surance premiums. (clear)

The sentence

> Some countries have exceptionally high mountain ranges, such as
>   Nepal.

makes sense to someone who knows that Nepal is not the name of a high mountain range. The rule of proximity requires

> Some countries, such as Nepal, have exceptionally high mountain
>   ranges.

(*d*) *Not only . . . but (also)* . . . should be followed by grammatically equivalent sentence components.

> The reorganisation entailed hard work not only *by the secretarial staff* but also *by senior executives*.

is correct, but

> The reorganisation entailed not only *hard work by the secretarial staff* but also *senior executives*.

is loose because the italicised phrases are not parallel: the first consists of *noun + prepositional phrase*, the second does not.

> The war resulted not only in the Treaty of Versailles, but also the rebirth of German militarism can be traced to the resentment caused by the Treaty.

should be

> The war resulted not only *in the Treaty of Versailles* but also *in the rebirth of German militarism*, which can be traced to . . .

(*e*) In an expression introduced by *either . . . or* . . . and *neither . . . nor* . . ., the two halves must balance each other (e.g. two phrases, two infinitives, two clauses) as parallel constructions.

> Incorrect: We shall either *call tomorrow* or *the day after*.

The true alternatives are *tomorrow* and *the day after*, and *call* belongs to both; it should therefore be placed outside the *either . . . or* . . . construction.

> Correct: We shall call either *tomorrow* or *the day after*.

Any words preceding *either* and *neither* apply equally to the words after *either* and *neither* and to the words after *or* and *nor*. The alternatives must correlate.

> Incorrect: He has neither *written* nor *has he telephoned*.
> Correct: He has neither *written* nor telephoned.

(*f*) If carelessly used, *more* and *less* may lead to ambiguity.

> The hospital is having to deal with more serious casualties.

may mean *more casualties that are serious* or *casualties that are more serious*.

> This year's programme contains less modern music.

may mean *less music that is modern* or *music that is less modern*.

> Girls like maths more than boys.

may be true, but what is meant is probably

> Girls like maths more than boys do.

(g) The adjective *unlike* is used correctly in

> Unlike me, he enjoys housework.

and incorrectly in

> Unlike France and Scotland, central control of the sport does not exist in England.

Here, *France and Scotland* are contrasted with *central control* (the opening adjectival phrase attaching to the nearest noun) whereas the intended contrast is between *France and Scotland* and *England*.

> Unlike France or Scotland, England does not have any centralised system for controlling the sport.

There must be similar care with *like*.

> *Like most people*, I prefer peaceful methods of solving problems.

correctly places the adjectival modifier next to the word it belongs to. This is not so in

> Like most people, peaceful methods of solving problems appeal to me.
> Like most people, it seems to me that . . .

(h) Both *owing to* and *because of* may be used to introduce independent or 'absolute' phrases which do not need to be grammatically related to any adjacent word. The same is not true of *due to*, which is adjectival and needs a noun/pronoun to modify.

Correct:	The accident was due to carelessness.
	Due to carelessness, an accident occurred.
Incorrect:	Due to carelessness, he suffered an accident.
	The river burst its banks due to heavy rain.

These last two sentences, taken literally, mean that *he* was due to *carelessness* and that the *banks* were due to *heavy rain*. It is necessary for *due to* to link two nouns, or their equivalents, when one is *due to* or *caused by* the other. In fact, *due to* is only correct if it can be replaced by *caused by*.

Safe alternatives to *due to* exist in the multi-purpose *owing to* and *because of*, which are not restricted to adjectival use as *due to* is. Sentences with *due to*, especially at the beginning, are often found to be wrongly constructed.

(i) Many verbs are often used with a particular preposition or adverb, e.g. *look in, come on, set up, leave out, open up, peg away, put down, hang back, throw away, pull through*. These are usually called **phrasal verbs**. Sometimes the two words cannot be separated (e.g. *give in* meaning *surrender*; *hold with* meaning *agree*) but if the parts of a phrasal verb are separated, the separation should be brief.

> *Take* the cork *out*. *Cut* the vegetables *up*.

are acceptable, but

> *Take* the clothes we shall need for the night *out*.
> *Cut* the vegetables that are to be heated *up*.

are clumsy (and ambiguous):

> Take out the clothes we shall need for the night.
> Cut up the vegetables that are to be heated.

As is so often the case in English, words that go together should be placed together.

(*j*) Though an adverb generally modifies a verb, adjective or other adverb, some adverbs may be used absolutely.

> They have obviously got lost.

does not mean that they have got lost in an obvious manner, but

> *It is obvious* that they have got lost.

Adverbs that may be used in this way include *clearly, presumably, understandably, (un)fortunately, regrettably, luckily* and *apparently*. Thus

> Regrettably, he does not know the answer.

means

> It is regrettable that he does not know the answer.

In other words, the adverb, *regrettably* is not performing its usual job of enlarging the meaning of the verb (*know*); it is commenting on the entire main clause.

The recent importation of *hopefully*, in the sense of *it is hoped*, has led to its widespread adoption in this absolute sense:

> Hopefully, he died instantaneously.

Careful writers avoid this use, partly because it is unnecessary, partly because it is fashionable, mainly because it is confusing to have the same word meaning *it is hoped* and *in a hopeful fashion*, the traditional meaning. The word is best reserved for this sense:

> They began digging hopefully.

Thankfully and *regretfully* are increasingly used in the same way as *hopefully*, with the meaning of *it is a matter for thankfulness/regret*. It is advisable to avoid this use of *thankfully*, which is subject to the same objections as *hopefully*. The use of *regretfully* to mean *it is a matter for regret* is indefensible because *regrettably* already has this meaning.

(*k*) Most monosyllabic adjectives and adverbs can take the endings

-er and *-est* to denote higher degrees of their qualities. The difference between *great/greater/greatest* is that *greater* indicates a higher degree of the quality of being *great*, and *greatest* indicates the highest degree. The *-er* form is called the **comparative** and the *-est* form the **superlative**. Longer adjectives and adverbs, including most of three or more syllables, form the comparative and superlative by having *more* and *most* placed before them. Some words have two comparative forms (*lovelier, more lovely*) and two superlative ones (*loveliest, most lovely*). A few words have irregular comparatives and superlatives (*good, better, best; bad, worse, worst; much/many more, most* etc.). In theory, adjectives and adverbs expressing absolute qualities cannot have degrees of comparison (e.g. *infinite, unique, absolutely, entirely*), though in practice many of them are used with *more* and *most*, sometimes at the risk of absurdity:

> The white whale is the most immortal of all its species.

(where the intended sense is *most long-lived*).

The comparative form is used when two people or things are compared, and the superlative when more than two are compared: *the better of the two, the best of the three, the lesser of two evils, the least of all our problems*.

The double comparative or superlative is illiterate: *more pleasanter, most latest*.

Care should be taken not to compare something with the class it belongs to:

> Nuclear weapons are more destructive than any weapons of war.

implies that nuclear weapons are not a weapon of war, or that nuclear weapons are more destructive than themselves.

> Nuclear weapons are more destructive than *any other weapons of war*.

correctly excludes *nuclear weapons* from the category they are being compared to.

(*l*) Two negative modifiers cancel each other out.

> I don't want none of that. I don't know nothing about it.

although typical of some colloquial expressions, have the logical sense

> I do want some of that. I do know something about it.

If the first part of a sentence is in the negative, it may have a carry-over effect which is the opposite of that intended.

> No repairs will be possible while the floods last, but will be started as soon as the water level returns to normal.

The grammatical subject of *will be started* is *No repairs.*

> It isn't a matter of hoping that your reader will catch your drift, but of ensuring that he does.

is probably clear, but the logical construction is

> It is a matter *not of* hoping . . . *but of* ensuring . . .

Double negatives such as *not unlike* and *no little* have a shade of meaning or tone that *like* and *great* do not have, but over-use of this device can become tiresome. It should not be used unless there is an identifiable nuance, or if the understatement has some other purpose.

Sentences with several negatives or words with a negative meaning place unnecessary demands on the reader.

Verbs

4.5 (*a*) Some verb forms ending in *-ing* may be used in what are called absolute constructions.

> *The strikers having decided to return to work*, the dispute was officially ended.
> *The strike being over*, the men were reinstated.

The italicised phrases are not adjectival modifiers requiring clear attachment to a noun/pronoun outside the phrase (as described at **4.3**(*c*) on page 48 and **4.3**(*d*) on page 49). The participles clearly belong to nouns within the phrases: *having decided* attaches to *strikers*, and *being over* goes with *strike*. The phrases themselves stand on their own with the force of clauses meaning

> Because the strikers had decided to return to work . . .
> As the strike was over . . .

There is an important difference between such constructions and the following ones:

> The strikers, having decided to return to work, now hope for fresh negotiations.
> The strike, being over, should be forgotten as soon as possible.

where the phrases, placed parenthetically between commas, are adjectival modifiers correctly related to the nearest nouns, which are the subjects of the main verbs *hope* and *should be forgotten*.

A comma is usually needed before or after an absolute construction, but not before *and* after:

> The pitch being waterlogged, the match was abandoned. (*correct*)
> The pitch, being waterlogged, the match was abandoned. (*incorrect*)

The pitch, being waterlogged, was impossible to play on. (*correct – adjectival modifier*)

The match was abandoned, the pitch being waterlogged. (*correct*)

(*b*) A verb often consists of more than one word:

I have taken; I should have taken; I will take; I am taking

These compounds consist of:

(i) *auxiliary verbs* – the different parts of *be*, *do*, *have*, *may*, *will*, *shall*, *can*, *must* – which help to form tenses, negative forms, interrogatives and other verb-forms;

(ii) the verb that expresses the main action (*take* in the above examples). This has a different form depending on the auxiliary: are *taking*, had *taken*, should *take*.

In a construction such as

I can and will do it.

two auxiliaries with different senses (*can*, *will*) are applied to the same verb (*do*). The sentence is short for

I *can do* it and I *will do* it.

This is correct when the different auxiliaries require the same form of the main verb, as they do here (both *can* and *will* require the form *do*). However, in

I can and often have repaired it myself.

the auxiliary *have* is correctly followed by *repaired*, but the auxiliary *can* requires *repair* (we say *I can repair it*, not *I can repaired it*). The sentence is incorrect because *can* does not agree with the only main verb in the sentence, *repaired*. It is necessary to rewrite

I can repair it, and often have repaired it, myself.

so that both auxiliaries are correctly equipped with the appropriate form of the main verb *repair*.

He always has and always will be stubborn.

Here, *will be* is correct, but *has* . . . *be* is not; *has* requires *been* and cannot be left incomplete:

He always *has been* stubborn, and (he) always *will be* (stubborn).

A final example:

Incorrect: This has not and must not deter us.

Correct: This has not deterred and must not deter us.

When two auxiliaries are linked to the same verb, each of the auxiliaries must agree with that verb.

(*c*) Some verb forms ending in -*ing* may be used as nouns.

Smoking is bad for your health.

has a verbal noun acting as the subject of the sentence.

> *Smoking cigarettes* is particularly harmful.

has the same verbal noun demonstrating its verbal ability to have a direct object, *cigarettes*, while itself forming part of a phrase which is a subject.

When such a verbal noun has a modifier, the modifier should be in the possessive (i.e. adjectival) form:

> Please excuse *my* mentioning it.
> She didn't approve of *his* staying up late.

Instead, it is common to find the direct object form:

> Please excuse *me* mentioning it.
> She didn't approve of *him* staying up late.

even though the direct object of *excuse* is *mentioning*, and what is disapproved of is not *him* but the *staying up late*. There is no alternative with *that*, which has no possessive form:

> There is no chance of that (*not* that's) happening.

This common practice of not using the possessive form before verbal nouns may cause ambiguity:

> For education authorities, who have to foot the bill, difficulties are caused by students living at universities a long way from home.

This implies that it is students who cause difficulties; the intended meaning is that their living at universities does. The problem is solved by using the possessive *students'* (as the possessive *their* was used in the previous sentence), or by avoiding the *-ing* form:

> . . . difficulties are caused by the costs of students who . . .

The dropping of the possessive form has long been common in speech, and is rapidly becoming (or has already become) acceptable in writing, though many people still find it loose if not incorrect. Its retention, especially with pronouns and people's names, is recommended in formal writing.

(*d*) To express the future tense, *will* is used in all cases except for *I shall*, *we shall*.

> They will be home before we are.

but

> I shall be fifty next birthday.

These are statements, or rather predictions, of what is to happen in the future.

To express intention, determination, will, obligation or strong wish, *shall* is used in all cases except *I will*, *we will*.

You shall (i.e. must) do no such thing.

but

We will not sell it.

These are expressions of determination.

In practice, this distinction (which never applied to English as used in Scotland, Ireland or America) has become blurred, with the assistance of the contraction *'ll* which is used for both *will* and *shall* in all their meanings except *shall not* (shan't) and *will not* (won't). Though there are occasions when a useful distinction may be drawn between a statement of what is to happen in the future and an expression of determination, there are more occasions when no such distinction is possible:

I shall see you on Friday. (plain future)

and

I will see you on Friday. (determination, intention)

mean the same to most people, and are bound to if expressed as

I'll see you on Friday.

as both of them may be.

It is now common to find *will* used indiscriminately, with all pronouns and nouns, to express both futurity and intention, while *shall* persists only in questions:

Shall I draw the curtains? Shall we go for a walk?

(Even here, *shall* is not used to ask a question about the future but about the present wishes of the person addressed.)

With this exception, it is now safe to use *will* for all the purposes for which *shall* has traditionally been reserved, as described at the beginning of this paragraph. The careful writer should still use *I/we shall* to express the future tense, however. He may find other occasions when the traditional *will/shall* distinction is worth observing in the interests of clarity, but he may equally find that few readers will appreciate his subtlety.

(*e*) It is normal to use *should/would* to express futurity from the standpoint of the past:

He felt (*in the past*) that his bid would succeed (*at some later time*).

Conventionally, *would* is used with all persons except *I/we should*; this usage is parallel to that of *will/shall* expressing the future tense. However, *would* seems likely to displace *should* in this sense, if it has not already done so.

To express obligation, *should* is invariable with all persons as a weaker alternative to *ought to*:

I should have known better. *He should* lose weight.

Note the difference between

> He wondered whether he would arrive before tea-time. (future in the past)
> He wondered whether he should arrive before tea-time. (= ought to)

In clauses beginning with *that*, after verbs expressing surprise or wish, *should* is used:

> I regret that he should misunderstand me.
> His intention is that the wall should be demolished.

though alternatives are possible if these sound too formal:

> I regret that he misunderstands/misunderstood me.
> His intention is to have the wall demolished.

Clauses beginning with *if* often have *should*:

> If you should phone him, tell him I'll be in touch.

though simpler forms are often preferred:

> If you phone him . . .

Would is used to express determination

> He said he wouldn't make the same mistake twice.
> I wouldn't spend that much on a holiday.

habitual action

> He would always read before going to sleep.

or willingness

> If I had time I would do it myself.

Requests or suggestions sound politer if expressed with *should/would*:

> I should say/think that . . . (instead of *I say/think that* . . .)
> Would you please . . . (instead of *Will you* . . .)

In such cases, *should* is used with *I/we*, and *would* with other persons:

> *I should* be grateful if *you would* . . .

is preferable to the more imperious

> I shall be grateful if you will . . .

(*f*) The infinitive has four forms:

present   – to thank, to see
past   – to have thanked, to have seen
continuous   – to be thanking (present), to have been thanking (past), to be seeing (present), to have been seeing (past)

passive   – to be thanked (present), to have been thanked (past), to be seen (present), to have been seen (past)

The present infinitive, including the continuous present and the passive present, is used to indicate an action that takes place at the same time as or later than the action of the preceding finite verb:

> I want (*now*) to thank (*now*) . . .
> I wanted (*then*) to thank (*then*) . . .
> I had wanted (*then*) to see (*later than then*) . . .
> I should like (*now*) to see (*in the future*) . . .
> I should have liked (*in the past*) to see (*later than then*) . . .

Use of the past tense often attracts a subsequent infinitive into the past tense automatically:

> Incorrect: I should have liked *to have seen* . . .
> They would have liked *to have thanked* . . .

This error normally occurs because past tenses formed with *have* appear to need a following infinitive formed with *have*. This is not so.

The past infinitive, including the continuous and passive past, is used to refer to an action that takes place *before* the action expressed by the preceding finite verb:

> I should like (*now*) to have thanked (*in the past*) . . .
> I seem (*now*) to have been tricked (*in the past*) . . .
> I seemed (*in the past*) to have been tricked (*further in the past*) . . .
> They believed him (*in the past*) to have gone abroad (*further in the past*)

but

> They believed him (*in the past*) to be abroad (*at that time in the past*: see above)

(g) There is no 'rule' forbidding the split infinitive, i.e. the placing of an adverb or adverbial phrase between *to* and the verb, as in *to completely destroy*.

Splitting may produce a clumsy effect, but to avoid splitting – for fear of appearing ignorant of the 'rule – may also produce clumsiness:

> The jury took five hours to convict unanimously the defendant.

Ambiguity may result from an attempt to avoid splitting an infinitive:

> It is not easy always to keep one's temper.

where the adverb *always* may look back to *is not easy* or forward to *to keep*, producing different meanings. In these cases, split infinitives would be both clear and natural:

> The jury took five hours to convict unanimously the defendant.
>
> It is not easy to always keep one's temper.

The safest rule is to avoid splitting the infinitive with a lengthy adverbial phrase, but to split if the alternative is awkwardness or ambiguity. It will usually be found that clarity and naturalness may be achieved without splitting – and the 'rule' is still sufficiently believed in to justify attempts to satisfy its adherents.

(*h*) The auxiliary verb *may* expresses uncertainty, possibility or probability

> That may be true.

or permission

> You may take it away.

Though it is a present tense, *may* sometimes refers to the future

> It may be ready tomorrow.

The past tense is *might*

> He was worried that he might appear uncooperative.

but it does not always refer to past time: it can denote a greater degree of doubt, a more distant possibility or a greater diffidence than *may*.

It is also possible to use *may* to express a wish

> May all your troubles be little ones.

and *might* to express a request

> You might let me know what you think.

or complaint

> You might have warned me.

There is a difference between *may* and *can*, though the words are often interchanged in speech. *Can* means *have the ability or power*. Thus

> Can I help?

means

> Do I have abilities which are helpful in what you are doing?

and

> May I help?

simply asks permission to help. The distinction is helpful and worth preserving, though it is in danger of vanishing.

The past tense of *can* is *could*, but it does not always express past time. Like *might*, it is used to express more uncertainty. Compared with *I can help*, *I could help* implies that some condition, reservation or refusal will follow (e.g. *if I understood the problem*).

Conjunctions

4.6   Conjunctions that link two words, two phrases or two clauses are **coordinating** conjunctions:

> Tom *and* Jerry; firmly *but* politely; you *or* I
> Marching into heavy firing *yet* never faltering . . .
> They ran into the street *and* (they) showed their defiance.

Conjunctions that link subordinate clauses to main clauses are **subordinating** conjunctions. These include conjunctions that indicate time (*when, while, before*), reason (*because, why*), purpose (*so, that*), comparison (*than*) and conditions or supposition (*although, if, unless*).

(*a*)   Coordinating conjunctions must link grammatical equivalents. In combinations such as *both . . . and* and *between . . . and*, the words that follow *and* must balance those that follow *both* or *between*.

> He was both successful at golf and cricket.

is incorrect because *both* is followed by an adjectival phrase and *and* by a noun. Nothing between *both . . . and* can be 'understood' after *and*. The correct versions are

> He was successful / both *at golf* and *at cricket*.
> He was successful at / both *golf* and *cricket*.
> He was / both *successful at golf* and *accomplished at cricket*.

This rule not only makes for tight and logical construction; it also helps to avoid ambiguity.

> The child was spoiled by both his relations and by his parents.

is correct only if the child has just two relations.

There must be a similarly exact correspondence in both halves of constructions introduced by *either . . . or . . .* and *neither . . . nor . . .* (see **4.4**(*e*) on page 53) and *not only . . . but also . . .* (see **4.4**(*d*) on page 53).

(*b*)   As a subordinating conjunction, *while* expresses time:

> He learned Italian while he was in hospital.

It is sometimes used to express condition, as an alternative to *even though* or *although*:

> While I agreed at the time, I now wish I hadn't.

There is a danger of ambiguity in this usage:

> While he was under pressure, he shouldn't have thrown the typewriter
> out of the window.

The reader is kept in two minds until he reaches the main clause: is *while* intended to mean *although* or *during the time when*? Almost certainly the former, though the fastidious reader will enjoy the implications of the latter.

While is sometimes found as a coordinating conjunction equivalent to *and*:

> He likes a quite life while his wife prefers to be more active.

Again ambiguity or absurdity is possible:

> My wife mixed the cement while I spread it on the wall.

These uses of *while* in place of *although* and *and* are idiomatic, but avoidable and unnecessary. In view of the strong temporal associations of *while*, it should not be used in these other senses without care.

(c) The construction *conjunction* (e.g. *and, but*) + *relative pronoun* (*who*, *whom*, *whose*, *which*, *that*) + *subordinate clause* should be used only when there is a preceding construction consisting of *relative pronoun* + *subordinate clause*.

> Correct: He has written a book *which* is full of excellent advice
>   *and which* deserves to be widely read.
> Incorrect: He has written a book full of excellent advice *and*
>   *which* deserves to be widely read.

because the *and which* clause is not balanced by and linked to a preceding *which* clause.

> He was a thinker much respected in parliament but who was little
> known by the public.

should have *who was much respected* . . . as a balancing clause (or *but little known* . . . as a balancing phrase).

> The club, without a win since the beginning of the season, and which
> has recently been losing money, will have to sell some players.

needs *which has been without a win* . . . so that *and which has recently* . . . is properly coordinated (see **4.6** and **4.6**(*a*) above), or should be reworded:

> The club, without a win . . . , has recently . . . *and* will have . . .

so that the subordinate clause, previously uncoordinated, is eliminated; the sentence now consists of *main clause* (subject word *club* + modifier + verb) + *coordinating conjunction* (and) + *parallel main clause* (subject understood + verb *will have*).

There is no need for the relative pronouns (*who* and *which* in the above examples) to be identical:

> The townsfolk *whose* houses were destroyed *and who* needed immediate evacuation were accommodated in a local school.

What matters is that there should be two relative pronouns introducing two subordinate clauses if they are to be linked by a coordinating conjunction.

(*d*) After *the same*, use *as* (not *that* or *which*) before a clause. *Same . . . as* indicates a comparison.

> Correct: I still use *the same* car *as* I bought five years ago.
>   I still use the car that I bought five years ago. (same meaning: different construction)
> Incorrect: I still use *the same* car *which* I bought five years ago.

(*e*) Adjectival phrases beginning *as* must follow the normal rules for modifiers.

> *As a painter*, *nothing* was more important to him than the quality of light.

should be either

> Nothing was more important to *him*, *as a painter*, than the quality of light.

or

> *As a painter*, *he* found that nothing was more important . . .

There is a difference between

> Do you see him as often as me?
> Do you see him as often as I?

In the first, *me* (object form) is parallel with *him* as the object of *see*, and the meaning is therefore

> Do you see him as often as (you see) me?

In the second, *I* (subject form) is parallel with *you*, the subject of *see*, and the meaning is

> Do you see him as often as I (see him)?

The ambiguity in

> He hates television as much as his wife.

must be resolved by

> He hates television as much as his wife does.

or, if need be,

> He hates television as much as he hates his wife.

Before a clause, *as* is often used as a conjunction-cum-relative pronoun:

> He was embarrassed, as you could see from the way he talked.

Here, *as* means *and this* or *which fact*, the antecedent of the pronouns *this* or *which* being the main clause in general. In such contexts, *as* (not *which*) is correct:

> History repeats itself, *as* has been frequently demonstrated.

In phrases including *as . . . as* (e.g. *as much as*, *as many as*), the second *as* must not be mistakenly replaced:

> Incorrect: There were twice as many casualties last year *than* in the year before.

Care must be taken when saying that something is *as good as*, *if not better than* something else. The first part of this expression – and similar ones – is sometimes left incomplete:

> Petrol is as cheap if not cheaper *than* it was last year.

The *as . . . as* construction must be finished off, not left in the air or converted into an unidiomatic *as . . . than*:

> Petrol is *as* cheap *as*, if not cheaper *than*, it was last year.

or the less formal, but correct

> Petrol is *as* cheap *as* it was last year, if not cheaper.

The initial *as . . . as* comparison should be completed before a modifying phrase (*if not*) is introduced.

(*f*) Traditionally, *like* has not been accepted as a conjunction, capable of being followed by a clause, and *as* (which may be used as a conjunction) has been regarded as the correct alternative:

> Incorrect: He thinks like I do.
> Correct: He thinks as I do.

However, *like* is often used as a conjunction in colloquial speech:

> The new publican is popular, like the previous one was.

Even so, it is still best to avoid the use of *like* before a finite verb, and to write *as if* instead of *like* in

> She looked like she'd seen a ghost.
> It looks like it's going to be fine tomorrow.

In time, such usage may become generally accepted, partly through the pressure of American English which sees nothing wrong in

> He walked in like he owned the place.

and partly through the bother of having to remember that

> Cut it like this.

is right because *like* is used as a preposition but

Cut it like I showed you.

is wrong because *like* is used as a conjunction. For the moment, a handy rule is to use *like* only before single words or phrases, not before finite verbs (i.e. clauses). In this way, its use as a conjunction will largely be avoided.

It is perfectly safe to use *like* as a preposition

I wish I had a garden like this.

as long as the rule of proximity is observed when a prepositional phrase beginning with *like* is used as a modifier:

Incorrect: Like the previous boss, the job proved too much for him.

Correct: Like the previous boss, he found the job too much for him.

(*g*) There is no rule that a sentence may never begin with *And* or *But*. Special emphasis may be added by using conjunctions in this way, but such emphasis will be weakened by over-use.

A sentence beginning with *And* should introduce a new idea, and not just be an extension of the previous sentence. In other words, an initial *And* must have a more emphatic function than its usual linking one.

The journalistic habit of omitting the subject in sentences beginning with *And* has no place in formal writing:

She has just bought a new house. And decorated it herself.

(*h*) As a conjunction, *than* is most frequently used to introduce the second element in a comparison:

Blood is thicker than water.

When *than* is followed by a pronoun, problems may occur. *He is taller than I am* is correct. *He is taller than I* is correct but a little artificial. *He is taller than me* (where *than* is a preposition followed by the object form) was formerly shunned but is now acceptable. However

He likes her more than me.

means

He likes her more than (he likes) me.

and if the required meaning is

He likes her more than I do.

the sentence must be stated in that form.

One must always say *than whom*, not *than who*, if it is necessary to say it at all.

Note the plural verb after *than* in

More deer are killed than are allowed to live to breed.

and the singular verb in

More children were born than was expected.

which is short for *than (it) was expected (there would be born)*.

More children were born than were expected.

means that some mothers did not know they were expectant.

5

Common Errors

ain't is a dialect word and should have no place in correct speech or writing.

alright should be *all right*.

also is not a conjunction. Add or substitute *and* in *I left my umbrella, also my coat* and in similar expressions when **also** is used to introduce additional information.

alternative used to be applied to one of only two possibilities; it is no longer so limited. It does imply choice, however, and it is illogical, though common, to use it when no genuine choice is implied (*There is no other alternative*) or when *other* would be correct (*When North Sea oil runs out, we shall need an alternative supply*).

any *Soccer is more popular than any sport in the country* is wrong because *any sport* includes soccer, which cannot be more popular than itself. Say *any other sport*.

aren't I? is colloquial, and *am I not* (as in *Am I not right to say . . . ?*) should be used in writing.

as how should be *that* in *I can't say as how I agree*, or simply *how* in *He didn't see as how he could help*.

as if should be used instead of *like* in such expressions as *It looks like it's going to rain* and *It seemed like he would never stop talking*.

This use of *like* is an Americanism which is regarded as incorrect in British English.

averse, aversion must be followed by *from*, it is sometimes argued, because *from* has the sense of *away from* which is appropriate to words expressing dislike. But *averse from* is so rare as to sound unnatural; *averse to*, and *aversion to* or *for*, are normal.

barely   see **hardly**.

between   There used to be a 'rule' that **between** referred to two and *among* to more than two. This distinction is no longer observed.

between . . . and, not *between . . . or*. One may choose meat *or* fish, or between meat *and* fish, but not between meat or fish.
   In long sentences there is sometimes a temptation to write *between . . . and between* (*There is a difference between Wordsworth's view of nature, which . . . and which . . . , and between that of Keats . . .*). This is incorrect.

between each (other) is to be avoided in such contexts as *Leave a space between each paragraph / each of the paragraphs*. Because *each* is singular, and logically 'something' cannot be between one, it is safer to write *between each paragraph and the next* or *between (the) paragraphs*.

between you and I should always be *between you and me*.

blame means *find fault with* (*He blamed me for it*). The common *He blamed it on me* is loose.

bored with or **by**, not *of*.

both should not be used of more than two people or things.
| Correct: | *The journey was both long and difficult.* |
| Incorrect: | *The journey was both long, difficult and expensive.* |

broadcasted, forecasted appear in dictionaries, but *broadcast* and *forecast* are much more common as past tenses.

but, as a preposition, is normally followed by the object-form of a pronoun (*everyone but me*) but there can be no objection to using the subject-form if what immediately follows is the verb of which the pronoun appears to be the subject (*Everyone but she arrived on time*). *Everyone but her* is actually the subject, but usage permits *she* because *her arrived* sounds odd.

As a conjunction, *but* introduces a contrasting statement, and should not be used when there is no contrast.

can denotes ability (*Can you come tomorrow? Can you play the piano?*); **may** denotes permission (*May I come in?*) or possibility (*I may go away for the weekend*). In speech, **can** is often used instead of **may** (*Can I go out tonight?* is a request for permission, not an enquiry about one's physical ability), but the correct distinction between the two words is worth preserving.

can't seem, as in *I can't seem to get it right*, is meaningless. Say *I seem unable to get it right* or, more directly, *I can't get it right*.

centre round is bad English. A discussion may *centre in* or *on* a subject, or *revolve around* it, but not *centre round* it.

circumstances. As the prefix *circum-* means *around* (circumference, circumscribe, circumvent), there is an argument that *in the circumstances* is correct, *under the circumstances* incorrect, because you are in, not under, whatever surrounds you. Only purists now press the argument, and *under the circumstances* is established, perhaps implying slightly greater pressure than *in the circumstances*.

class   see **kind**.

compare to means *liken to*; **compare with** means *estimate similarities or differences*.

In the sense of *bear comparison with*, the correct form is always *compare with* (*This meal doesn't compare with the one we had last time we came here*).

Comparable to and *comparable with* should be similarly distinguished.

comprise of is incorrect; the *of* is superfluous. (*The symphony comprises four movements* or . . . *consists of / is composed of / has four movements*).

different from, not *different than* or *different to*.

doubt that is correct in negative sentences (*I don't doubt that the decision is wrong*), and **doubt whether** in positive ones (*I doubt whether the figures are accurate*).

each other   It used to be thought correct to restrict **each other** to references to only two people or things, and to use **one another** for more than two. The terms are now used interchangeably.

each other's is never punctuated *each others'*.

easy is not an adverb except in a few idiomatic expressions (*go easy, easy does it, take it easy, stand easy, easy come easy go, easy-going*). In other cases (*I can get there easy in five minutes*) use **easily** as the adverb.

e.g. means *for example*, and should not be confused with **i.e.** (*that is to say*) which introduces a rephrasing or clarification of the previous statement.

either of means *one or the other of two* and should not be used when more than two people or things are referred to.

Correct:	*I didn't see either of the two.*
Incorrect:	*I didn't see either of the three.*
Correct:	*I didn't see any of the three.*

Either of must be followed by a single verb: *Either of the two is suitable*.

equally as is an example of duplication of meaning.

Incorrect:	*He is equally as successful as his brother.*
Correct:	*He is as successful as his brother.*
	He and his brother are equally successful.
	(or *He is just as successful as his brother.*)
Incorrect:	*He is equally to blame as his brother.*
Correct:	*He and his brother are equally to blame.*
	He is (just) as much to blame as his brother.

Equally and **as** have the same meaning. Use one or the other, not both. If **equally** is used, never add **as**.

essential deserves to be regarded as an absolute, having no degrees:

either something is essential or it is not. If words like *fairly*, *rather*, *very*, etc. fit the required sense, it is better to use *important*, *useful* etc.

etc. means *and other things*, and should not be applied to people. It should be spelt with a full stop; there is no need to add a second full stop if *etc.* occurs at the end of a sentence. *And etc.* is incorrect.

Use *etc.* only when there is no doubt about what it refers to. It is a common fault to use it as a lazy substitute for clear or specific statement.

ever is used as an emphatic adverb (meaning *possibly*) after the interrogative *how? what? when? where? who?* (*How ever did it happen? What ever can it mean?*). It usually comes immediately after the interrogative, but not necessarily (*How did it ever happen?*)

Confusion is possible because *ever* is also used as part of *however, whatever, whenever, wherever, whichever* and *whoever*. These words have a less definite sense than *how, what, when* etc. on their own. (*He comes whenever he can* has a more general sense than *He comes when he can*.)

There is therefore a difference between *how ever / however*, *what ever / whatever* etc. If *ever* is capable of repositioning (*How ever did it happen? How did it ever happen? When ever did he say that?*) it is used, and must be written, as a separate word.

fed up (slang) is followed by *with*, not *of*.

fewer is applied to number (i.e. to what is counted); *less* is applied to quantity (i.e. to what is measured).

Incorrect: *The falling birthrate means we shall need less teachers.*
Correct: *The introduction of seat-belts has led to fewer accidents.*

The common error is to use *less* where **fewer** is needed.

first two, **first three**, etc., as in *the first two chapters*, is better sense than *the two first*, etc.

forever is the American spelling; the English is **for ever**. The American version is harmless enough, but it is unnecessary. *Forever and ever* is ungrammatical.

former, **latter** must be applied only to one of *two* people or things.

The terms are often used loosely, in a way that sends the reader back to the preceding sentence to work out what they refer to. This discourtesy may be prevented by rephrasing to avoid their use.

In *She decided to clear out the attic. The latter was filled with junk*, **latter** is not applied to one of two, and must be replaced by *This* or . . . , *which*.

If it is necessary to refer to the first or last item in a list of more than two, use *first mentioned* or *last mentioned*.

Better, rephrase to avoid such cumbersome terms.

guess does not mean *think*, and there is no good reason for adopting the American *I guess I'll go to bed* unless guesswork is needed.

hardly should be followed by *when*, not *than*, when the sense is *no sooner . . . than* (*The game had hardly begun when the fog descended*).

Hardly has a negative meaning and needs no other negative: *I couldn't hardly believe it* is wrong. Say *I could hardly believe it* (or *I couldn't believe it*). The same is true of **barely**.

how is sometimes used instead of *that* unnecessarily and ambiguously. *They told the press how they had been held captive for several days* is acceptable if they explained *in what way* they had been held. If *how* means *that*, use *that*.

however should be **how ever** when the meaning is interrogative (*How ever did that happen?*). See **ever**.

if may be used to mean *whether* (*Ask them if they mind*), but ambiguity may result. *Please let me know if you would like to come* may mean that the writer wants a reply whether or not the invitation is to be accepted, or that he wants a reply only if the invitation finds favour. *If you would like to come, please let me know* is unambiguous: it requires an answer only under a certain condition.

It is safe to use *if* to introduce a condition, and *whether* to introduce an indirect question. *Please let me know whether you would like to come* implies that an answer is expected *whether or not* the invitation is to be accepted.

in order that should be followed by *may* or *might*.

> Incorrect:　. . . *in order that the roof would not leak.*
> 　　　　　　　. . . *in order that they could finish early.*

The less formal *so that* has no similar restriction.

into is a preposition (*The car ran into the wall*), but **in to** is correct when *in* is an adverb and *to* a preposition. (*Take the tray in to her*) or *to* is part of an infinitive. (*They went in to ask about it*). In the sense of *interested in* (*He's into greyhound-racing*), **into** is colloquial and should not be used in formal writing or speech.

kind is singular, so *this kind* and *that kind* are correct; *these kind* and *those kind* are not. The same is true of *sort*, *type* and *class* (or any other singular word used with an incorrect plural *these* or *those*).

less see **fewer**.

like is followed by pronouns in the object-form (*like you and me*, not *like you and I*).

literally means *precisely in accordance with the meaning* of the word to which it is attached, e.g. *He literally became hysterical* means that he became hysterical in the dictionary sense of the word, and that the statement is not an exaggeration. To say that someone was *green with envy* is a legitimate figure of speech; to say he was *literally green with envy* is nonsense.

　　Literally is very often used in this way as an emphatic adverb meaning no more than *almost*. It is a useful word in its correct sense, and does not deserve to be weakened by misuse. Expression is strengthened – and unintended comedy avoided – by its omission from *The audience was literally glued to its seats*; *They literally screamed their heads off*; *By over-spending, the newspaper is literally bleeding to death.*

much less is often used when **much more** is needed. In *It is difficult to learn to speak a foreign language, much less to write it* the writer means that it is *much more* difficult to write a language. It will generally be found that *much more* is needed in affirmative sentences and *much less* in negative ones. Thus *It is not easy to learn to speak a foreign language, much less to write it* (where *much less* means *much less easy*).

neither of means *not one nor the other of two* and should not be used when more than two people or things are referred to.

Correct: *I saw neither of the two.*
Incorrect: *I saw neither of the three.*
Correct: *I saw none of the three.*

Neither of must be followed by a singular verb: *Neither of the two was satisfactory*.

neither . . . nor . . . nor . . . is acceptable, whatever some grammar books may say about restricting *neither . . . nor* to only two alternatives.

no-one is the best spelling when *no person* is meant, so that **no one** may be reserved for such cases as *no one* (i.e. single) *book covers the whole subject*. *Noone* is correct, but looks odd.

nor is correct after *neither* (*neither rhyme nor reason*). Both *nor and or* are possible after *no* (*no time* (*n*)*or energy*) and *not* (*has not written the minutes* (*n*)*or the agenda*); *or* is better because the negative force of *no* and *not* carries over to the words after the conjunction *or*, and so there is no need to repeat the negative by using *nor*. But *nor* is not incorrect.

no sooner . . . than, not . . . *when* or . . . *that* (*No sooner had the band started to play than the lights fused*).

of is sometimes used instead of *have* or its contraction *'ve* (*I shouldn't of said that*; *he could of hurt himself*). This is wrong: *of* is never a verb.

off of (as in *He fell off of his bike*) is illiterate.

on account of means *because of*, not *because*. *I stayed at home on account of I was feeling ill* is wrong. The correct version is . . . *because I was feeling ill* (or *on account of feeling ill*).

onto is not yet regarded as normal. *On to* is preferred. Do not use *on to* if *on* is sufficient. Never use **onto** when *on* is an adverb and *to* a preposition (*Keep right on to the end of the road*) or part of an infinitive (*He went on to say . . .*).

ought has the negative form *ought not*. The common *didn't ought* is wrong; *shouldn't* is available as a (weaker) replacement for *didn't ought to*, but *ought not to* is better.

perfect is an absolute: there are degrees of quality, but the highest degree, perfection, cannot itself have degrees. Therefore *more perfect*, *most perfect*, *less perfect* are ungrammatical.

point of view is responsible for many clumsy expressions:

> *The play was good from the acting point of view* / . . . *was well acted*
> *The position looks promising from the economic point of view* The economic position looks promising
> *Oil companies are happy from the supplies point of view* / . . . about supplies

A point of view is the place where one stands to look at something. One has or sees a *view*, not a point of view. *From his point of view* is correct; *he gave his point of view* should be *he gave his view(s)*.

prefer   One may prefer tennis *to* golf / swimming *to* riding / to play *rather than* to watch. One may not prefer tennis *than* golf.

preferable to, not *preferable than* or *from*. Avoid *more preferable* / *most preferable*, because *preferable* means *better liked* or *best liked*, so that *more/most* are as ungrammatically redundant as they would be in *more better* or *most best*.

protest is used as a transitive verb in a few expressions (*protest one's innocence/ignorance*), when it means *affirm*. When it means *complain*, the current fashion for the Americanism *protest the bomb*, *protest war* etc. should be avoided in favour of *protest against* . . .

quite means both *completely* and *fairly*. The tone of voice will make clear which sense is meant when saying *I am quite happy*; in writing, there is a need to be more specific, or ambiguity may result.

rarely ever should be *hardly ever* or just *rarely*.

reason being is that . . . should be *the reason is that* . . . or *the reason being that* . . .

> Incorrect: *We won't be able to come. The reason being is that the car's broken down.*
> Correct: *. . . The reason is that the car's broken down.*

or: *We won't be able to come, the reason being that the car's broken down.*

or: *. . . because . . .*

reason . . . is that, not *. . . is because* or *. . . is due to.*

Incorrect: *The reason he phoned was because he was worried.*
Correct: *The reason he phoned was that he was worried.*
                (or *He phoned because he was worried.*)
Incorrect: *The reason for the accident was due to carelessness.*
Correct: *The reason for the accident was carelessness.*
                (or *The accident was due to carelessness.*)

In *the reason . . . was because/due to*, the words *because* and *due to* repeat the sense of *reason*. Such duplication of the sense is ungrammatical.

There used to be objections to *reason why* on similar grounds, i.e. *the reason why it collapsed* should be *the reason that it collapsed* (or *the reason for its collapse*). But *reason why* is now accepted idiom.

relationship to applies to degree of relation; **relationship with** applies to manner of relationship. *What's your relationship to the boy? I'm his father* but *What's your relationship with him? Very good on the whole.*

scarcely should be followed by *when*, not *than*, when the sense is *no sooner . . . than* (*I'd scarcely finished mending the roof when the rain started*).

Scarcely has a negative meaning and needs no other negative word: *I scarcely never see him* should have *ever*.

seeing as should be *seeing that*, but the simpler *as* or *since* is neater.

seldom is an adverb (*he seldom loses his temper*), not an adjective. *His visits are seldom* should read *. . . infrequent.*

sort see **kind.**

so that, not *so* or *so as*, is used to introduce a subordinate clause expressing purpose.

Colloquial: *He drove quickly so he might arrive early.*
Incorrect: *He drove quickly so as he might arrive early.*
Correct: *He drove quickly so that he might arrive early.*

An infinitive expression may be introduced by *so as*: *He drove quickly so as to arrive early*.

such is followed by *as* before an infinitive (*He's not such an idiot as to believe that*) or an adjectival clause (*It was such a gale as we'd never known before*) but by *that* before an adverbial clause expressing result (*He's not such an idiot that he'll believe that*).

such as is followed by a pronoun in the subject-form when the antecedent of **such as** is a subject. In *Women such as she are only interested in their careers*, the antecedent of *such as* is *Women*, which is the subject of *are interested*. Accordingly the pronoun *she* (subject-form) is needed.

In *It's best to avoid people such as him* and *I have respect for people such as him*, the antecedent of *such as* is *people*, which is the object of the verb in the first sentence and of the preposition *for* in the second. By the normal rule of agreement, the object-form *him* is required in both sentences.

suffer with, as in *He was suffering with a cold*, is colloquial. Use *suffer from*.

superior to, not *than*.

theirs is never spelt *their's*.

theirselves does not exist. *Themselves* is correct.

try and is often used instead of *try to* in speech; *try to* is better in writing.

type   see **kind**.

unequal to, not *for* (*He was unequal to the task*).

unique means *without equal*. It is an absolute: there can be no degree of uniqueness (something is either unique or not), and so *quite unique*, *rather unique*, *very unique* etc. are illogical and ungrammatical expressions. (Say *quite rare* etc.) It is possible for something to be *nearly unique* or *almost unique* if it is extremely rare, but it is a pity to blur the uniqueness of *unique* by qualifying it in any way.

use to, used to are often misspelt because they sound alike. *Used* is the past tense; *use* is the infinitive after *did*.

> Statement: *I used to like jazz.*
> Negative statement: *I used not/didn't use/usedn't to smoke.*
> Question: *Did you use to play hockey?*
> *Used you to live in Scotland?*
> Negative question: *Didn't you use to keep chickens?*

The adjectival form is *used to*, meaning *accustomed* (*I'm not used to so much noise*). The noun is *use* (*Is this any use to you?*).

well, when used with a participle as part of a compound adjective, is usually hyphened (*a well-known singer*, *a well-built house*), but not when used as a straightforward adverb (*She became well known*; *he is well intentioned*).

were is better than **was** in *If I were to do it . . .*; *if he were to decide . . .*, etc.

what is an illiterate substitute for *which* or *that* in *These are the books what I have just read.*

whilst is an unnecessary word. It means no more than *while* and because of its archaic flavour seems destined to drop out of use.

wouldn't know is a pointless expression if the intended sense is *don't know* as it is in the common reply *I wouldn't know.*

yours is never spelt *your's.*

6

Words Used Wrongly

academic   scholarly. The meaning of this word has gradually shifted from *abstruse/theoretical* to *remote from real life* to *unimportant/irrelevant* (as in *The majority is so large that the voting figures are academic*). There are enough synonyms for *unimportant* without misusing a serviceable word.

aggravate, in its sense of *irritate*, is well established but thought to be colloquial. The word is best reserved for the sense of *make worse* (*Walking may aggravate the injury*).

alibi   a defence by an accused person that he was elsewhere when an alleged offence was committed. There is no good reason for weakening this useful word by using it as a showy replacement for the perfectly adequate word *excuse* (*The Government's alibi for high unemployment is the state of the international economy*).

allergic   unusually sensitive to the effects of certain foods, pollens etc. This useful medical term may be used jocularly (*He's allergic to hard work*) but it is in danger of driving out *hostile, averse antipathetic, sensitive* and other alternatives with helpful shades of meaning. It should not be used to express mere dislike; medically, one may like something yet be allergic to it.

ambivalent   having opposite feelings about or attitudes to the same person or thing.
   Loosely used of mixed feelings (instead of opposite or irreconcilable ones), and even more loosely as a high-sounding alternative to *vague, undecided, indecisive*, or even to *ambiguous* and *devious*, all of which are better.

anticipate   consider or take action in good time (*They anticipated what our needs would be*); forestall. Commonly, unnecessarily and wrongly used as a synonym of *expect* or *foresee*, as in *We do not anticipate many problems*.

appreciate   esteem highly, be grateful for, estimate value of, be sensitive to. It is a pity to weaken this word by using it when a word with less feeling (*realise*, *understand*) will do (*I appreciate that two coats of paint will be needed*).

approximate   near to the actual; **approximately**   nearly exactly. The common expression *very approximate(ly)* means *very rough(ly)*, i.e. not approximate(ly) at all, and should therefore be avoided, as should any use of **approximate** to mean *rough* instead of *almost precise*.

auspicious   conducive to success; prosperous. Sometimes wrongly used to mean merely *special* in the phrase *auspicious occasion*.

beg the question does not mean *avoid the question* or *fail to give a straight answer*, but *assume the truth of something that needs proof*. A group of people may be called *terrorists* or *freedom-fighters* depending on one's point of view: arguments are full of such *question-begging* words.

breakdown   collapse, failure (*the breakdown of law and order*); statistical analysis (*the breakdown of the accounts* e.g. into separate headings of expenditure). There are times when ambiguity may occur (*the breakdown of economic growth*) unless this (over-used) expression is handled circumspectly.

categorical, categorically   No denial, statement, promise, undertaking or assurance, especially by a politician, is nowadays ever given without being **categorical** or made **categorically**. Those who know that **categorical** means *unconditional*, and **categorically** means *in plain words*, are likely to be more careful.

charisma   divinely gifted so as to inspire devotion or enthusiasm. A powerful word, not to be abused by being made a substitute for weaker adjectives such as *popular* or *attractive*. Nor should **charismatic** be similarly cheapened: it does not mean merely *glamorous*.

chronic　lingering, lasting, constant. It is both inaccurate and slangy to use it in the sense of *severe, bad, intense*. In the medical sense, **chronic** is the opposite of **acute** (*coming sharply to a crisis*), not a synonym.

comparative, comparatively are often used as elaborate alternatives to *rather, very* or *fairly*; they should be confined to occasions when comparisons are being made. Prefer *The store was fairly busy* to the more impressive *The store was comparatively busy* unless a comparison is intended with other stores or with the same store at other times.

compound　mix; settle a matter by agreement; refrain from prosecution, in return for payment.

Its widespread use as a synonym for *make worse, complicate* (as in *the difficulties were compounded by* . . .) should be resisted because the original meaning of the word is useful and the new meaning is adequately expressed by existing words.

contemporary　(person, thing) belonging to the same time. It means *modern* (i.e. of our own time) only if no other time is mentioned. A person who writes or speaks of his liking for *contemporary music* is referring to that of his own time; *medieval music performed on contemporary instruments* is played on medieval ones, not modern ones.

counter-productive　having an effect opposite to the intended one. Not to be loosely used as a fashionable alternative to *unhelpful*, as it often is.

crescendo　a gradual increase in loudness; gradual progress towards a climax. It is correct to refer to a *crescendo of noise* or *a crescendo of protests*, but not to say *Protests reached a crescendo* or *The noise rose to a crescendo* because *reached* and *rose to* are part of the meaning of *crescendo* itself. Say *Protests reached a climax / came to a head* and *The noise rose to a peak*.

criteria is the plural of **criterion** and should not be used as a singular word (*this criteria; the criteria for success was* . . .).

data is not a singular word, but the plural of the little used **datum**. It is therefore wrong to write *This/that data* or *The data is* . . . If the singular form is needed, say *one of the data* (or *the datum*).

decimate reduce by one tenth (originally, to execute one in ten of mutinous or cowardly soldiers to set an example); to destroy a tenth or a small proportion.

It is therefore illiterate to use the word to mean *exterminate, almost wipe out, destroy completely or nearly completely*.

destined has to do with *destiny*, not *destination*.

Correct: He was destined to die before completing the work.
Incorrect: The army intercepted arms destined for the rebels.
(The arms were *intended* for the rebels, and *destined* to be intercepted).

differ from means *be different* (*Olive oil differs from sunflower oil*) or *disagree (with)* (*He differed from his colleagues*), though *differ with* is common in this latter sense.

dilemma position in which one must make a choice between two (*the horns of a dilemma*) or more possibilities that are equally unwelcome. The word is far too handy and precise to deserve ignorant misuse as a synonym of mere *difficulty, problem* etc.

doubtless, no doubt, undoubtedly, indubitably mean *without doubt*, and should not be used – as they often are – to mean *probably*.

eke out supplement; make something more tolerable, serviceable etc. by adding to it. (*The refugees eked out their meagre rations with what they could beg*). It has come to mean *make something last longer* (as in *They eked out their pocket money for a few more days*) or *make or manage with difficulty* (*They eked out their retirement in poverty*), but this misuse should be avoided.

enhance intensify; make more valuable or attractive. Only things can be enhanced.

Correct: He enhanced *his reputation* by . . .
                 His popularity was enhanced by . . .
Incorrect: Success enhanced *him*.
                 She was enhanced by . . .

euphoric means *in a state of euphoria*, which is a feeling of well-being, especially one stemming from over-confidence or over-optimism. It does not mean merely *hopeful*.

fascination is the exercise (not the experience) of enchantment. It is correct to speak of *the royal family's fascination for* the press, but not of *the press's fascination for/with the royal family* (unless the sense is that the royal family are *fascinated by*, i.e. charmed by, the press).

feasible   able to be done. It may therefore mean *possible* in some contexts, but that is no excuse for using it always as a synonym for *possible*, *probable* and *plausible*.

first, firstly   Either of these words may be used at the beginning of a sentence or paragraph which is first in an enumeration. It is sensible to follow the sequences *First . . . Second . . . Third . . .* and *Firstly . . . Secondly . . . Thirdly . . .* , not to mix the two forms.

fraction   a quantity that is less than a whole number. A fraction may be small (one hundreth) or large (ninety-nine hundredths). The word should therefore not be used as if it meant only a small part (*It cost only a fraction of what I expected*; *I paid fractionally more than I planned*). Use *small part*, *a little* etc., and leave fractions to mathematics.

ilk occurs only in a few Scottish titles. It does not mean *sort* or *type* (*people of that ilk*), nor is there any good reason for using it as if it ought to.

inculcate   *We inculcate* (i.e. impress) things, such as habits, ideas, manners, etc., *on* or *in* a person or his mind. We cannot *inculcate* somebody, nor can he be *inculcated* with something, though we can *indoctrinate* him so that he is *imbued* with it.

irony   saying the opposite of what is meant; an event that is contrary to what is expected, desirable or fit.
    The word is weakened if used as a synonym for *sarcasm*, or for an event that is a mere coincidence. Similarly, *ironically* does not mean *coincidentally* or *oddly enough*.

leading question   question so worded as to *lead* to the answer which the questioner wants (especially in a court of law, where barristers may not ask such questions).

More often used, wrongly, to mean a difficult, unfair or pointed question.

leeway   literally, the sideways drift of a ship to leeward (i.e. downwind) of its desired course; figuratively, any deviation into *unwanted* position. One can therefore *make up leeway* (recover from a bad position, make up lost time etc.); one cannot *leave oneself some leeway* or *have some leeway*, as if leeway was something desirable. Use *room for manoeuvre* in such senses.

majority   greater number or part. Best reserved for number, and not used of volume, amount or quantity. Use *most* or *the greater part* instead of *the majority of the industry*, *the majority of the time*, and in similar expressions having to do with amount.

Majority does not mean *almost all*: 51% is a majority.

It is possible to speak of *the great majority* (i.e. almost all) but illogical to speak of the *greater/greatest majority* as if there could be more than one majority, one *greater* than the other, or one *greatest* of all.

As a collective noun, majority may take a singular or plural verb. The plural is normal when *majority* means a group of people: *The majority were in favour* (but *The party's majority is small*).

marginal   at or close to a limit, edge, border. A *marginal constituency* is one where the number of an MP's votes is close to the dividing line between majority and minority. A firm with *marginal profits* is close to deficit. The *marginal advantages* of a scheme are incidental and additional to the main ones.

These meanings are weakened when *marginal* and *marginally* are popularly used to mean no more than *slight* or *slightly*.

materialise   means *make or become material*, not *happen*, *arrive*, *occur*, *turn up*, *take place*.

maximise   increase to the greatest possible extent. It is therefore nonsensical to say *maximise a little* or *to a certain extent*.

The word does not mean *increase*. It is also over-used.

means is plural when it is used in the sense of *money. (His means are not sufficient to . . .).* In the sense of *method* it can be singular (*It is a means to an end*) or plural (*The means do not justify the end*).

media, the collective word for newspapers, television, radio and other means of communication, is a plural word (the singular is **medium**). It should be always used with a plural verb (*The media have criticised . . .* , not *The media has . . .*) and as a plural noun (*experimental media*, not *an experimental media*) despite its widespread misuse as a singular.

minimal means *least possible*, not merely *small* or *slight*. Likewise, **minimum** means *smallest amount possible*, not *small amount*.

minimise   reduce to (or estimate at) the smallest possible amount. *Minimised to a certain extent* and *minimise a little* are therefore nonsensical.

   The word does not mean *decrease, lessen, reduce, underestimate*, and will lose its valuable shade of meaning unless people who use it show more regard for accuracy and less for fashionable jargon.

minority   smaller number or part. It does not mean *a few*: 49% is a minority. A minority may be small or large: *only a minority of customers pay by cheque* indicates a number between 1% and 49%, and if the writer means *only a few* he should say so.

moot   debatable (*a moot point*); raise for discussion (*The idea was mooted at last year's conference*). Often mispronounced to rhyme with *cute* (instead of *hoot*) and wrongly written as *mute*.

mutual   between two. The word is correctly used in *our mutual affection* (our affection for each other), *a mutual understanding* (an understanding between two people), *they are mutually dependent* (each depends on the other), *the feeling is mutual* (each feels the same way about the other).

   When more than two are referred to, use **common**. To say *I believe you and I have friends in common* or *have common acquaintances* means that the friends/ acquaintances are common to you and me, i.e. the relationship is three-way, not two-way.

Common is therefore correct: *mutual friends/acquaintances* would have been wrong.

optimum means *most favourable*, not *maximum*.
Optimum use is the best use, not the most use.

phenomena is not a singular word; it is the plural of **phenomenon**.

plethora unhealthy excess. Both aspects of this definition have been lost by careless over-use and misuse of the word, which now seems destined to be no more than a fancy substitute for *abundance*. There are enough synonyms for *abundance* and *superabundance*, and careful writers retain *plethora* for occasions when both unwholesomeness and glut need to be signified.

plummet fall rapidly. Wrongly believed by some journalists to mean *move rapidly* or even *shoot upward* (*The team has plummeted to the top of the league*; *the youngster who has plummeted to stardom*).

presently soon. In Scotland and the USA it means *at once* and also *at present*; this latter sense is gaining ground in British English (*We are presently experiencing some difficulty*). One word should not be expected to carry so many different meanings, and it may be wise to avoid *presently* in favour of *soon/at once/at present/currently* until the confusion dies down.

pressurise Except in the sense of *maintain normal atmospheric pressure in* (an aircraft cabin etc.), this means no more than **pressure** (*The Council has been pressured by public opinion*) which has the advantage of being shorter.

profession a self-governing body of people employed in a particular occupation, and controlling their own standards and admission or qualifications. Hence *the learned professions* (the Church, medicine, the law). Now it is a swanky all-purpose word for any occupation (*a professional criminal*). Careful writers will restrict its use (e.g. *a full-time criminal*) but the original meaning – or even any distinctive meaning – is probably lost for ever as all trades, businesses and ways of making money have taken over the word to dignify themselves.

protagonist   chief person in play, story or affair. *Chief protagonist* is therefore tautological. Contrary to popular belief, the meaning of the word is not *advocate, champion, supporter, proposer,* etc., nor should it be confused with **antagonist**, which means *adversary*.

refute   prove false. There is a world of difference between this and **deny**, which means merely *declare* (not prove) *to be false*. Many people -- notably politicians, very frequently -- use *refute* when they mean *deny* (*I refute that suggestion*) probably because *refute* sounds stronger and *deny* is too readily understood. But you 'cannot refute anything by mere assertion, only by proof.

reiterate   repeat more than once. Frequently, and wrongly, used to mean simply *repeat*. If a grander word than *repeat* is required use *iterate*, and keep **reiterate** for *repeat two or more times*.

relative, relatively should be used only when someone or something is being viewed *in relation to* another. *They left the district relatively recently* (relative to whom or what?) should have *fairly* or *rather*. See **comparative**, **comparatively**.

strata is the plural of **stratum**. *A strata of society* is therefore ungrammatical.

substitute (verb)   put person or thing in place of another. (*We shall have to substitute margarine for butter*). The substitute is the person or thing used.
  The word does not mean *replace, replacement* (*We substituted butter with/by margarine*). Football journalists insist that a player has been *substituted* when they mean the opposite (*replaced*): the player who is *substituted* is the one sent on, not the one brought off.

surprise   If one is expecting rain, it is logical to say *I shouldn't be surprised if it rains* (or *I should be surprised if it doesn't rain*). The more common *I shouldn't be surprised if it doesn't rain* is illogical, though acceptable as a colloquialism.

susceptible to   easily affected by (*susceptible to flattery*); **susceptible of**: admitting of (*That law is susceptible of more than one interpretation*).

transpire   become known (*It transpired that the letter was a forgery*).

The word is popularly misused as an impressive substitute for *occur*, *happen*.

7

Unnecessary Words

The golden rule of effective English is to say what one has to say in the fewest possible words.

'The most prevalent disease in present-day writing is the tendency to say what one has to say in as complicated a way as possible. Instead of being simple, terse and direct, it is stilted, long-winded and circumlocutory; instead of choosing the simple word it prefers the unusual, instead of plain phrases the cliché.' The authors of *Plain Words* wrote this for those who use English in administration, notably in the Civil Service. It applies equally to English used in other contexts.

The purpose of communication is to engage the reader's attention. This is more likely to be held, and writing is more likely to be read with respect, if the reader's time is not wasted. If he has to pick his way through numerous superfluous words to make out the sense, the writing has been ineffective. The reader may even be led to conclude that woolly wording reflects imprecise thinking.

The words listed in this chapter exemplify the fault of verbosity, the use of more words than are needed. Several categories of verbosity may be identified.

7.1 Meaningless intensification The handiest example of this vice is the incessant abuse of the word *very* in both speech and writing:

> *I am very grateful/very sorry/very worried/very pleased/very happy/very glad/very upset/very tired.*
> *That was very good/very nice/very interesting/very exciting/very funny/very enjoyable.*

Most people would be hard pressed to explain the difference between their being *sorry* and *very sorry*. The addition of *very* is to emphasise, not to add to the meaning. Unfortunately, *very* has become so habitual (*A very good night*; *A very good morning* say the radio and TV announcers) that it has become meaningless, almost a commonplace flavouring:

> *That's very true/very unlikely/very possible/very inconvenient/very probable/very necessary/very important/very useful.*
>
> *He's very pleasant/very friendly/very hard-working/always very cheerful/very talkative/very helpful/very kind.*

Having lost its force, *very* has been supplemented by other intensifying adverbs (*really, terribly, awfully, extremely, exceptionally, considerably*) which are also in danger of losing their weight because of unthinking over-use. They often attach themselves almost automatically to certain adjectives – *absolutely* vital, *basically* untrue, *vitally* necessary – almost as if the adjective is felt to be indecently explicit without some conventional protective clothing, however flimsy.

Adjectives themselves may act as meaningless intensifiers, and it is important to ask what precise meaning they bring to the following common expression: *real* threat, *serious* crisis (what crisis is not serious?), *definite* decision, *closely guarded* secret, *undue* haste, *active* or *careful* consideration (would anyone ever offer to give inactive or careless consideration to a suggestion?), *complete* surprise, *paramount* importance, *considerable* risk, *essential* link, *appreciable* amount (how appreciable?), *invariable* habit (what else is habit?), a *particular* problem, *monotonous* regularity. There are times when such adjectives do convey meaning (a *real* threat is distinguished from an imagined one, and a *particular* problem is different from a general one) but very often they are mere padding, clogging the sense instead of allowing the nouns to carry their own weight.

This use of adverbs and adjectives (see also **11.5** on page 137) clutters speech and writing with second-hand expression. If any words can be omitted without changing the sense, omit them. Writing will be found to gain strength and exactness by their removal.

7.2 Prepositional elaboration is a preference for prepositional phrases when single words suffice. This fashion is hard to explain: there must be a widespread misconception that little prepositions are somehow unworthy – lacking dignity or impressiveness – to do the required work. A few illustrations show what economies may be made:

> He phoned *in connection with* . . . (about)
> Misbehaviour *on the part of* spectators (by)
> Prices change *in relation to* the season (with)
> The improvement *in terms of* output (in)
> Payments *in respect of* overtime (for)
> *In such a manner as to* (to)
> *On the basis of* what he said (from)
> I am writing *with reference to* (about)
> *In the vicinity of* (near)

Similar elaboration occurs with conjunctions (*until such time as* (until); *in the eventuality of* (if); *during the time that* (while)) and with other parts of speech (*a considerable amount of* (much)).

The pruning of such dead wood will allow the main sense of sentences to stand out more boldly.

7.3 Dignity words are long words that demonstrate the writer's erudition and are felt to be more striking than shorter ones with identical meanings. There may be occasions that call for *discontinue* (stop), *declared redundant* (sacked), *ameliorate* (improve), *eventuate* (happen, occur), *terminate* (end), *adjacent to* (near), *converse* (talk), *accommodate* (hold), *commencement* (start), *acquaint* (tell), *initiate* (begin), *requirement* (need), *reside* (live), *endeavour* (try), but the observant writer will be aware that polysyllabic proliferation causes indigestion as readily as paronymous superfecundation (using too many words) does.

7.4 Tautology is needless repetition. For example, as *requisite* means *something required*, and *necessary* means *required*, to describe something as a *necessary requisite* is tautological. Likewise *unexpected surprise*, *prejudge in advance*, *new innovation*, *final completion*, *cooperate together*. One can forgive football commentators their lapses in the heat of the moment ('*After a goalless first half, the score at half-time is nil-nil*'), but such errors in writing stem from a simple failure to use words whose meanings are understood.

7.5 Circumlocution is roundabout expression: thus *teachers with an inexpressive classroom-behaviour orientation* (boring teachers). There are occasions when circumlocution is needed in the interests of politeness, to avoid giving offence or to deliver an unpalatable idea in the least hurtful way. In other circumstances, directness and economy are to be preferred.

Further examples

about often creeps in unnecessarily: *He told us about how the plan would work*; *He explained about what he was going to do.*

active is pointless in *under active consideration*.

actual adds nothing to *in actual fact*.

actually may usually be omitted without altering the sense. Omission often strengthens, not weakens, an expression.

again is tautological in *recur again*, and after any verb (e.g. *reorganise*, *reassert*, *revisit*) in which the prefix *re-* means *again*.

ago and **since** should not be used together.

Correct: *It happened five years ago.*
                    It is five years since it happened.
Incorrect: *It is five years ago since it happened.*

all of is not incorrect, but the *of* is superfluous except before personal pronouns (*all of us*).

and additionally is tautological.

as   The first *as* is redundant in *As much as I dislike him, I value his advice* / *He can't afford it, as cheap as it is*, and in similar cases when the sense of *although* is intended. The *as . . . as* construction implies comparison (*It wasn't as severe as we thought*), not concession.

as a matter of fact   It is usually enough to state a fact without stating also that it is a fact.

as at means *at* in *The information was true as at the time of publication*.

as far as . . . is/are concerned is a cumbersome phrase that can usually be avoided: *It makes no difference as far as I'm concerned* (*. . . to me*); *As far as long-term prospects are concerned . . .* (*In the long term . . .*).

as from means no more than *from* (*as from Monday*; *comes into effect as from today*).

as of means no more than *from* (*as of now*). The phrase *as of right* is more plainly expressed as *by right*.

as to is often unnecessary before *how, why, whether, who, what*: *There was some doubt* (*as to*) *whether* . . . ; *He informed them* (*as to*) *how they should apply*. It is legitimate in *He's not so stupid as to think* . . .
    As to is commonly used in place of more exact prepositions: *He advised us as to* (on) *the best materials to use*; *information as to* (about) *his qualifications*.

at a time when is long-winded for *when*.

at this moment in time is an extraordinary circumlocution, fast becoming a cliché, meaning no more than *now* (or, if emphasis is needed, *at this moment*).

back is unnecessary after *return, reverse, revert, re-export* and any other word which includes the sense of *back* in its definition.

basically is an overworked intensifying word that may be omitted from most sentences without loss of meaning and with a gain in sharpness. It means *fundamentally*, which is preferable because *basically* is in danger of losing its meaning through repetition.

basis is a frequent cause of wordiness: *on a regular basis* (regularly), *on a voluntary basis* (voluntarily), *on a part-time basis* (part-time), *on a temporary basis* (temporarily), *on a weekly basis* (by the week).

both is redundant in *both the shopkeeper as well as the customers*; *the two houses are both alike*; *both of them are equally responsible* (They are equally responsible); *stitch them both together*.

both of is not incorrect, but the *of* is usually superfluous except before personal pronouns (*both of them*).

but, as a conjunction, introduces a statement which contrasts with the preceding one. It is therefore unnecessary to add *however* (in the sense of *nevertheless*) which has a similar effect: *We thought it would be a quiet village, but when we got there, however, we found it was a small town.* Either omit *however* or put a semi-colon in place of *but*.

For similar reasons, do not use *nevertheless* or *yet* with *but*.

but what has a surplus *what* in *I never go out but what I forget something*.

case often leads to roundabout expressions:
> *If that is the case* / If so
> *In many cases, people ignore . . .* / People often ignore . . .
> *In the case of handicapped people, they may . . .* / Handicapped people may . . .
> *Prices are higher than was the case last year* / . . . than they were
> *That was not the case* / . . . not so

check out has become accepted in the sense of *pay one's bill and leave, record one's departure*, but not in the sense of *test* (*The police are checking out the evidence*), which is American: *check* alone suffices in this sense.

check up on means *check*.

consensus general opinion. It follows that *the general consensus was that . . .* and *the consensus of opinion is that . . .* are tautological. Omit *general* in the first, and *of opinion* is the second.

consult with Example of the modern trend towards never using one word when two will do the same work.

currently is high-sounding for *now* (or *nowadays*).

due to is redundant in *The reason for the postponement is due to illness* / *The cause of the error was due to carelessness*, where *due to* repeats the sense of *reason* and *cause*. Delete either *due to* or the first three words of both sentences.

Due to the fact that is wordy for *because*.

earlier on is colloquial. In writing, omit *on*.

end up does not need the *up*.

enough is tautological in *adequate enough* or *sufficiently enough*. Use one word or the other, but not both.

face up to means no more than *face*. The argument that *face up to* carries an extra implication of defiance or determination does not carry weight.

fact that is common and often unnecessary. *His early arrival* is less cluttered than *The fact that he arrived early*. Similar economies are possible in *I object to the fact that we have to* . . . (I object to our having to . . .) and *The fact that the shipyard has closed means that* . . . (The shipyard's closure means that . . .)
   Despite the fact that means *although*.
   In view of the fact that means *as*.

field as in *He is working in the field of computer software* may usually be omitted without loss: *He is working in/on computer software*.

finalise, a recently coined word, is now firmly fixed in the language, much to the regret of those who can detect no shade of meaning not already present in *finish*, *complete*, *conclude* etc.

hand down, as in *The judge handed down severe sentences*, is an Americanism which has no advantages over *pass*.

if and when   One or the other is usually sufficient, and the phrase is often used tautologically.

in colour, in size, in shape, in number are tacked on surprisingly frequently when they add nothing to the sense (*The tent is rectangular in shape; the crowd was small in number*).

inevitably merely repeats the sense of *must* in the common expression *must inevitably*.

in excess of   *more than* is shorter.

in fact is often superfluous.

in order to may often be shortened to *to*.

inside of (or *outside of*) is acceptable in *They painted the inside of the house*, but *of* is unnecessary in *Wait for us outside of the library* or

Inside of the airing-cupboard you'll find some towels. In other words, *of* is permissible after *inside*, *outside* when they are nouns, but not when they are prepositions.

in spite of the fact that means *although*.

integral necessary to the completeness of a whole. Do not use the common expression *integral part* unless the part in question is truly *integral*.

just may mean the same as *exactly* and one of the two is therefore redundant in *It is just exactly six years ago that he died* and *The time is just exactly four o'clock*.

kind of is common in speech as a meaningless addition (*The house is kind of long and low*) but should have no place in careful speech or writing.

lose out Prime example of the American fondness of tacking on words to verbs that do not need them.

meet with, an American expression meaning *confer with*, is nosing its way into English usage, and should be resisted by those who object to (*a*) unnecessary prepositions, (*b*) expressions which merely duplicate existing ones, (*c*) the possibility of confusion with established expressions: in English, *meet with* means *experience*, as in *They met with an accident*.

meet up, **meet up with** are examples of a perfectly serviceable verb (*meet*) decorated with unnecessary prepositions.

miss out on means *miss*.

mutual, in its correct sense of *between two*, is redundant in *They agreed on a policy of mutual cooperation* / *We hold each other in mutual regard/esteem/affection* / *There is a mutual understanding between us* (*two*) / *Jack and Jill are mutual friends* (i.e. of each other). See **mutual** on page 88.

necessary, **necessity** and **essential** are absolutes i.e. something is necessary/essential or it is not; there cannot be degrees of necessity (*Careful planning will be rather essential*) though there can be degrees of *helpfulness*, *usefulness* etc. The qualifying adverbs are therefore spurious or tautologous in the common expressions *most/absolutely essential* and *strictly/very necessary*.

one sometimes intrudes unnecessarily. *The answer is a simple one* wastes two words compared with *The answer is simple*.

otherwise in its sense of *or else* does not need a 'second' *or*. In *We must hurry, or otherwise we shall miss the start*, omit either *or* or *otherwise*.

overall is an exceptionally popular word, often used unthinkingly when it adds nothing to the meaning: *he has overall control / an overall majority / the overall cost / the overall picture / overall responsibility / in overall command / my overall feeling is*. The writer who is tempted to use *overall* can invariably find a fresher substitute, or (better still) omit the word altogether.

personal(ly) is pointless in *I don't personally believe that / Personally, I'd rather stay at home / a personal friend /* but it has some point when *If you want my personal opinion* implies *as distinct from my official one, the one I have to hold as representative of an organisation etc.*

position is preferable to the omnipresent **situation** but is sometimes a cause of vagueness or circumlocution:
> *The position was soon reached where there was no more . . . /* Soon there was no more . . .
> *The position in regard to schoolchildren is that they should . . . /* Schoolchildren should . . .
> *We have arrived at the position when we must . . . /* We must now . . .

prerequisite means *something essential*, and so the common expression *essential prerequisite* is tautological.

previous to means no more than *before*.

prior to is pompous for *before*.

proportion   *A large/small proportion of the spectators* is long-winded for *many/few*.

question as to whether, as in *the question as to whether she ought to have done that*, does not need and should not have *as to*. Likewise *the question as to who was responsible* is wordy for *the question of responsibility*.

real, really are very widely used for emphasis (especially in television advertisements) – so widely that they have become almost automatic, to the extent that statements would be toughened by their omission.

regard is a frequest cause of prepositional elaboration in such phrases as *in regard to*, *as regards* and *with regard to*. A shorter and more direct preposition is usually available:
>*His duty in regard to the supervision of the building* / His duty to supervise the building
>*Problems with regard to* or *as regards recruitment* / Problems in recruitment

regarding, like *concerning*, is too often preferred to the simpler *about*.

respective, respectively are so often used unnecessarily that it may be best to avoid them completely. Their correct use is to show the exact relationship between the individual members of two groups: *my son and daughter spent their holidays in Dorset and Yorkshire respectively* means that my son was in Dorset and my daughter in Yorkshire; without *respectively* the sentence means that son and daughter were together in both places.

>**Respective(ly)** adds nothing to *Each of the guests made his respective way home*; *he belongs to the cricket and the rugby club respectively*; *we have a right to our respective opinions* (where *own* is needed).

separate out Another example of the superfluous *out*.

sort of is very common, almost habitual, in speech (*It means sort of* . . .) not to convey sense but to give the speaker time to think what to say next. The expression is too vague to deserve a place in writing.

subsequent to means *after*.

together is redundant in *mix together, cooperate together, combine together* and after any other verb whose definition includes the sense of **together**.

totally is so much used as an intensifier (*totally wrong, totally unacceptable, totally unsuitable*) that expression would often gain emphasis by its excision.

transportation is unnecessarily long for *transport*.

ultimate end is tautological because *ultimate* means *final*.

undue means *more than is necessary* or *appropriate*.
    It is correct to say *He showed undue alarm* (more alarm than was warranted) or *He was unduly concerned* (more concerned than he needed to be), but there is a danger of tautology in negative constructions e.g. *There is no need for undue haste* (There is no need for more haste than there is need for), *We should not be unduly worried* (We should not be more worried than we should be).

up until, as in *up until the present*, needs no *up*, though *up till now* and *up to now* are idiomatic.

utilise, utilisation rarely, if ever, mean more than *use*.

vainly, in vain are unnecessary before *but*.
    Incorrect: *He tried in vain to open it, but could not.*
    Correct: *He tried to open it but could not.*
    (or simply: *He tried in vain to open it.*)

well   One of the most common openings to a spoken sentence, especially in answer to a question. The habit is worth breaking, and has no place in writing.

what is superfluous in *We are doing better than what we did last year / Printing costs have risen more than what is generally believed / The market handles twice as much fish as what it used to.*

whether or not is needed when two alternatives are referred to. The *or not* is redundant when *whether* means *if* (i.e. when only one possibility is referred to): *I wonder whether the meeting's been postponed.*

while is superfluous in *The car was worth while repairing*. Correct forms are *The car was worth repairing* or *The repairs were worth while*; *worth* needs only one object, which may be *while*, (i.e. worth the expense of time) or some other word (here, *repairing*) but not both.

win out is Americanism for *win*.

with the result that uses four words when a simple *and* normally suffices: *They reduced the prices with the result that they sold more tickets*.

you know Very common, often automatic, in speech, to give the speaker a breathing-space while he searches for a word. Silence would be preferable.

8

Tired Words

Words come at us from all directions, from newspapers, magazines and books, incessantly from television and radio, down the telephone, across the desks of offices, in cinemas and theatres, at meetings, through the letter-box, in conversations wherever we are. They are used to inform, persuade, entertain, advise, sell, educate, transact business, ask questions, establish relationships, express or influence emotions. They chatter out by the billion every day in offices, factories, schools, streets, shops and homes, on air-waves, cables and satellite links, on computer screens and telex machines, on typewriters and visual display units, and over uncountable hectares of paper.

It is not surprising that some words give way under the strain. Savaged by people who do not always understand their meaning, stretched to breaking-point by advertisers and other persuaders, thrust into startling headlines and shrill news reports by journalists in pursuit of sensation, strait-jacketed into the private languages of sociologists, economists, salesmen and art critics, drained of meaning by sloganising politicians and others who live by evasion, once-colourful words grow pale, losing their power and often their very sense.

In order to be effective, vocabulary needs to be as fresh as possible, free from limp words, tired expressions and over-worked devices denoting ready-made thoughts. This chapter lists some examples to watch: most belong to one of four main categories.

8.1 Cliché: an expression, once original and lively, which has become stale by over-use. Not all heavily-used expressions can

reasonably be described as clichés. Everyday life would be impossible without *What's for lunch? How's the family? What time is it?
Good morning! What'll you have to drink?* Many rather more
colourful common phrases may also be defended on the grounds
that they are more concise and no more objectionable than their.
alternatives: *fall between two stools, thin end of the wedge, swings
and roundabouts, white elephant, in a nutshell, get down to brass
tacks, part and parcel, food for thought,* though some would regard
them as clichés and others would feel them more appropriate to
colloquial speech than to formal writing.

But there are many expressions that are obviously drab and give
writing a feeble, stereotyped air: *in this day and age, conspicuous by
their absence, last but not least, first and foremost, too funny for
words, leave no stone unturned, that's what it's all about, green with
envy, moment of truth, slowly but surely, stand up and be counted,
like the plague, few and far between, step in the right direction, fast
and furious, long arm of coincidence / the law.* A writer who leans on
such terms is not only insensitive to the impression his words will
make: he has stopped thinking.

8.2 Conventional modifiers: *sadly* lacking, *fondly* imagine, *bit-
terly* disappointed, *gallant* losers, *psychological* moment, *tender*
mercies, *bated* breath, *calculated* risk, *forlorn* hope, *marked*
contrast.

8.3 Vogue words There are fashions in words as there are in
clothes or popular music. Some words are suddenly heard on all
sides, are quickly wrung dry, and then return to their former status.
Others linger, especially on the lips of those who do not listen to
what they say: *escalate, confrontation, situation, environment,
rethink, catalyst, arguably, productivity, decision-making, commitment, restrictive, credibility gap, permissive, underpriviliged, in-
depth, cost-effective.* Vogue words are usually useful, which is why
they are in vogue, but they should not be used merely because they
are fashionable; there is always an alternative.

8.4 Faded images Many expressions have meanings that may be
used both literally and figuratively. The phrase *off the ground,* for
example, probably originated with aviation: the literal use is seen in
The aircraft was too heavy to get off the ground. Figuratively, it may
be used in contexts which have nothing to do with the real ground,
as it is in *The project failed to get off the ground* or *His election*

campaign has finally got off the ground. Here the meaning has to do with successful development, not height.

Though there can be no objection to figurative use of this kind, problems occur if a writer fails to remember the literal origins of an expression. *The Channel Tunnel has failed to get off the ground* is a case in point; in unthinkingly reaching for a popular expression to mean *failed to develop successfully*, the writer has not observed that enough of the original literal meaning is still present in the image to put the reader in mind not only of an undeveloped tunnel but a flying one.

Many such popular images become clichés: examples include *blueprint, bottleneck, track record, breakthrough, target, acid test, spring-board* and *fine-tooth comb* (not to mention the mysterious *fine tooth-comb*). Once newly-minted, they have become devalued by too much use. Worse, what little life they have left is sometimes squeezed out by writers unresponsive to the original visual image that made the expressions vivid and effective. A *target*, for instance, is something we aim at, hit or miss, yet we encounter *spending targets* that are *met, achieved* or even *overtaken*. Likewise we may read of *traffic bottlenecks*, which need to be widened, being *reduced* or *ironed out*; of *spring boards* for *climbing*, not diving, to success; of milestones that are *broken* or *overtaken*, not passed; and of the *fruits* of one's work being *harnessed* instead of harvested, reaped or enjoyed. A journalist describing the end of the Olympic Games informed his readers that the *Olympic Flame has been put into cold storage for another four years*. Thus do serviceable expressions pass through cliché into ridicule because of failure of imagination.

Further examples

absolutely is a conventional pairing in *absolutely incredible, absolutely essential, absolutely necessary, absolutely confident, absolutely awful* etc. and has thus come close to losing its meaning. The same is often true of **absolute**, as in *absolute necessity, absolute priority* etc.

and/or may be useful shorthand in business writing, but should be avoided elsewhere. For *trains and/or buses* write *trains or buses or both*.

arguably is in vogue as a showy and inaccurate substitute for *possibly*, *perhaps* or even *probably* (*Arguably the most advanced car of the 80's*). It means *disputably*, not *almost indisputably*, and is to be used only when argument is intended. The same is true of **arguable** (*Whether it is his best film is arguable*).

awful in the sense of *bad* (*awful weather*) and **awfully** in the sense of *excessively* (*awfully boring*) are colloquial and loose. Fresher and more precise alternatives are usually available.

background is worth resting in favour of *origins*, *history* (*the background of a problem*) or *experience* (*the background of the applicants*). It is sometimes tautological (*the background history*) or wordy (*It can only be explained against the background of* (i.e. by) *rising unemployment*).

board is found in two vogue expressions which are becoming clichés: **right across the board** means *for everyone*, as in *wage increases right across the board*; **take on board** means *adopt* or *consider*, as in *He promised to take the idea on board*.

carry out is a popular all-purpose verb which deserves an occasional rest, as in *carry out instructions* (follow), *carry out orders* (obey, implement), *carry out research* (do), *carry out repairs/a search* (make), *carry out an investigation* (hold).

ceiling is a tired metaphor in *prices reached a ceiling*, and becomes an absurd one if a writer forgets that he may reach, raise, lower or even go through a ceiling but not increase, top, amend or reduce one.

commence, **commencement** are formal words (*The meeting will commence at . . .*) which sound rather pompous compared with *start* or *begin(ning)*.

compact is sales-talk for *small*.

confrontation is the act of meeting face to face, especially in a hostile or defiant manner.
    In political circles it is often a modish and dishonest euphemism for *unprovoked aggression* or *intimidation*.

considerable and **considerably** are over-used emphasisers and have the addition disadvantage of being imprecise. Their omission usually improves emphasis, increases clarity and leaves the sense unaltered.

definite, definitely are examples of words used so frequently or automatically to give emphasis that they have lost their force. An expression is likely to be strengthened rather than weakened by their omission.

diametrically tends to attach itself automatically to *opposed* and *opposite* (*Their views are diametrically opposed*). It means *completely*, *directly*, like opposite ends of a diameter. *Diametrically opposite/opposed* has the flavour of a cliché, and should only be used in reference to complete opposition, not partial dissent.

economical is advertising jargon for *cheap*.

escalate, escalation Vogue words meaning *increase*, popular among those who never use two syllables when three or four are available.

explore every avenue   Cliché. There are plenty of plain alternatives to **explore** (*examine*, *study*, *consider*, *analyse*, *look into*, *investigate*, *discuss*). And who wants to explore in an avenue?

factor in the sense of *anything contributing to a result* is a very general term, and therefore attractive to the lazy writer (*a key factor, one of the factors in his decision, an important factor in his mind, a factor in the problem, some of the factors behind the policy*). The discriminating writer will look for a less reach-me-down word, such as *element, feature, circumstance, constituent, influence, fact.*

far be it from me to . . . is hackneyed.

feedback in the sense of *information gained in response to a stimulus* (e.g. an inquiry, a questionnaire) is a good example of tired metaphor.

get occurs in numerous expressions, many of them colloquial. It cannot be completely avoided, but its ubiquitousness may tempt the unwary into over-using it monotonously.

great is a slang word when used, as it popularly is, as an all-purpose expression of approval, and should be replaced by a more precise word in formal speech or writing.

head up is a vogue American import meaning *head* (*He has been appointed to head up the new company*).

heavy is over-used (*heavy losses, heavy demands, heavy burden, heavy fine, heavy reductions, heavy security*). There are several interesting and more subtle alternatives.

hopefully is driving out *I hope* (*Hopefully he will soon get better*) and *it is hoped that* (*Hopefully there will be no further price increases this year*), to the dismay of those who believe that it is an adverb meaning *full of hope* (*They waited hopefully*) and needing to be grammatically related to a verb. See **4.4.**(*j*) on page 55.

horrendous   A formerly rare word now enjoying a sudden vogue as a replacement for *horrifying, horrible, frightful*. Its meaning is in danger of being thinned to *surprising/excessive* by over-use.

interface   Place where interaction occurs between two processes. It is over-used as an impressive substitute for *point of contact, meeting-place, common frontier, connection, liaison*.

involve is extremely popular because of the numerous meanings it has acquired. The lazy writer uses it frequently, to save himself the trouble of thinking of a more precise word. The careful writer therefore avoids it – which is easy:
The cost involved will be . . . / The cost will be
Four lorries were involved in the accident / were in the accident
The plan involves the demolition of . . . / entails, necessitates
We are involved in discussions about . . . / We are discussing
Trades Unions should be involved in negotiations / included
Several people are involved / taking part, affected

leave severely alone does not need the threadbare *severely*.

legendary in the popular sense of *remarkable enough to be a subject of legend* is colloquial. The word has a useful meaning, weakened by journalistic over-use when *remarkable* is all that is meant.

low profile, as in *maintain/keep/adopt a low profile*, meaning *stay/become inconspicuous*, has rapidly been made into a cliché.

major is the opposite of **minor** in *major war*, *major road*, *major speech*, *major accident*. It is in danger of losing its force through prolonged over-exposure, and should not be used when less powerful words like *important*, *noticeable*, *significant* or *leading* would suffice.

massive   An over-popular all-purpose word (*massive dose/indifference/heart attack/assault/number/thunderstorm/building/reputation*). There are several and more specific alternatives.

meaningful is the opposite of *meaningless*. Its over-use as a fashionable substitute for *useful*, *significant*, *fruitful* (often in contexts when the sense would be unchanged by its omission) is to be avoided.

nice is perhaps the most popular adjective in the language for signifying approval, and for that reason should be avoided in any writing or speech that aspires to clarity and freshness of expression.

not to put too fine a point on it   Perhaps not quite a cliché, but certainly a long-winded way of saying *frankly*.

ongoing is the sort of word that has set people's teeth on edge through trendy over-use. It means *continuing*, and is often used superfluously.

orientate, orient   Direct towards. *To orientate oneself* is to get one's bearings. *A disoriented person* is confused about what he should be doing, and a *customer-orientated service* is a service for customers.
    A prime example of a vogue word run riot. Avoid it, or at least use the shorter version (*orient*, *oriented*).

parameter has a precise mathematical meaning, but has become extremely popular as a showy substitute for *limit* or *boundary* (by confusion with *perimeter*?), *framework* (*the parameters of the problem*) or *characteristic*, all of which are better because they do not invite a reader to wonder why a writer has felt it necessary to reach for such an impressive-looking and probably unnecessary word.

paranoia Mental derangement in which the victim feels himself persecuted or famous. It is a strong and useful word with a technical meaning. The language is weakened if the word is too much used to mean an abormal, or even a mild, tendency to suspect someone or something, when *obsession* or even *preoccupation* would be more accurate.

particular Relating to one as distinct from others; special. Expression is weakened if the word is used superfluously, as it often is after *this/these* and *that/those*. Omit it unless it adds something particular.

percentage is too much used as a dignified substitute for shorter words: *a high percentage of burglaries* (most), *only a small percentage of offices* (few). It does not make good sense to refer to *a percentage of votes* (some) without saying what percentage. The word is best reserved for occasions when the relationship between two numbers is expressed.

pipeline, in the pipeline A very popular expression (*schemes in pipeline, mortgages in the pipeline*) meaning *in the process of being produced*. It is close to becoming a cliché. Carelessly used, it invites merriment (*In the 1990's, an increase in the number of children of secondary-school age is in the pipeline*).

plus is a trendy substitute for *and* (*I've polished the car, plus I've vacuumed the inside*; *He's a professional tennis player, plus he's an economics graduate*). The usage is unnecessary and ugly.

quality, used as an adjective meaning *of good quality* (as in *a quality car, a quality newspaper*) is commercial jargon. It is possible for quality to be bad, and *quality* should not be used as a synonym for *good quality* only.

re is avoidable commercial jargon for **about**.

realistic has a frank, honest ring about it, and is therefore much used in the language of persuasion in place of subtler words like *reasonable, workable, sensible, practicable, fair, frank, suitable, probable* and *appropriate*.

relative to and **relating to** may often be replaced by a more economical word like *about* or *in*.

-ship is a source of abstraction (*the membership, the leadership, hardship*) when more concrete words (*the members, the leader, suffering*) may be preferable.

significant(ly) deserves an occasional rest in favour of *important(ly), appreciable(-ly), considerable(-ly), marked(ly)*.

situation   Perhaps the most over-worked word in the language. It can usually be avoided (*position, circumstances*) and often omitted:

> *We are into a loss situation* / We are losing money
> *in the classroom situation* / in the classroom
> *They were in a no-win situation* / They could not win
> *we are in a situation where we find it difficult* / we find it difficult
> *talks are in a breakdown situation* / talks have broken (are breaking) down
> *men and women in the prison situation* / prisoners
> *we are in a situation where we cannot* / we cannot

syndrome   A group of symptoms occurring together in a disease. It is not itself a disease. As a fashionable metaphor in a non-medical sense (*the education system suffers from the examination syndrome* i.e. from too much emphasis on exams; *society experiencing the unemployment syndrome* i.e. suffering from the effects of unemployment) the word is too much used by those who do not understand it. Not being a disease, neither a syndrome nor a symptom is *suffered*, though both may be observed, expressed, etc.

thing is too imprecise a word to deserve any prominent place in correct expression.

to all intents and purposes is trite, and wordy: it means *virtually*.

trauma is a strong word indicating an injury, or the shock produced by it, or – in psychology – mental or emotional shock. Together with its adjective **traumatic** it is in danger of losing its force through over-use when weaker words indicating mere unpleasantness or surprise would serve.

viable is a fashionable substitute for *workable, practicable, feasible,* and is much loved by those who reach for unfamiliar words in order to fudge: *The plan is not economically viable* (We can't afford it).

watershed A tired metaphor meaning *turning-point,* avoided by those who know what the literal geographical meaning is.

-wise has enjoyed considerable vogue, being tacked freely onto nouns (*The cost staffwise, moneywise and frustrationwise will have been worthwhile*). The fashion is passing and deserves oblivion.

9

Spelling

In the last resort, the weak speller must resort to learning words parrot-fashion. The following rules will help him to discern patterns, but he must remember that most of them have exceptions.

9.1 Words with a single final consonant double it before an ending beginning with a vowel (e.g. *-ing*, *-ed*, *-er*, *-able*, *-ous*, *-ible*, *-en*)
(*a*) if the word is a monosyllable with a short vowel:

> fat – fatten, fatter, fattest; fit – fitted, fitting, fitter

(*b*) if the word has more than one syllable and the stress is on the final syllable:

> begin – beginning, beginner; refer – referred, referral, referring

There is no doubling of the single final consonant
(*a*) if the word is a monosyllable with a long vowel or a double vowel:

> seat – seated, seating; look – looking, looked

(*b*) if the word has more than one syllable and the stress is before the final syllable:

> benefit – benefited; totter – tottering, tottered
> Exceptions: handicap – handicapped, handicapping; kidnap – kidnapper etc.; worship – worshipped etc.

Words ending in *w*, *x*, *y* or in double consonants never double the final letter.

9.2 Words ending in a single *-l* preceded by a single vowel double the *-l* before an ending that starts with a vowel (irrespective of where the spoken stress falls):

cancel – cancelling, cancellation, cancelled
control – controller, controlled, controlling
Exception: parallel – paralleled

The -*l* is not doubled if it is not preceded by a single vowel:

cool – cooler, cooled, cooling, coolest
snarl – snarling, snarled
Exceptions: wool – woollen; dial – dialled, dialling

The doubling rule does not apply before endings that start with a consonant:

instal – installed, installation *but* instalment
rival – rivalling, rivalled *but* rivalry

Double the -*l* if you want to add -*y*:

loyal – loyally; normal – normally
Exception: oil – oily

Thus adjectives ending -*ful* (never -*full*) form adverbs ending -*fully*.

9.3   Nouns ending -*our* form adjectives ending -*orous*:

humour – humorous; vigour – vigorous

9.4   The letter *q* never stands by itself, and is always followed by *u* and a vowel.

9.5   A silent -*e* at the end of a word is

(*a*)   retained before an ending that starts with a consonant:

definite – definitely; move – movement
Exceptions: argue – argument; hate – hatred; true – truly; nine – ninth

(*b*)   dropped before an ending that starts with a vowel:

become – becoming; fame – famous; value – valuable
Exceptions: whole – wholly; mile – mileage; sale – saleable; rate – rateable

Words ending -*ye*, -*ee*, -*oe* retain the final -*e* before the ending -*ing*:

eye – eyed *but* eyeing; agree – agreeing

9.6   With words ending -*ce* and -*ge*, the final -*e* is

(*a*)   retained before an ending that starts with a consonant:

strange – strangely; discourage – discouragement

(*b*)   retained before -*ous* and -*able*:

outrage – outrageous; service – serviceable

(*c*) dropped before other endings:

> notice – noticing, noticed (*but* noticeable);
> ice – icy, de-icer, icing, icily

9.7 Words ending *-ie* change the *-ie* to *y* before *-ing*:

> tie – tying (*but* tied); lie – lying; die – dying

9.8 No English words end in *v*, *j* or *i* (except taxi)

9.9 To distinguish between *ie* and *ei*, remember that *i* comes before *e* except after *c* if the desired sound is *ee*:

> belief, relieved *but* conceit, ceiling
>
> Exceptions: seize, species.

This rule does not apply on the many occasions when *ie* and *ei* are *not* pronounced *ee*:

> neither, weird, neighbour, variety, friendship, pierce

9.10 The sound *seed* at the end of words is spelt *-sede* in only one case (supersede), *-ceed* in only three (proceed, exceed, succeed) and *-cede* in all other words.

9.11 Words ending *-c* add *k* before endings beginning with *e*, *i*, or *y*:

> panic – panicked, panicking, panicky

9.12 Words ending in *-y* preceded by a consonant change the *y* to *i* before all endings except *-ing*:

> easy – easier, easily, easiest; dry – drier, dries, dried but drying
>   (exception: dryness); occupy – occupier, occupies, occupied *but*
>   occupying; copy – copier, copies, copied *but* copying
>
> Exceptions: shy – shyness, shyly; sly – slyly

9.13   Words ending in *-y* preceded by a vowel retain the *y* before an ending:

> convey – conveyed, conveying, conveyance;
> delay – delaying, delayed.
>
> Exceptions: pay – paying *but* paid; say – saying *but* said; gay – gaily

9.14   The endings *-ise* and *-ize* are often interchangeable. The *-ise* ending is usually safe (but note *prize*) and is more common. Those who wish to use *-ize* must remember that certain spellings are invariable (e.g. compromise, revise, supervise).

The formation of plurals

9.15 Most nouns form the plural by adding *s*.

9.16 Nouns ending in *-s*, *-ss*, *-x*, *-z*, *-ch*, *-sh*, *-o* add *-es*:
> bonuses, potatoes, dishes
> Exceptions: photos, radios, kilos, twos, solos, zeros, studios, dynamos

9.17 Nouns ending in single *-f* or *-fe* change these endings to *-ves*:
> half – halves; life – lives
> Exceptions: chiefs, roofs, beliefs, proofs

9.18 Nouns ending in *-y* preceded by a consonant change *-y* into *-ies*:
> party – parties; factory – factories
If the *-y* is preceded by a vowel, simply add *s*.

9.19 Some nouns ending *-is* change the *-is* to *-es*:
> basis – bases, axis – axes, emphasis – emphases, crisis – crises

9.20 Many words of foreign origin have irregular plurals:
> phenomenon – phenomena
If dictionaries offer a choice between a foreign plural and an English one (ultimatum – ultimata, ultimatums), choose the English one.

9.21 In hyphened compounds, only the appropriate noun takes the plural:
> brothers-in-law, passers-by
If there is no noun, add *s* at the end:
> lay-bys, go-betweens, stand-bys, take-offs
It is now normal to place *s* at the end of
> bucketfuls, pocketfuls, spoonfuls.

List of words commonly misspelt

absence	across	apparatus
abysmal	address	appearance
accessible	advertisement	argument
accidentally	already	arrangement
accommodation	although	attach
acquaint	amount	awkward
acquire	annual	

basically
because

beginning
believe

benefited
business

choose
chose
college
commitment
committed

committee
comparative
comparison
conscience
conscientious

conscious
consensus
control
criticism

daily
decisions
defence
definite
description
desirable

desperately
detached
develop
development
different
difference

diminution
disappear
disappointed
discipline
dissatisfied

eighth
efficient
embarrassment
equipment
exaggerate
exceed

excellent
excessive
excite, exciting
excitement
exercise
exhilarating

existence
expense
extraordinary
exuberant

favourite
February

fortunately
forty

fulfil
fulfilled

gauge
glamorous
government

grammar
grateful
grievous

guarantee
guard

harass
hare-brained
height

honorary
holiday

humorous
humour

idiosyncrasy
immediately
incidentally

independence
install
instalment

interested
irrelevant

jewellery (jewelry)

knowledge

liaison
leisure

loose

lose

maintain

medicine

miscellaneous

maintenance   miniature   mischievous
marvellous

necessary   ninth   noticeable
neighbour

occasion   occurred   omit
occasionally   occurrence   opportunity
occur

panicked   precede   procedure
parallel (ed)   preceding   proceed
parliament   prefer(red)   profession
particularly   prejudice   prominent
pastime   premises   publicly
playwrite   preparation   pursue
possess   privilege

queue

receipt   refer(red)   relevant
receive   recognise   repetition
recommend

secretary   sincerely   supersede
seize   skilful   suppress
sentence   strength   surprise
separate   succeed

temporary   tragedy   twelfth
tendency   truly   tie, tied, tying

undoubtedly   unnecessary   until
unmistakable   unparalleled

vicious   vigorous

weird   wilful   woollen

10

Words Sometimes Confused

The words listed here may have other meanings besides the ones given. Only those meanings which are a possible source of confusion are quoted.

adapt   adjust, modify, alter (*The shop is being adapted to provide more display space*).
adopt   take up, accept (*We ought to adopt their suggestion*).
    The corresponding nouns are **adaptation** (not *adaption*, which does not exist) and **adoption**.

adhesion and **adherence** both mean *sticking* (*to*), but **adhesion** is used in the literal sense (*the adhesion of tiles to the wall*) and **adherence** in the sense of sticking to a plan, belief or cause (*adherence to one's principles*). The corresponding adjectives are **adhesive** (*adhesive tape*) and **adherent**. Both of these may be used as nouns: an **adhesive** is a sticky substance, and an **adherent** is a supporter (of a political party etc.). The verb is **adhere**.

admission and **admittance** mean *permission to enter*, but **admission** is the more normal word, **admittance** the more formal and official one normally used in negative senses (*He was refused admittance to the building. No admittance except on business*).

adverse   opposed, unfavourable. An *adverse reaction* to a proposal is one that is hostile.
averse   unwilling, reluctant, disinclined (*He's not averse to the*

idea). Both words are followed by *to*. Note that **averse** cannot be applied to a noun: *adverse comment*, not *averse comment*.

affect (verb)   influence, act on (*How has his death affected her?*); pretend (*He affected not to be concerned*).

effect (verb)   bring about, achieve, accomplish (*To effect an escape*).

effect (noun)   result (*His warning had no effect*); state of being operative (*To put a plan into effect*).

    The common mistake is to use **effect** (verb) for **affect**. Either *Ill health has affected* (not *effected*) *his career* or *Ill health has had an effect on his career*. There is no noun *affect* in common use.

already   before a particular time (*When we arrived the show had already started*).

all ready   all prepared (*The cutlery is all ready on the sideboard*).

alternate (adj.)   first one, then the other, in turn (*The two care-takers work the night-shift on alternate weeks* i.e. each has one week on, then one week off).

alternative (adj.)   available in place of another; affording a choice (*There is an alternative method*).

    The same distinction applies to the corresponding adverbs **alternately, alternatively**.

altogether   completely; on the whole (*I forgot altogether*).

all together   all at the same time or in the same place (*Parcel them all together*).

always   at all times (*He is always helpful*).

all ways   (in) every possible way (*We've tried all ways*).

amiable   friendly and inspiring friendliness. (Applied only to people.)

amicable   in a friendly spirit. (Applied to things e.g. *an amicable agreement, meeting, arrangement* etc.)

anyone   any person (*Has anyone seen my pen?*)

any one   any single (thing) (*Any one of those styles would suit you*).

appraise   form a judgement about. *To appraise a problem* is to evaluate it.

apprise   inform. *To be apprised of a problem* is to be told about it.
   The former is sometimes used when the latter is needed. The expression *to appraise oneself of* (intended to mean *to inform oneself about*) is nonsensical. *To apprise oneself* is needed.

aural has to do with hearing or the ear, **oral** with speaking or the mouth, and **verbal** with words.
   It is common to speak of a *verbal message* or *verbal agreement* when one means a message or agreement by word of mouth (e.g. by telephone) rather than in writing. Prefer **oral** if there is any danger of confusion with the meaning of **verbal** in its more general sense.
   Aural and **oral** have the same pronunciation.

beside (prep.)   by the side of (*Sit beside the fire*).

besides (prep.)   in addition to, except (*No-one was there besides us*).

besides (adv.)   moreover, otherwise (*It will take too long. Besides, I don't think it'll work*).

censor (verb)   remove undesirable parts of (book, film etc.).

censure (verb)   blame, condemn.
   The same words act as nouns with corresponding differences of meaning.

ceremonial (adj.)   having to do with ritual or ceremony (*a ceremonial occasion*, *ceremonial uniform*).

ceremonious   very formal, polite, punctilious; addicted to ceremony. Found mainly in **unceremonious(ly)**, meaning *without politeness*.

circumvent   avoid (*to circumvent a problem*).

circumnavigate   sail around (*to circumnavigate the world*).

classic (adj.)   of the highest class; outstandingly typical (*a classic example of bureaucracy*).

classical (adj.)   characteristic of the literature or art of ancient Greece and Rome (*classical civilisation*). The word is also applied to serious music.

classic (noun)   thing of the highest quality (*This novel is a classic*). But **the classics** are the literature of classical antiquity as well as distinguished works of art of other countries or periods.

cohesion and **coherence** both mean *sticking together*, but **cohesion** is usually used of people or things, both in its literal sense (*the cohesion of groups of atoms*) and in the figurative sense (*The team lost its cohesion*).

   Coherence is usually applied to thoughts or words, in the sense of *capacity to be understood* or *consistency* (*the plan lacked coherence*).

   The corresponding adjectives are **cohesive** and **coherent**.

compare   note the similarities and differences (*compare notes*); liken (*He should not be compared to his brother*). See **compare to** on page 72.

contrast   show differences on comparison (*contrasting colours*).

compliment   expression of praise (*pay a compliment*). In the plural, it means *greetings*.

complement   thing that completes. The *complement of a ship* is the number required to man it completely.

supplement   thing that is added (to make up a deficiency). (*His earnings from part-time work are a supplement to his pension*).

   These three words are also verbs with similar differences of meaning.

consecutive and **successive** mean *following on one behind the other*, but **consecutive** refers to logical or uninterrupted sequence (*three consecutive numbers*) and **successive** to any kind of sequence (*three successive accidents*).

consequent (**on**)   following (from) as a result (*The storm, and the consequent damage . . .*).

subsequent (to)   following (*The storm, and the subsequent fine weather . . .*).

contemptible   deserving contempt; despicable. *A contemptible remark* is one that causes the hearer to feel contempt for it.

contemptuous   expressing contempt. *A contemptuous remark* is one that shows the speaker's contempt for someone or something.

continual   always or frequently happening. A car's *continual breakdowns* occur often but are (necessarily) separated by periods of normal functioning.

continuous   happening without any interruption. A *continuous flow of water* is incessant.

council   assembly, as in *Town Council, council house*.

counsel   advice, as in *counsel of perfection* i.e. ideal but impracticable advice. The word is also applied to a barrister (*counsel for the defence*) and is used as a verb meaning *advise*.
Similar distinctions exist between **councillor**, **counsellor**.

credence   belief, trust, acceptance. *Give credence to* means *believe*.

credibility   quality of being believable. Anything that *lacks credibility* lacks the qualities in which we normally place belief.

credulity   readiness to believe anything. The opposite to **incredulity**, refusal to believe.
The common error is to confuse **credence** and **credibility**.

credible   believable. The opposite is **incredible**.

creditable   bringing credit or honour, as in *a creditable achievement*.

credulous   too ready to believe anything. A *credulous person* is one who is easily taken in. An **incredulous** person is unwilling to believe.

defective   having a defect. *Defective brakes* are faulty.

deficient insufficient, lacking, incomplete (*Their diet is deficient in carbohydrates*).

delusion false belief. *He is under the delusion that . . .* means that he has a false opinion or impression.

illusion misapprehension. *He has no illusions about his chances of promotion* means that he perceives them clearly.

In the general sense of *mistaken belief* the words are synonymous, but **illusion** specially refers to deception by something which is not what it appears to be.

allusion (indirect) reference (*He made no allusion to his illness* i.e. he did not mention it).

demur (at) raise objection (to). Rhymes with *recur*.

demure quiet and serious. Rhymes with *secure*. The first is sometimes wrongly pronounced as if it were the second.

dependent (adj.) relying on (*He is dependent on drugs to control his illness*).

dependant (noun) person who depends on another for support. One's *dependants* are *dependent* on one.

deprecate express (or feel) disapproval of (*Everyone deprecates violence*).

depreciate diminish (in value) (*Cars depreciate rapidly*).

Confusion may arise because **depreciate** also means *belittle*: one may therefore *depreciate* (be disparaging about) or *deprecate* (disapprove of) a person's achievements.

derisive mocking, ironical. *Derisive cheers* or *laughter* express derision.

derisory so inadequate as to be ridiculous. *The management's derisory wage offer* invites derision.

detract from take away from, depreciate (*Electricity pylons detract from the beauty of the landscape*).

distract draw (attention) away from; sidetrack, divert the attention of (*The examinees were distracted by the noise of passing* *traffic*). The word carries the sense of interruption, confusion or perplexity in the mind.

disinterested impartial, free from self-interest. *To take a disinterested view of a matter* is to have no regard for one's personal interest (i.e. advantage).

uninterested not interested. *To be uninterested in a matter* is to be indifferent to it.

It is a common error to use **disinterested** to mean the opposite of **interested**.

distinct clearly perceivable or distinguishable. A *distinct smell of burning* is a definite, unmistakable one.

distinctive distinguishing, characteristic, peculiar to one thing. The *distinctive smell of gas* distinguishes gas from anything else.

disused no longer in use. A *disused factory* implies that it is no longer serviceable.

unused not used, not yet used. *Unused machinery* implies that it is serviceable. In this sense, the *s* is pronounced *z*. The word may also be pronounced with the *s* sounding *s*; the meaning is then *unaccustomed*, as in *We are unused to long holidays*.

economic having to do with the science of economics, the study of the production and distribution of wealth. Thus *economic growth, economic recovery, economic problems* etc.

economical thrifty, avoiding unnecessary waste. The *most economical way* of doing something is the way that saves most money, time, effort, etc.

effective having an effect. *Are nuclear arms an effective deterrent?* asks whether they bring about the desired result.

efficacious has the same meaning (and may safely be ignored, as may its noun **efficacy**). It is normally applied to words like *treatment, remedy*.

effectual is another synonym, normally found in the negative (*not very effectual, ineffectual*) to denote human ineffectiveness.

efficient having a good effect; businesslike, successful.

All these words share the basic meaning of *producing an effect*; only the first and last have useful shades of meaning.

elder is applied to the more senior of *two* persons, usually close relations (*his elder brother*), **eldest** to the most senior of more than two (*He is the eldest of the three children.*) An *elder statesman* is a person of long and respected experience, and *one's elders* are people who are older than oneself.

    Older, oldest mean the same as **elder, eldest**, which are now used mainly of one's own children.

emotive   arousing emotion. An *emotive issue* gives rise to strong feeling.

emotional   expressing emotion. An *emotional meeting* is filled with strong feelings.

ensure   make certain (of). We may *ensure the success* of a venture by *ensuring that everything is fully prepared*.

insure   guarantee against risk, harm or loss by paying **insurance**.

assure   make (person) sure or confident (*I was assured that there was nothing to worry about*).

especially   in particular, particularly, pre-eminently (*This room is especially beautiful* i.e. more beautiful than the others).

specially   for a special purpose (*The room has been specially decorated* i.e. for a specific purpose).

    There is no such distinction between **especial** and **special**; the latter is more common.

everyday is adjectival (*An everyday occurrence*).

every day is adverbial (*Milk is delivered every day*). Two words are always needed when *every* is an adjective and *day* a noun (*Every day brought worse news*).

everyone is used to refer to people (*Everyone was doing his best*).

every one is used to refer to things (*Every one of the shops was closed*). It is used of people when the meaning is *every single one*, as in *Every one of the competitors was awarded a prize*.

exceptional   unusual (*The heat was exceptional*).

exceptionable   open to objection (*His behaviour was not exception-able*). The more usual form is **unexceptionable**, not open to objection, as in *His behaviour was unexceptionable* i.e. no-one could take exception to it.

further and **farther** are synonymous when referring to distance, as are **furthest/farthest**, though the most commonly used forms are **further** and **furthest**.
   Further also has the senses of *additional* (*until further notice*), *in addition* (*He has nothing further to say*), and *advance* (*to further a cause*).

fictional   belonging to fiction, i.e. to literature. A *fictional character* is a person in a novel etc.

fictitious   not genuine. A *fictitious name* is an assumed one.

flaunt   display conspicuously; show off, as in *flaunt one's wealth*.

flout   treat with contempt, as in *to flout the rules* or *to flout someone's authority*.
   The first is sometimes used when the second is required, as in *to flaunt the law*.

formerly   in the past (*He was formerly a teacher*).

formally   as required by convention or rules, especially those of politeness (*He was formally dressed*).

forward and **forwards** are synonymous adverbs (*to move forward(s)*) though **forward** is more common. Only **forward** is possible as an adjective (*forward movement*) and verb (*to forward a letter*).

historic   noteworthy, so as to deserve a place in history (*a historic victory*) or having a long history (*historic houses*).

historical   concerned with history (*a historical novel*) or relating to history rather than legend etc. (*a historical character*).

hoard (noun)   (secret) store. The word is also a verb meaning *save and store up*.

horde   large crowd of people or insects (*hordes of demonstrators*).

imply   suggest indirectly; hint (*The Prime Minister's speech implied that tax changes were being considered*).

infer   deduce (*MP's inferred that tax changes were being considered*).

The common error is to use **infer** instead of **imply** (*The Prime Minister's speech inferred that* . . .). A writer or speaker implies: a reader or hearer infers.

industrious   hard-working.

industrial   related to industry in its sense of trade or manufacture (*an industrial dispute*; *the Industrial Revolution*).

inedible   not able to be eaten because of its nature. Poisonous plants are **inedible**.

uneatable   not able to be eaten because of its condition. Meat which is **edible** may be **uneatable** through being over-cooked.

inquire/inquiry are interchangeable with **enquire, enquiry**, but it is usual for the *en-* forms to be used of asking questions, and the *in-* forms of making investigation. To *make an enquiry* is to ask for information; to *hold an inquiry* is to make an (official) investigation.

lay (transitive verb)   place down (*lay a carpet*, *lays hands on* etc.). The past form is *laid* (*He laid/had laid a trap*) and the present participle is *laying* (*The hurricane is laying waste the whole area*).

lie (intransitive verb)   recline, rest (*lie sunbathing*, *lies down*). The past tense is *lay* (*The ship lay at anchor*), the past participle *lain* (*She has lain awake all night*) and the present participle *lying* (*I found him lying there*).

The common error is to use *laid* instead of *lay* (e.g. in *He laid down on the bed*) or *lain* (*He had laid in wait all night*). Being part of a transitive verb, *laid* must always have a direct object.

lend is the verb, **loan** the noun. In America, **loan** is a verb meaning *lend*, and this use is becoming well established in Britain, perhaps on the grounds that *Can you loan me a pound?* sounds less blunt than *lend*.

licence (noun)   permission (*driving licence*); abuse of freedom.

license (verb) grant permission (*licensed premises* are those which have been granted *a licence* that alcoholic liquor may be served).

may be is a verb; **maybe** means *perhaps*. Thus *Maybe the fuse has blown* but *It may be that the fuse has blown*.

metre unit of length (*Fifty metres long*).

meter instrument used to measure something (*Parking-meter*).

mitigate alleviate, moderate, lessen (*His apology mitigated her anger*). *Mitigating circumstances* are those that make an error or crime seem less severe.

militate (against) operate, have effect (against) (*The scandal has not militated against* i.e. had an adverse effect on *his popularity*).

It is a common error to use the nonsensical expression **mitigate against** instead of **militate against**.

official having authority. An *official letter* comes from a person holding office, in a position of authority.

officious giving unwarranted advice. An *officious letter* is meddlesome, likely to be bossy in tone.

onwards exists only as an adverb (*to march onwards*) but **onward** is both adverb and adjective (*onward transmission*).

In most cases, neither word means more than *on*.

outward and **outwards** are interchangeable as adverbs (*to move outward(s)*), but only **outward** may be used adjectivally (*his outward appearance*).

partially not completely (*They were partially successful*).

partly in part (*The sculpture was partly in wood, partly in metal*).

practicable capable of being done. *A practicable scheme* is one that can be put into practice. The opposite is **impracticable**.

practical concerned with practice (not theory). *A practical man* is good at doing things; a *practical examination* requires you to do or make something. The opposite is **unpractical** (usually applied to people) or **impractical** (not useful in practice).

practice is a noun (*to make a practice of doing something*) which may· be used as an adjective (*a practice match*).

practise is a verb (*to practise the piano*).

The difference may be remembered by analogy with **advice** (noun) and **advise** (verb), where the pronunciation helps.

precipitate (adj.)   hasty, rash (*a precipitate departure* or *action*).

precipitous   very steep (*a precipitous slope*).

The second is sometimes used when the first is needed (*He acted precipitously*).

principal (adj.)   chief (*one's principal source of income*). It may be used as a noun (*a college Principal*).

principle (noun)   basic truth; rule of right conduct (*I objected on principle* i.e. as a matter of moral code).

prise (prize)   force with a lever (*to prise open a container*).

pry   look or ask inquisitively or impertinently (*to pry into other people's business*).

Ludicrous expressions like *pry open the lid* are sometimes found.

prophecy is the noun, **prophesy** the verb.

recourse (noun) is found mainly in *have recourse to*, seek help in.

resort is both noun (*in the (as a) last resort*, when everything else has failed) and verb (*resort to*, have recourse to).

resource (noun)   source of help; expedient (*Surrender was their only resource*).

It is wrong to say *have resource to* or *in the last resource*, though *as a last resource* is correct.

relationship   state of being related.

relations   ways in which one is related.

In practice the difference is often immaterial (*How's your relationship with your neighbours? How are your relations with your neighbours?*) but *relationship to* implies family relationship, and *relationship with* is used of other connections e.g. social, business.

restive refusing to be controlled. A *restive crowd* is impatient and irritated.

restless unable to rest.

review (noun) survey, examination (*The report is a review of the company's progress*).

revue entertainment consisting of songs and short acts.

sociable liking company. A *sociable person* is friendly and communicative.

social having to do with society or the community. A *social function* is one where people gather (though it may not necessarily be very *sociable*).

stationary is the adjective, **stationery** the noun. Remember *a* for adjective in *-ary*.

suit and **suite** are used of a set of matching things. **Suit** is applied to clothes (and to clothing for a particular purpose, as in *space suit*) and playing cards (hence *follow suit*). **Suite** (pronounced *sweet*) is applied to furniture, rooms, pieces of music, and people forming a group of attendants.

wake cease to sleep. The past tense is **woke** and the past participle **woken** (*He woke (up) early. He had woken early*).

awake (awoke, awoken) has the same meaning.

waken, awaken also have the same meaning, but they have the past tense and past participle **wakened, awakened**.

Wake is the most usual form, and is the only one that can be followed by **up**.

11

Style

The purpose of writing is to communicate – to transfer thoughts and feelings to another person so that he experiences them as precisely as the writer does.

Because the writer feels the need to communicate, it does not follow that the reader feels the same need to be communicated with. The writer must therefore express himself not only accurately and correctly but in a *manner* that is best calculated to catch the reader's attention and interest, and make the process of communication a stimulating one. This manner is what is known as 'style'.

A stimulating style is not the same as a journalistically punchy or racy one (though journalists have something to teach us: they write for a living, and will not succeed if they are dull). Nor is it the same as a familiar or chatty style, full of colloquialism, slang or loose expression, similar to the way many people speak. There are times when such styles are appropriate, just as there are times for seriousness, humour, formality, persuasion, provocativeness or firmness – all of which affect the manner of writing. Good style is having something to say, having it clearly formulated in the mind or feelings, and saying it, in one's natural voice, in a way that suits the occasion, the purpose and the reader. The effective writer knows, from his reading, study and practice, not only what words mean and what fine shades they are capable of, but also how they may be arranged in different patterns to make different effects.

Some people will argue that style cannot be taught: budding novelists, playwrights or poets, if they are any good, will have their own natural, instinctive, untaught style, acquired as mysteriously as genius always is, whether in writing, music, art or any other creative activity. But most people use English for a more humdrum purpose, perhaps in their daily work – and even if what they send to their readers has to be read as a matter of business or duty, that is no excuse for humdrum writing, flat and lifeless. This chapter is about some practical ways in which the ordinary user of English can put together his words so that their effect is more likely to be fresh, alive and interesting, not feeble, flavourless and boring.

11.1   Avoid the abstract whenever possible; the concrete or pictorial is more visual and tangible, familiar and striking, more readily able to appeal to the mind's eye.

The following illustrations show how some abstractions (italicised) in common use may be easily avoided, not necessarily by replacing them with concrete terms, but simply by cutting them away. They are often used unthinkingly, out of a habit related to the modern fashion for using more words than necessary. Pruning abstractions eliminates much vagueness and leaves writing sturdier. The pruning is easy, proving how little work some abstractions do. Many words are saved – and, as has been said before, the fewest words usually make for the most effective writing.

a speech of a controversial *nature*	(a controversial speech)
work on a voluntary *basis*	(voluntary work)
in the *majority* of *cases*, breakages occurred . . .	(most breakages occurred . . .)
a certain *amount* of difficulty	(some difficulty)
is not a practical *proposition*	(cannot be done)
the *nature* of the problem is such that	(the problem is that)
should *circumstances* arise in which	(if)
the *trend* is towards earlier marriages	(people are marrying earlier)
a more modern *type* of	(a more modern)
in *respect* of	(about)
the *extent* of the damage	(how much damage)
complete *lack* of	(no)
a greater *measure* of	(more)
of a different *sort*/*character*	(different)
police *involved* in patrolling	(patrolling police)
an inadequate *level* of	(low)
families without an adequate *level* of income	(poor families)
from an educational *standpoint*	(educationally)
a considerable *proportion* of children	(most children)
a high *degree* of support	(strong support)

we are in a *situation* where we	(we)
an important *factor* to take into *account* is the weight	(the weight is important)
the school's performance in *terms* of exam results	(measured by)
the *situation* with *regard* to spare parts is that they are . . .	(spare parts are . . .)
there is a good *deal* of uncertainty in *connection* with the *overall position*	(nobody knows what's happening)

In many of these examples, eliminating abstractions means preferring single words to phrases.

11.2 Prefer the active to the passive (see **1.5** on page 4 for an explanation of these terms). A sentence in which the subject or 'doer' is dominant rather than submissive is likely to be stronger in its effect.

The passive is used, often in official or commercial writing, when the writer wishes to be indirect. Such lack of explicitness may stem from a polite wish to be unemphatic:

> Your application *was not felt* to be justified.

instead of

> Your application was not justified.

In a large organisation, the anonymity provided by a passive construction may be customary (or convenient):

> A refund *is not considered* appropriate.

instead of

> *We* will not make a refund.

though the 'house style' that some large companies now instruct their staff to follow insists on the active because it is more direct and natural, less wordy and stilted.

The passive is useful when the 'doer' of the verb is unknown or irrelevant.

> The road *has been dug* up.
> The land is *to be sold*.

or when a writer wishes to give more prominence, at the beginning of a sentence, to the recipient than to the doer:

> This version of the New Testament *was published* by an obscure group of fanatics, but its appearance aroused great interest.

In the absence of such justification the use of the passive may simply become a monotonous bad habit reflecting a diffident cast of mind. The following examples show how it may also be ugly, flat, unnatural and long-winded:

The certificate states what guns *are allowed to be acquired*, and how much ammunition *is allowed to be used*.	(. . . what guns you may acquire and how much amunition you may use)
Sufficient air *must be permitted* to circulate.	(Allow sufficient air to circulate)
Action *must be taken* by social workers to ensure . . .	(Social workers must ensure . . .)
It *is thought* by many critics that . . .	(Many critics think that . . .)
What *is being proposed* is . . .	(The proposal is . . .)

11.3   The personal is preferable to the impersonal. That is to say, personal pronouns such as *I* and *you* have more life than the impersonal *it* or *one*.

There is a convention – in academic writing, for instance, and in some officialese and business writing – that *I* and *you* should be hidden behind *it* (not *I suggested* but *it was suggested*). This is because personal pronouns are felt to obtrude too personal a flavour on writing which should be cool and detached because the emphasis is on facts, argument or the collective voice of 'the firm'. There is also an old-fashioned, rather aristocratic convention that *one* is less vulgarly direct than *I* or *you*, so that *one doesn't like* is preferable to *I don't like*, and *one should always* to *you should always*.

Too much use of *I* and *you* may, it is true, become overbearing; certainly too many sentences beginning *I* (an easy habit to fall into) may have a monotonous effect, even a pompous one. Conversely, any straining after impersonality may breed colourless writing, particularly if it entails the repetitive use of the artificial *one*. But the commonest trap is set by *it*. Beginning too many sentences with *It* is not only boring but weak: *it* encourages the passive form (*It is thought that* . . .), and the common use of *it* as an anticipatory subject holds up the true subject, often unnecessarily or wordily:

It may be that the phone's out of order
(Perhaps the phone's out of order)

(For other problems with *it*, see **4.2**(*k*) on page 45.) For these reasons, the impersonal *it* should be used carefully and sparingly:

It appears to me that . . .	(I think that . . .)
It is to be regretted . . .	(Unfortunately)
It will be observed	(You will see)
It should be obvious that	(Of course,)
It has been argued	(People have argued)
It may be true that	(Possibly)
It is often the case that	(Often)
It should be pointed out that	(Please note that)

11.4 The assertive is stronger than the unassertive. Words like *could, would, may, might, should* are indispensible, but they are often used unthinkingly, suggesting a degree of reservation or vagueness that is neither intended nor needed. Their omission in such circumstances improves readability and vividness:

It could have been more fully explained	(It wasn't fully explained)
I should also like to suggest that	(Moreover)
The danger would seem to have . . .	(The danger seems to have . . .)
You might not have known	(Perhaps you didn't know)
He may be under the impression	(Possibly he believes)
I should not like it to be thought	(Please don't think)

This last example brings together *should, it* and a passive construction, all of them weak and avoidable.

Other unspecific words include linking verbs (e.g. *appear, seem* – *seem* – see **1.5** on page 4) and vague terms such as *thing, nice* and *real*.

11.5 Some intensifying adverbs are so commonly used that they are in danger of losing their power to intensify; they include *definitely, tremendously, inevitably, extremely, undoubtedly, positively, really, absolutely, necessarily, perfectly, essentially, significantly, simply, intensely, particularly, terribly, certainly, completely, immensely, practically*. Such words occur frequently in couplings: *absolutely incredible, practically nothing, extremely serious, intensely boring, simply not true, immensely grateful, not necessarily, terribly worrying, perfectly clear, differ significantly, vitally important, definitely wrong*.

Not only do such commonplaces come close to cliché, they are often used so unthinkingly that they fail to carry weight; if anything, these adverbs weaken utterance instead of strengthening it, and sentences would usually be clearer and stronger if they were omitted, or replaced by more original adverbs.

The same is true of other habitual modifiers such as *actually*, *clearly*, *in fact* and *obviously*.

11.6 Though the negative (*not at all bad*, *no little concern*) and the double negative (*not unlike*, *not unreasonable*) have their uses, the positive is more direct and economical.

11.7 Nouns and verbs carry more weight than adjectives and adverbs. Modifiers bring important colour, originality, flavour and meaning to a sentence, but it is what they modify – nouns and, above all, verbs – that are the sinews of a sentence. A well chosen verb on its own is better than a weak one propped up by a showy adverb: one vivid noun is preferable to a nondescript one adorned by adjectives.

Of course, adjectives and adverbs cannot and should not be entirely excluded, but special importance should be attached to the selection of strong nouns and verbs, which may then be found to stand in no need of embellishment. Unbalanced writing – richly decorated but without substance at the centre – is indigestible and ultimately unsatisfying.

11.8 The natural pleasure of acquiring new words should not be matched by a determination to use unfamiliar words unnecessarily. The familiar is likely to carry more weight than the unfamiliar, which may irritate or patronise the reader.

11.9 Choose the short word in preference to the long. Sentences stuffed with polysyllabic words are likely to be turgid, pretentious or heavy-going for the reader. Short words are usually livelier than long ones, and there is good sense in the old recommendation that the word of Anglo-saxon root is stronger than the Latinate.

The main reason for choosing one word rather than another must always be the appropriateness of its shade of meaning; if no such reason exists, the shorter word is best for clarity, economy, and immediacy of comprehension. Passages of great literature often derive strength from monosyllables:

> That time of year thou mayst in me behold
> When yellow leaves, or none, or few, do hang
> Upon those boughs which shake against the cold,
> Bare ruined choirs where late the sweet birds sang.
>
> (Shakespeare, Sonnet 73)

Consider the lilies of the field, how they grow;
they toil not, neither do they spin; and yet I say
unto you that even Solomon in all his glory was
not arrayed like one of these. Wherefore, if God so
clothe the grass of the field, which today is, and
tomorrow is cast into the oven, shall he not much
more clothe you, O ye of little faith.
(St Matthew, Chapter 6)

Lilies that fes'er smell far worse than weeds.
(Shakespeare, Sonnet 94)

We are such stuff
As dreams are made on, and our little life
Is rounded with a sleep.
(Shakespeare, *The Tempest*)

Even two-syllable words like *glory*, *arrayed*, *fester* and *rounded* are given special emphasis here by virtue of their generally monosyllabic surroundings. The ordinary writer of English can learn a useful lesson from this: an important word of two or three syllables may gain a subtle shade of extra weight from being carefully placed among shorter words.

Polysyllabic words cannot be avoided, nor should they be: variety is important. But as a general rule, writers should go for the short word as often as they can.

11.10   The use of nouns as adjectives (*goods* train, *road* works) is one of the particular flexibilities of the English language, but it should be treated with moderation.

Headline-writers like the device because *Poll Selection Shock* is more striking than *Methods of selecting candidates for the election have shocked people*; journalists prefer *car-body assembly-line workers* to *workers on the assembly line for car bodies* because it uses fewer words. Politicians and management scientists follow suit: *public sector borrowing requirement* sounds safer than *state deficit*, and *the export sales management control function* looks more scientific than *the job of supervising people who sell things abroad*.

Normal people do not talk like that; they use pronouns and prepositions. Not more than two successive nouns should be used as adjectives (*road fund* licence, *home insurance* policy); more than that is unnatural if not baffling.

11.11 Avoid ugly repetition of the same sound:

> loud sounds are bound . . .
> the company's consequent cost-cutting
> tighter site-security might have frightened . . .
> several successive sentences
> flooded farmers face shortages of fresh fodder

Unthinking repetition of a word is also clumsy:

> He let slip that he had let them . . .
> In my view, he views the prospect . . .
> They put themselves out to put a stop . . .
> Taking into account the time taken
> He makes a living by making furniture
> Considering the attendance, the event was considered . . .

11.12 Sentence-openings should be varied. The normal pattern of *subject* + *verb* + *object/complement* is capable of several permutations:

Object before verb	That much I can understand.
Complement before verb	That this should ever have happened is a serious indictment of the authorities.
Verb before subject	Rarely have ethnic minorities . . .
	Do it they must.

Other variants:

Modifier before subject	Grim-faced, the mourners filed past.
Omission of elements	When (he was) young, he travelled . . .
	The guard (who was) in charge of the train . . .
	The food was good but (it was) expensive.

The opening of a sentence may be emphasised by inversion of the normal word-order to give prominence to a negative:

> Nor *is it* easy . . . (instead of the more conventional *It is not easy*)
> Never again will the Emperor . . .
> Not for nothing did the inventor . . .
> Nowhere are better examples found . . .
> At no time has it ever . . .
> In no circumstances could they . . .

Adverbs may be placed at the beginning of a sentence to change the normal pattern

> Seldom has there been more ill-feeling . . .
> Hardly had he sat down . . .

or for strong effect:

> Infrequently though it may happen . . .
> Suddenly the atmosphere changed (*Compare* The atmosphere changed suddenly)
> Quickly the call was answered.

In these examples, the shifting of the adverb to an early position from its normal one – after the verb – draws attention to it.

Sentence-openings are important in catching the reader's attention.

> The return of Parliament today means that the Home Secretary will soon find himself having to defend his changes.

The author (a newspaper leader-writer) obviously wants to strike a 'newsy' note, and so he begins by referring to a topical event (*the return of Parliament*), placing the words at the front of the sentence as its subject. Had he chosen, he could have reshaped his sentence to emphasise a different subject, such as the Home Secretary

> *The Home Secretary*, after today's return of Parliament, will soon find himself . . .

or his changes

> *The changes* made by the Home Secretary will soon have to be defended, after today's . . .

or both

> *The Home Secretary's changes* will soon have to be defended

or neither

> Today, with the return of Parliament, *the time* draws nearer for . . .

There are usually several ways in which a sentence may be begun; the writer should take care to choose the most effective one. It is easy to fall into a rhythm of beginning sentences in the same way. The pattern of openings should be varied.

11.13 In speech, emphasis is injected by laying stress on key words. In writing, emphasis has to be communicated by placing key words in strategic positions so that the shape and rhythm of sentences make it quite clear that certain words are intended to be more important than others. (The underlining of words for emphasis is to be avoided; it easily becomes a bad habit, like too much use of the exclamation mark, bludgeoning the reader.)

The most effective place for emphasis is at the end of a sentence which has been carefully constructed to lead the reader, with an increasing sense of expectancy, to a final climax – rather like what comic writers call the 'pay-off' or 'punch-line'. The next most prominent place is the beginning of a sentence. In consequence, weak or unemphatic words placed at the beginning or end of a sentence make for unemphatic writing.

These are the grounds for avoiding passive forms (*She was thought to have* . . .), impersonal constructions (*It is intended that we should* . . . instead of *We intend* . . .) and other low-key words or expressions at the beginning of sentences. Likewise, unemphatic adjectives, adverbs, prepositions or pronouns should not be placed in positions of advantage at the ends of sentences unless a dying fall is deliberately intended. There is no rule against ending a sentence with a preposition, but to do so is unemphatic: *a system we have confidence in* has less force than *a system in which we have confidence*, and *the answer they came up with* tails off in comparison with *their answer*; in both cases the nouns *confidence* and *answer* carry more meaning and therefore conclude the expressions more weightily than the prepositions *in* and *up with*.

> In spite of what people may say, they have nothing to fear.

has more impact, because the main statement is placed last, than

> They have nothing to fear, in spite of what people may say.

11.14 Even if no special emphasis is required, a writer should try to distribute interest by varying his sentence-structure so that the reader is not bored by repetitive sentence-shapes. To the reader's inner ear, sentences rise and fall, quicken and slow down, exactly as they do when spoken or read aloud. A writer needs to be aware of this, and compose his sentences so that their effect is similarly alive.

The following illustration shows how just three successive sentences (from a journalist's column) have been structured so that their main interest (i.e. what they are about) is placed at different points in the sentence-pattern. The first sentence, conventionally enough, reveals what it is about in the first few words (subject and verb); the rest of the sentence adds further information. This is in conformity with normal speech-patterns.

> Mr Bangs has recently had his rates increased, and is, understandably enough, displeased in consequence.

The second sentence, however, adopts a different pattern and defers the subject and main verb (italicised):

> When, therefore, a large and official-looking car passed him, in which he saw a gentleman in colourful, not to say ridiculous, clothes, *he suited* his actions to his feelings . . .

The sentence continues with a second main clause, but the main interest is deliberately held back until the very end:

> . . . and extended the first and second fingers of his right hand, knuckles outwards, in its direction, believing that the gorgeously caparisoned traveller was the Mayor.

The following sentence holds the reader in suspense until half way through:

> In this, it speedily appeared, he was mistaken, for the man at whom he had made his rude gesture was not only blameless in the matter of the rates; he was Mr Justice Lawson . . .

and the remainder of the sentence, instead of coming to a further climax, is allowed to tail away:

> . . . on his way to clock in for the morning shift at Teesside Crown Court, and what is more he was accompanied by his oppo, Mr Justice Mays by name and rank.

This brief example shows that variety is not just a matter of mixing sentence-ingredients (main clauses, subordinate clauses etc.) in different ways, but of placing the main weight of meaning and interest in varying positions, sometimes at the beginning, sometimes in the middle and sometimes at the end of sentences, so that the style is always fresh, keeping up the reader's interest.

11.15 For normal purposes it is unwise to veer sharply between a formal and an informal style – between the high-flown and the vernacular, or between standard English and the colloquial. That may puzzle the reader, draw attention away from matter to manner, and suggest that the writer is not in secure control of his medium.

The sentences quoted in the previous section illustrate a legitimate use of stylistic inconsistency, however. The general tone is formal, even literary – *displeased* is arch understatement, *gorgeously caparisoned* is high-flown, *speedily* and *blameless* are a little out of the ordinary, and *in the matter of* is almost legal terminology. After nearly a paragraph in this careful style, the writer unexpectedly throws in the colloquial *clock in* and the slang *oppo*, and applies the factory worker's *shift* to a session at the Crown Court. In the context of a description of the law's majesty, the effect is comic and deliberately deflationary; the justification is, as the rest of the article goes on to make clear, that the writer's intention is to puncture the pomposity of some judges.

11.16 Main clauses are more important than subordinate clauses. Main clauses should therefore be reserved for main statements, subordinate clauses for less important material, and parentheses for the least important of all.

Writing which consists largely of simple sentences, or of main clauses linked by conjunctions, is likely to be all on the same level, as in this letter published by a local newspaper:

> We have at last been told about the Area Authority's plans. Two local hospitals are to close. There will be no maternity hospital in the centre of the town, and the nearest geriatric hospital will be seven miles away. I ask all your readers to sign our petition and make the strength of local feeling known. Come to our protest meetings and write to your MP. The Prime Minister has said that cuts will be small, and the Health Minister has promised that essential services will be safeguarded. These are not small cuts, and essential services are not being safeguarded. Expectant mothers will have to travel from the centre of town, and fathers will have to make the same journey after a day's work.

This is serviceable and clear, but it would have been more interesting and persuasive if there had been a balance of main and subordinate clauses to reflect the difference between salient points and less important ones:

> Now that we have at last been told about the Area Authority's plans, we know that two local hospitals are to close. Not only will there be no maternity hospital in the centre of town; the nearest geriatric hospital will be seven miles away. By signing our petition, coming to our protest meetings and writing to your MP, your readers can make known the strength of local feeling. Whatever the Prime Minister may say about the cuts being small, and the Health Minister about the safeguarding of essential services, expectant mothers will have to travel from the centre of town, as will fathers after a day's work.

11.17 Another common type of construction is the loose sentence in which phrase is heaped on phrase:

> Many people have been frustrated in the past few years by landowners allowing paths to become overgrown or deliberately obstructing pedestrian ways, including some established centuries ago, despite local councils having statutory obligations to clear obstructions and keep routes open for the benefit of walkers wishing to take advantage of opportunities to visit the open countryside near their homes, or within easy reach by car, for exercise or recreation, as is their right.

Again, this is reasonably clear, but too many such sentences would be indigestible. It is important to vary sentence-type, by mixing in occasional questions, exhortations or exclamatory statements along with a judicious blend of simple, double and complex sentences, to prevent the sameness of style that can lull a reader into inattentiveness.

11.18 Variety in the length of sentences is equally important. Too many short sentences may have a jerky or over-emphatic effect: too many long ones may tax or confuse. A careful mixture is best.

There can be no rule about how long a sentence should be: the length is governed by the thought or feeling that is to be expressed. But thoughts and feelings come in different shapes, sizes and weights; if they are accurately perceived by the writer, they will be reflected in the varying types, structures and lengths of his sentences.

Short sentences are quickly absorbed, which gives them a special vitality, an immediacy of impact on the reader's mind. This is useful in certain types of writing. Novelists and short-story writers sometimes introduce a number of short sentences one after the other to build up a sense of excitement, expectancy or drama, for example. Speech-writers or people who write prose which is intended to persuade know that a short sentence coming after an involved one, or following a passage of several longer sentences, can neatly clinch a point. But short sentences, because of their very shortness, cannot express intricate thought, nor can they offer the variety – the rise and fall, the different speeds and emphases of voice – that the construction and punctuation of more complex sentences can provide.

Even so, long sentences cause more problems than short ones, for the reader who has to absorb them as for the writer who has to construct them correctly. Many long sentences are, in fact, shorter ones needlessly yoked together by semicolons and conjunctions when full stops would have provided useful breathing-spaces. As a general rule, many writers would do well to check that their semicolons and conjunctions are justified, and to cultivate shorter sentences, provided always that they do not lapse into too level, uninteresting or repetitive a style.

11.19 Parentheses, whether between brackets, dashes or commas, are best kept short and infrequent. If they are long, they may lead the reader too far from the main sense, so that he can return to it only with difficulty. If they are frequent, they may obscure the sense with qualifications and reservations, and give the impression of writing so stuffed with afterthoughts that the writer would have done better to think before putting pen to paper.

The paragraph

11.20   A paragraph is a unit of thought comprising a group of sentences. Its essential feature is that the sentences are related to a single topic, so that a paragraph has unity and coherence.

The topic may be anything a writer chooses to make it. Most typically, it is a stage in an exposition, description or argument, or a step forward in a narrative. In turn, the topic is related to that of the previous paragraph and the following one, and all are organically related to the subject of a chapter, essay, short story or whatever larger unit the paragraphs are part of.

The topic is usually announced early in the paragraph, as a signal that the reader is, for example, being led into another aspect of the topic of the previous paragraph or into a completely new aspect of the more general theme. Often the topic is stated in the opening sentence or clause, after which it is enlarged, explained or illustrated. In the following examples, the topic is italicised:

> *Certain movements or events stand out in the history of English*: the settlement in this island of Jutes, Saxons, and Angles in the fifth and sixth centuries; the coming of St Augustine in 597 and the subsequent conversion of England to Latin Christianity; the Scandinavian missions in the eighth, ninth, and tenth centuries; the Norman Conquest in the eleventh; the revival of learning in the sixteenth; and the migration of English-speaking people to North America, Australasia, and South Africa mainly in the eighteenth and nineteenth centuries.
>
> Of all these movements *the first was clearly the most decisive*. Our knowledge of it is derived from . . .

> *English is not static* – neither in vocabulary nor in grammar, nor yet in that elusive quality called style. The fashion in prose alternates between the ornate and the plain, the periodic and the colloquial. Grammar and punctuation defy all the efforts of grammarisms to force them into the mould of a permanent code of rules. Old words drop out or change their meanings; new words are admitted. What was stigmatised by the purists of one generation as a corruption of the language may a few generations later be accepted as an enrichment, and what was then a common currency may have become a pompous archaism or acquired a new significance.

> To a visitor *they are understandably depressing, these massed proletarian areas*; street after regular street of shoddily uniform houses intersected by a dark pattern of ginnels and snickets (alley-ways) and courts; mean, squalid, and in a permanent half-fog; a study in shades of dirty-grey; without greenness or the beauty of sky; degrees darker than the north or west of the town, than 'the better end'. The brickwork and the woodwork are cheap; the wood goes too long between repaintings

– landlords are not as anxious to keep up the value of the property as are owner-occupiers. The nearest park or green open space is some distance away, but the terraces are gap-toothed with sour and brick-bespattered bits of waste-ground and there is a piece of free ground half a mile away, called 't'Moor'. Evocative name: it is a clinkered six-acre stretch surrounded by works and grimy pubs, with a large red-brick urinal at its edge.

While such 'front-loaded' paragraphs are probably the most common, and have the advantage of taking the reader along step by step, other patterns are possible and desirable. In the next example, the main point (again italicised) is introduced in the middle, the two opening sentences being devoted to groundwork:

The English, in their splendid isolation, used to regard foreigners as either a comic turn or a sexual menace. To learn a European language was, at best, to seek to acquire a sort of girl's-finishing-school ornament, at worst, to capitulate weakly to the enemy. Things are not very different now, but an uneasy awareness is dawning that *linguistic isolation is no longer possible*, that the tongues of these damned Europeans may have to be taken seriously if they persist in pretending not to understand English. Unfortunately many educated Europeans *do* understand English and are very ready to speak it to English travellers and write it to English business firms, thus soothing that uneasy awareness back into island complacency. But, in their soberest moments, most English people will admit that the attitude of 'Let them learn our language, blast them' will no longer do.

Another option is to defer the most important point to the end of the paragraph:

The schools have been held to blame for this (violence). But if they are indeed to blame, it is neither because of their lax discipline or because of the use of modern methods. The cause can only be that their curricula and teaching methods have not been fully adapted to the needs and interests of a potentially delinquent population; and above all that the areas where delinquency is common often have schools which are the least well served in terms of buildings and staff. Here social policy would surely dictate *an immense increase in the number of highly qualified staff and a substantial provision of playing-fields and out-of-school activities*, to compensate for the lack of elementary social provision in the area.

The shape of a paragraph reflects the shape of the writer's thought. If the thought is interesting and lively, it is likely that his paragraph-shapes will be interesting and lively in their variety. Too many 'front-loaded' paragraphs, for example, may fall like hammer blows. Variety of paragraph-shape, like variety in sentence-structure, is an important feature of style.

The coherence of a paragraph stems not only from its having a clearly recognisable topic, but from the ordering of sentences within a paragraph. In narrative, the order of sentences is naturally determined by the chronology of events. If an argument is being presented, logic or the deployment of pro's and con's will govern the disposition of sentences. Whatever the circumstances, the paragraph should develop smoothly, leading the reader confidently towards the next stage and giving him a sense that he is being steered by an orderly mind.

No rules can be given about how long a paragraph should be: all depends on the nature of the topic, and some topics are meatier than others. The only rule is that paragraphing, like punctuation, should help the reader by indicating new stages in the thought and by providing a sort of breathing-space. Just as a full stop signals the end of one unit of sense and the beginning of another, the start of a new paragraph on a fresh, indented line is the heaviest punctuation of all, marking the beginning of a more important new phase.

What can be said is that too long a paragraph may over-tax the reader. Moreover, in the hands of an inexperienced writer, the longer a paragraph goes on, the more likely it is to break down or offend against the principle of unity. Conversely, if a paragraph is very short – a mere sentence or two – what it contains may not be important enough to justify the prominence of a separate paragraph. Short paragraphs are not to be ruled out: carefully placed, they can be very effective – in providing a punchy opening to a piece of writing, for example, or as a strong contrast after a long paragraph. A succession of short paragraphs may be needed (though not very often) because the sense demands a jagged or assertive effect. But such brevity has to be justified by context and function. A business letter making three quick separate points needs three paragraphs of not more than a sentence or two, whereas three equally brief paragraphs would appear perfunctory in a letter of condolence.

As with paragraph-shape, variation in paragraph-length reflects changes in pace and rhythm and is an important resource for the writer who is sensitive to the cadences of prose. If his subject-matter dictates that all paragraphs should be of about the same length, well and good, though there is no special merit in such uniformity: on the contrary, there is some danger of monotony. Generally, however, his material, whether narrative, description, reflection or argument, will have its important moments and its subsidiary ones, its twists and turns, its slower and quicker passages, and paragraphs will be shaped – or will shape themselves – to match.

If the writer's mind and purpose are clear, and his thought is organic and ordered, the paragraphing will look after itself: it will occur naturally because we naturally organise our thoughts into units. Paragraphing is not a matter of adherence to rules and recommendations (though one can always learn from studying the skill and subtlety of other writers' paragraphing as one can from all their stylistic techniques). It is a matter of allowing thoughts and feelings to express their own rise and fall, amplitude or terseness, smoothness or harshness or clash, and representing these in the almost infinite variety that responsive paragraphing allows.

Conclusion

11.21 Good literature is not only to be enjoyed; it repays study. If a piece of writing is strikingly enjoyable or successful, why is this so? The answer will often lie in the force, originality or beauty of the meaning; it may also lie in the choice and grouping of words, the architecture of sentences, the smooth progression of balanced and varied sentences, even the very sounds of words, or their rhythms. Reading aloud will often suggest some of the answers, just as reading aloud one's own writing may disclose awkwardnesses and prompt some improvements. The everyday user of English may never need the effects that fine writers achieve, but to ponder them will teach him something about effective English.

11.22 When all is said and done, one's own style (what was called the 'natural voice' in the opening part of this chapter) is always preferable to a style artificially concocted and applied like make-up. Style comes from within: everyone has his own style because everyone has his own thoughts and feelings to express, and no two people are alike.

Style is affected by *what* is said, *to whom* and *why*. If what is said is a humorous account of a personal experience on holiday, the style in which it is expressed will, by the operation of the writer's instincts, be different from that used for an account of a disturbing or distressing experience. Content, in other words, shapes manner. So does audience or occasion: the style of a letter to a friend will differ from that of a business letter, reflecting a difference in relationships. The purpose of writing also affects style: compare the style of a textbook, which is intended to inform, with that of a novel, which is intended to entertain or move.

Provided that the writer knows *what* he wants to say, and has thought carefully about the *to whom* and *why* (and not every writer does, by any means), the style will follow naturally enough. What makes for an interesting style is, in the last resort, the distinctive personality of the writer firmly in control of his material and therefore of his medium.

12

Types of English

People tend to use one tone of voice when talking to friends and another when among strangers. Likewise the vocabulary and grammatical forms we use in relaxed circumstances may differ from those we use on more serious occasions. The language we use at a job-interview or when speaking in public is not likely to be the same as that of conversation within the family. These are some of the differences between **formal** and **informal** English.

12.1   Formal English is that of the business letter, the news bulletin, the minutes of meetings, the examination essay, the official report, the text book, the serious novel, or the leader columns, news items and feature articles of newspapers. It is not formal in the sense of being stiff or dignified, though these qualities may be needed at times. It is simply the language of reasonably educated usage when the occasion – the subject and the reader or listener – requires or expects a certain vocabulary and style.

12.2   Informal English is more akin to the language of normal conversation. We are more likely to hear it in the television chat-show than in the documentary, and in a speech to friends at a wedding than in a lecture, sermon, political address or prepared talk. Letters or telephone calls to friends, and the chatty tone in newspaper gossip columns, are more likely to contain the colloquialisms, slang and contractions of everyday English. This is not to say that it is bad English; bad English is that which is incorrect, unclear, unnecessarily long-winded, or inappropriate in style to the purpose it is intended to serve. Informal English is perfectly acceptable if it suits the occasion.

12.3   Because of social developments in the second half of the twentieth century there is now far more informality in the use of English, as there is in English social life. Those whose business it is to communicate with us – people in commerce, politics, journalism, broadcasting, and the public service, for example – now use a language that is more popular and accessible than used to be the case. Whereas 'good' English used to be defined as a special, high-flown and rather artificial style thought to be suitable for public occasions, official correspondence and the like, it is now felt to lie in a more natural tone of voice. This trend has been reflected in novels, plays and poems, which are now written in a language much closer to people than was the more 'literary' style of those written in the earlier part of this century. One result of this trend is that the everyday user of written English must be on his guard to draw a line between natural plain English used as a tool in his job, or for some other important purpose, and the more jocular raw English that is now heard and read on all sides.

12.4   It is difficult – and perhaps unnecessary – to differentiate between **colloquialism** and **slang**: a word or expression may be characterised as *colloq.* in one dictionary and as *sl.* in another. There may be similar differences of opinion over whether a word is to be regarded as colloquial or as standard English: the word *cheek*, meaning *effrontery*, is listed in Eric Partridge's standard *Dictionary of Slang and Unconventional English* as *colloq.*, as it is in the *Shorter Oxford Dictionary*, though the *Concise Oxford Dictionary* places no such qualification against it. The writers of dictionaries, like other writers, can only use the best judgement they have when deciding whether a word, as generally used, is sufficiently informal to be regarded as colloquial rather than as received English, or so informal as to be regarded as slang. The problem is complicated by the fluidity of any living language: words often enter the language as slang, become generally accepted as colloquial, and with the passage of time lose their colloquial flavour and become established as accepted English. The word *mob*, according to Partridge, was slang from 1688 to 1750 or thereabouts, colloquial from then until about 1820, and thereafter standard English. Many such progressions could be quoted, as well as cases of words remaining at the colloquial or slang stage, or dropping out of the language altogether. A language as widely used as English is subject to flux and innovation. Dictionary-makers record, as best they can, how a word is used, not how they think it ought to be used. In the many cases when words hover on the borderline between one category of language and another, the user of English has to rely on his own ear and the sensitivity which comes from wide reading.

12.5 Colloquial English may be defined as that which is acceptable (i.e. regarded as correct and appropriate) in ordinary conversation, or in writing intended for friends and acquaintances, as distinct from speech or writing for more dignified occasions or for people one does not know, when the more reserved, conventional vocabulary and syntax of formal or standard English will normally be appropriate. Something of this difference may be seen in the following pairings: *have a go* / try; *haywire* / in disorder; *fantastic* / very enjoyable; *have pots of money* / be very wealthy; *get the message* / understand; *like a dream* / exactly as one would wish; *set-up* / structure of an organisation; *have a down on* / dislike; *clean up* / make considerable profit; *great* / enjoyable; *pass the buck* / shift responsibility; *go on* / complain; *play up* / annoy; *get across* / made understood; *get at* / imply; *get* / understand; *get by* / manage to survive; *send up* / mock, mimic; *on the go* / constantly moving; *go to pot* / lose quality; *tough luck* / unfortunate; *precious little* / very little; *headache* / problem; *dim* / stupid; *duck* / dodge; *half-baked* / inadequately thought out; *digs* / lodgings; *must* / thing that must be done, seen etc.; *throw* / disconcert; *boss* / person in authority; *dump* / abandon; *bloody-minded* / uncooperative; *cushy* / pleasant, easy; *shove* / put; *crack up* / collapse under strain.

12.6 The simpler, more vivid and often more pictorial nature of colloquial language is intensified in **slang**, which also includes oaths, obscenities and vulgarisms. Slang is the most informal type of language, used only among friends and acquaintances, often in closed circles like the armed forces, schools and particular occupations as a private language. It is vivid and colourful, often jocular and ephemeral, but its use in speech and writing should be restricted to contexts where there is no possibility that the user will appear inappropriately facetious or loose.

The flavour of slang is seen in *rip off* / defraud; *monkey-tricks* / mischief; *money for jam* / money easily obtained; *tear a strip off* / reprimand; *diddle* / cheat; *nitty-gritty* / basic facts; *take for a ride* / deceive; *sort out* / punish; *off the top of one's head* / impromptu; *take the mickey* / tease; *broke* / without money; *booze* / drink alcohol; *conk out* / break down; *fuzz* / police; *kids* / children; *fluff* / bungle; *nifty* / smart; *mug up* / learn by study; *nick* / steal, arrest, police station; *dicey* / risky; *go spare* / become angry; *grab* / appeal to; *tripe* / nonsense; *piece of cake* / something easy; *shut-eye* / sleep; *pie-eyed* / drunk; *a bit thick* / unreasonable; *wash-out* / failure.

12.7 **Idiom** is the way in which words, phrases and constructions are peculiar to a language and characteristic of general usage, even though they often defy logic or the rules of grammar. No native user of English is likely to be puzzled by the number of adverbs or prepositions that may follow the verb *turn*, for example: they include *down, in, off, on, out, over, round, to, up, against, about* and *away*. A foreigner may be forgiven for being bewildered that *down* and *up* express direction in *turn up the hill* / *turn down one's collar* but not in *turn up at the party* / *turn down the sound*; that *over* means one thing in *turn over the page* and another in a company's *turn-over*; that there are colloquial meanings for *turn on* (excite), *turn off* (cause to lose interest), *turn-up* (unexpected event) which are not always closely related to the non-colloquial meanings of these expressions; and that *turn in* may mean *go to bed, abandon* (work), *hand in, fold inwards* or *deliver*. *Turn out* is logical in *turn out the drawers*, less logical in *it's turned out nice again*.

Idiom dictates that we are *at* a loss but *in* a quandry, *out of* sorts but *in* low spirits, aware *of* but alert *to*, agreeable *to* but in agreement *with*, *on* our guard but *at* the ready. It is also studded with numerous vivid expressions drawn from all manner of sources: *off the beaten track, high and dry, the lion's share, lick into shape, bolt upright, under one's thumb, stone deaf, at a pinch, cross swords with, home truths, fly in the ointment, hell for leather, queer one's pitch, bury the hatchet, play second fiddle, knuckle under, ducks and drakes*, and many others. Despite their homely flavour, these are Standard English, not colloquialisms, and provide a rich store of interest for the student of English.

12.8 Many of these examples show the importance of the **figurative** use of language. If a plan gets *the thumbs up*, the people who have approved it have not *literally* or actually raised their thumbs, of course. The expression originates in the gesture of approval which used to be made to spare gladiators' lives at ancient combats; from this, the phrase passed into the language to signify any form of approval. To *take one's hat off to* someone is to feel respect for him, just as men used to physically (i.e. literally) remove their hats to greet a lady, for example. Notice the difference between the figurative

He's been very brave. I *take my hat off* to him.

and the literal

I *took my hat off* to mop my brow.

Many expressions have both a literal and figurative meaning: a cricketer may describe the state of the pitch as *a sticky wicket* (literal – the playing surface, drying after rain, is awkward for batsmen); a difficult situation, experience or prospect may be (colloquially) described as *a sticky wicket* (figurative – not physically sticky, nor physically a wicket, but awkward, uncomfortable or liable to put one at a disadvantage).

Figurative expressions of this kind are drawn from many activities: crime (*red-handed* / in the very act of doing something, not necessarily murder); sea-faring (*on the rocks* / short of money, breaking or broken down, served with ice); agriculture (*crop up* / appear, occur); military service (*soldier on* / persevere in the face of difficulties); theatre (*bring the house down* / give a tremendously popular performance); gardening (*thorny* / hard to handle); shooting (*target* / objective); health (*not to be sneezed at* / not to be regarded as unimportant); the Bible (*the salt of the earth* / the best of men); animals (*let the cat out of the bag* / disclose a secret); trades (*other irons in the fire* / other interests); hunting (*hunt for* / search for); cookery (*half-baked* / not thorough); birds (*feather one's nest* / acquire money for one's comfort); the weather (*under a cloud* / in disfavour); time (*the eleventh hour* / the last moment); movement (*jump to conclusions* / assume rashly); the human body (*see eye to eye* / agree); fishing (*hook, line and sinker* / completely), and many others.

12.9 The **emotive** use of language also needs to be understood. The effective writer must be sensitive to slight but important shades of meaning and differences of emphasis carried by words which have the same dictionary definition. These differences often stem from different degrees of feeling which have become associated with some words. All words convey sense, but some have emotive overtones which indicate the user's attitude to that sense. These overtones are particularly important in the language of persuasion, such as that of politics or advertising. The matter is dealt with more fully in the next chapter, but may be approached in a preliminary way by considering the differences in these pairs: thin/slim, mistake/blunder, well-known/notorious, strong-willed/domineering, unclear/muddled, faint-hearted/cowardly, freedom/licence, decisive/

ruthless, easy-going/feckless, meticulous/finicky, unconcerned/ apathetic, suspicious/paranoid, informal/casual, condemn/damn, imprudent/fool-hardy, careless/slack, repetitive/monotonous. The first word in each pair is neutrally toned; the second conveys an additional sense of approval or disapproval. For example, to describe a task as *repetitive* is to state a plain fact; to describe it as *monotonous* is to state that it is repetitive and additionally that it has a disagreeable effect on the person carrying it out.

12.10 Journalese and the language of advertising frequently exemplify this use of language. Newspapers, especially in their headlines, prefer colourful – usually short – emotive words to more accurate but duller ones: *shock* (surprise), *slash* (reduce), *soar* (increase), *probe* (inquiry), *dash* (rapid journey), *blast* (criticise), *quit* (resign, retire), *row* (disagreement), *rap* (rebuke), *bombshell* (unexpected event), *dramatic* (unusual), *epic* (very unusual). Such words make for lively, action-packed writing; in headlines they serve their purpose in attracting attention. Whether they accurately reflect the events they purport to describe, or over-sensationalise them, or whether useful, strong words are made to lose their power by being applied inappropriately, is another matter. (If a darts match is *epic*, what word is left for an important human struggle?) Effective English matches the word to the occasion, and respects both. The popular press believes that strong sensations expressed in strong language sell newspapers; the ordinary user of English would do well to copy the better features of journalistic writing: crisp, clear English, directness of statement, and sentences of digestible length.

Advertising is more often concerned to create an atmosphere, influence attitudes and project a product-style than to communicate factual information. The words *garden* and *country* in *garden peas* and *country-fresh eggs* are used dishonestly: they evoke the wholesome and pleasant outdoors while glossing over the fact that mass-produced peas do *not* grow in gardens, and that most hens never see a blade of grass, let alone the country. The words of advertisements, like the photographs, drawings and films they accompany, usually suggest a mood; they do not stand up to close examination, and are not intended to. There is something lulling in the advertisers' unending repetition of *modern*, *perfect*, *lasting*, *powerful*, *best*, *finest*, *smooth*, *luxury*, *exclusive*, *natural*, *stylish*, *new*, *real*, *improved*, *scientific*. We do language a disservice if we allow ourselves to be lulled, and stop thinking about what words mean. It is not pedantic to ask what *only* is doing in *only £99*, to

object that *French fries* are not French, to point out that *softer,*
whiter and *better* are meaningless unless they answer the question
than what?, to be suspicious of prices *from £150*, to note that *SAVE*
£50 means *SPEND* (just as Government *savings* sound worthier
than *cuts*), and to wonder why we should buy a *new, improved*
product from a company that was equally stridently advertising the
old, unimproved version a month previously. What is the evidence
behind slogans like *The world's favourite airline*; *Probably the best*
lager in the world; *The impossible is now possible*; *You can't beat the*
experience? In days when politicians and politics are packaged and
sold by the same people who promote cat-food, and in the same
way, we do well to be alert and critical. Words matter.

12.11 Jargon is the specialist language of a group of people,
usually those belonging to the same occupation. It is not intended to
be comprehensible to the non-specialist:

> This dichotomy is explored through multiplaner interjuxtaposition
> of bivalent (quasi-multivalent) tone clusters with neo-aleatoric
> material arranged in spaced points, occlusions, anti-points and
> reflexes . . . ambidilectic thematism is highlighted by the organic
> reantiorientation of paraorganic material.

This sort of closed language (from a book of musical appreciation) is
frequently found in the English of computing, psychology and
sociology, and to a lesser extent in all writing which is expert-to-
expert. It is mechanical and turgidly transactional, but it serves its
purpose. Probably *spaced points, occlusions, anti-points* and
reflexes could be expressed in language we could all understand, but
a large number of words would be needed, and specialist short-hand
is obviously justified in specialist writing.

It is much less justified when there is evidence that jargon has
been invented merely to make the ordinary sound impressive. All
the following examples are drawn from only three pages of job-
advertisements in two newspapers, and illustrate the jargon of
personnel management. The compilers of these advertisements
obviously believe that serviceable words like *job, office, factory* or
pay are uncomfortably direct or vulgar, and that high-sounding
gibberish will flatter the expectations of applicants for posts in
industrial management, and dignify a simple commercial transaction. The jargon words, with translations in brackets, include

> ENVIRONMENT: If you would like some indication of our environ-
> ment (*surroundings, region*); you will not find a more dynamic
> environment (*place to work*); expertise in a transportation environ-

ment (*in transport*); a fast-moving high technology environment; overseas experience in a multi-cultured environment (*used to dealing with foreigners?*); a friendly and enthusiastic working environment (*office*); the most stimulating environment (*work*) a graduate can enter; an assembly-based production environment (*factory*); some experience of work in the commercial environment (*in commerce*); candidates with expertise outside the oil and gas environment (*industries*) are invited to apply; experience within a truck sales management environment (*used to selling lorries* – though *trucks* are more fashionably American).

LOCATION: We will invite you to interview at our locations in Reading and Warrington (*factories*); the location is at our Head Office (*job*); assistance with relocation where appropriate (*removal*).

PACKAGE: a comprehensive benefits package; a healthy package of remuneration; flexible remuneration package; the remuneration package includes a salary (!); attractive emolument package; excellent remuneration package; a particularly generous relocation package.

INNOVATIVE: We require an innovative man or woman (*with new ideas*); a programme of technical innovation in our labour-intensive production-units; a career with an accent on innovation; developing innovative new (!) packages in liaison with airlines.

HIGHLY (meaning *very*, which is not grand enough): a highly informal loosely structured environment; a highly desirable benefits package; we are a highly innovative company; to tackle problem-solving within highly limited time frames (*very quickly*).

INTER-PERSONAL: You should have first-class inter-personal skills (*ability to get on with people*); inter-personal skills of the highest order; inter-personal (*good*) relations with staff and customers are the key to success.

OVERALL (meaning, as usual, almost nothing): a range of responsibilities within the overall infrastructive plan; the overall requirement is a high contribution to the improvement of efficiency; the apprentice will have overall responsibility for the division; to develop particular skills within the framework of overall business needs.

Jargon is least forgivable when used in writing intended to be read by laymen. The solicitor may be forgiven his *aforesaid*, *hereinafter* and *hereunder* on the (debatable) grounds that they ensure legal precision, but there is no such excuse for the unthinking 'officialese' sometimes found in letters from the tax-man that baffle and infuriate the reader they are intended to inform, and make him suspect he is being bamboozled:

The assessment raised for 1979–80 was duplicated in error and therefore one of these was vacated. The basis of assessment for Schedule D Case I and II, other than commencement and cessation, is what is termed a previous year basis. This means that where income is returned for example up to the 5 April 1979 i.e. 1978–9 it forms a basis of the 1979–80 assessment. Thus the year ended 5 April 1979 your assessable income less capital allowances as shown on your 1979–80 income tax return was, under the previous year basis of assessment operating, assessed 1979–80.

This sort of language is less common than it was, but too many public servants and others who have to write to or for the general public still forget that the jargon they use among themselves is incomprehensible to others, and therefore ill-mannered.

12.12   Because of British history, and the international nature of English in recent centuries, the language has been constantly diversified and enriched by words and expressions imported from all over the world. In recent years, **Americanisms** have been the most noticeable source of innovation; mainly through the influence of television, some lively, interesting and useful vocabulary has been adopted.

Some Americanisms deserve to be resisted – the unnecessary lengthening of words (*transportation*, *utilisation*), the habit of adding spurious prepositions (*consult with*, *meet with*) and the polysyllabic gobbledegook of the politico-military vocabulary and of business management. There are no good reasons for adopting expressions that merely duplicate existing ones, or for using Americanisms merely because of their novelty, to show off one's cosmopolitanism.

Nor should Americanisms be rejected merely because they are American. We should welcome additions to the language (e.g. the use of *host* as a verb meaning *act as host to*) if they serve a need, if we are sure they will be understood when we use them, and as long as we adopt them thinkingly.

12.13   Foreign expressions. Many words entering the English language from other languages have become so thoroughly naturalised that they are no longer thought of as foreign, or even recognised as such except through some un-English spellings (e.g. *manoeuvre*, *bureaucrat*, *café*) or pronunciations (*restaurant*, *bouquet*, *debris*). Other more obviously foreign expressions in common use have established themselves because they express a useful shade of meaning or have the advantage of being briefer than their English translations (*bona fide*, *sub judice*, *ad nauseam*, *fait accompli*). Less common expressions (*mutatis mutandis*, *a priori*, *prima facie*) may be justified if their user is confident of being understood, and may even be unavoidable in the technical jargon of music, ballet, opera, art or cookery. If they are used in other circumstances, they may lay the user open to a charge of bad manners if they are not readily understood, of rashness if they are wrongly used, of pomposity if there is an English equivalent, and of conceit if he is suspected of merely showing off.

The use of *per* is avoidable in *per annum* / a year, *per hour* / an hour, *per capita*, *per person*, *per head* / for each person, and *per se* / in itself. The use of *per pro* or *p.p.* (typed at the end of a letter to show that the person who signs it does so *on behalf of* a superior or an organisation) is rapidly giving way to the simpler *for*. Other traditional foreign expressions with simple English equivalents include *re*/about, *via*/by (way of), *viz.*/namely, and *inter alia* / among other things.

When foreign nouns have foreign plurals (*formula*, *formulae*; *terminus*, *termini*) and English ones (*formulas*, *terminuses*), the latter are increasingly preferred.

The use of foreign expressions to dignify (*cuisine*; *artiste*; a bathroom *en suite*) should be treated with suspicion. The safest rule is to stick with plain English unless a foreign expression has no exact or reasonably concise equivalent.

13

Words in Action

I am *firm*. You are *obstinate*. He is *pig-headed*. All three italicised words carry the sense of *unwilling to budge from one's opinion or course of action*. But that is not to say that they have the same meaning. They are not interchangeable. To describe someone as *firm* is to make a neutral observation, but to call him *obstinate* is to express disapproval. To say that he is *pig-headed* is to verge on the abusive.

From these simple examples we see that some words express not only sense but also shades of feeling. They convey not only information (e.g. that X is unwilling to change his mind) but also the writer's bias or attitude towards that fact (e.g. that X's stubbornness is deplored). Moreover, when we read words that express feeling, our own feelings will probably be stirred in response. Thus reading is not simply a mental activity dealing with facts or arguments, but an emotional activity as well. The same is true of writing. In speech, feeling may be expressed by the inflexion of the voice – angry, happy, excited or solemn, for instance. In writing, it is by the careful selection (and placing) of words, having regard to the overtones of feeling they convey, that the full richness of language is deployed.

We cannot use words effectively unless we grasp that their total meaning includes these two ingredients, sense and feeling. This chapter also illustrates other ingredients: *tone of voice*, by which is meant the way words are used to establish a particular relationship between writer and reader; and *intention*, the way a writer's choice of words is affected by his purpose.

These four elements, working together, tell us what a writer is trying to achieve. Unless we can understand what his objective is, we cannot estimate how successful he is in attaining it, i.e. how *effective* the writing has been.

13.1

(*a*) **Chicken roasted in foil**   Wrap the chicken in aluminium foil, making the join along the top. Roast in the oven (400°F, Mark 6) for one hour. Undo the join and loosen the foil, and roast for a further ten minutes to brown the chicken. Serve with the usual accompaniments.

(*b*). The surface tension of a liquid in contact with its vapour diminishes as the temperature rises, and becomes zero at the critical temperature, when the surface of separation between vapour and liquid disappears.

(*c*) Walkers can reach Rosthwaite without too much use of roads. From Watendlath there is a well-signposted, broad track which has beautiful views as one reaches the low pass overlooking Borrowdale. From Grange, there is a path to the west of the river, through a fine birchwood; this is generally flat, though the path crosses the shoulder of a hill before the descent to Rosthwaite. This was the route that used to be taken by quarrymen on their way to the top of Honister, where slate working still takes place.

These are examples of the use of language to provide information. The words are factual, simple and clear, though the writer of the first extract assumes a modest expertise in his reader – knowing what are the *usual accompaniments* to roast chicken – and the second writer assumes an understanding of technical terms such as *surface tension* and *critical temperature*. This apart, the language is readily accessible to the average reader; there are no long words or verbose expressions to obscure the sense. The intention is to give instruction or explanation, and the choice of plain words reflects that intention. It is noticeable that the authors are in the background; in the third passage, *beautiful* and *fine* briefly indicate the writer's personal opinions and feelings about the landscape, but otherwise the writers are unobtrusive and anonymous, their feelings, opinions and personality being irrelevant to the work in hand.

This is transactional English, the sort we find in news items, instruction handbooks, business letters, scientific treaties, technical reports, textbooks and the like. The appeal is to the reader's mind, not to his imagination or feelings, and so the tone of voice is correspondingly formal and unexcited, reflected in unemotional vocabulary and uncomplicated expression. Nothing is allowed to come between the reader and the sense he is to apprehend.

13.2

> Estate cars used to look like a cross between the baker's van and Ann Hathaway's Cottage. Quite a few still have the elegance of a suma wrestler. The Citroen Safari, in sharp and delightful contrast, might have been created for *Star Wars* or one of the other big-budget sci-fi epics. It will look good at the turn of the century when its 1984 rivals appear as quaint and dated as the old timber-framed dinosaurs do today. But that's typical. Citroens in general, and big Citroens in particular, have never been anything if not futuristic.
>
> The sleek, shark-like styling is not just an exercise in automobile cosmetics. It envelops a bumper bundle of appropriately advanced technology combined with the luxury of a five-seater limousine and a small truck's ability to swallow loads. A week with the latest CX25 TRI 5-speed variation on the Safari theme left me with no doubts about its right to be hailed as the thinking man's estate car. Where else can you exchange just under £11,000 for such a sophisticated cocktail of grace, speed, comfort, convenience, economy and versatility?

The author himself is more prominent here. He seeks to get on good terms with the reader by the jokiness of the first two sentences. The familiar tone of voice is continued in the slang of *sci-fi* and the colloquialism of *that's typical*. He makes a personal appearance in the penultimate sentence. His personal feelings are undisguised: instead of *in sharp contrast* he prefers *in sharp and delightful contrast*; for him the car's shape is not unusual, striking, surprising or startling but *eye-catching*, which carries the additional sense of attractive.

The reader's own attitudes to the subject are shaped by the choice of words. He is not invited to consider a mere car, but to think in terms of *automobile* and *limousine*, much grander words; nor is it a model but a *variation on a theme*, a term drawn from the art of music. The appeal to the reader is evident in *the thinking man*, flatteringly thought of as enjoying a *sophisticated cocktail* (even if a cocktail, whether of alcohol, fruit or explosives, normally has physical ingredients, not abstract ones like *speed* and *versatility*). Other words too shape the tone: the car has *styling* (not the humbler *shape*), it *swallows* loads so that they disappear, and it deserves – or rather has the *right* – to be *hailed* i.e. with acclamation, not just to be 'called' something. To acquire it, you do not vulgarly spend but *exchange* a sum of money.

We can identify the language of advertising even without being told that the extract is from a magazine published for a car company. The vocabulary is colourful and emotive, appealing to the reader's feelings. There are facts (*5-speed*, *just under £11,000*) but they carry little weight compared with the atmosphere of glamour established in words like *epic*, *futuristic*, *sleek* and *luxury*. This is not to say that the writing is bad. The author had a certain intention, different from that of the writers quoted in **13.1**, and he uses a different style of writing to match that intention. His success is to be measured by the extent to which he presents the car as a prestige product, interests us in it, and makes us feel favourably disposed towards it, not by the extent to which he uses one sort of vocabulary rather than another.

The sort of language examined here is that used in persuasion, whether by advertisers, salesmen or politicians. The handiest examples of it are found in television advertisements, which often tell us little that we can evaluate with our minds but which create moods (reinforcing what is called 'brand-image') to which we are expected to respond feelingly. The words used have little importance for the sense they carry; what matters is the vague, warm, suggestive, emotional overtone of carefully selected words, with the images and associations they evoke. It is a use of words to which we shall return later in the chapter, in a more literary context. For the moment, let us turn to another sort of persuasive language, from the leader column of a national newspaper, the *Guardian*, commenting on the French lorry-drivers' blockade of major roads in February 1984. Note that the writer's personality, emotions or prejudices are largely hidden: they are irrelevant to, and may even detract from, a dispassionate presentation of facts and argument in a matter of national importance. It is the public, collective voice of the newspaper that is speaking, not an individual's special or idiosyncratic voice. The authority of the article would be weakened if it was too obviously one man's personal view.

13.3

(*1*) The road network of western Europe has not experienced anything like it since the Battle of the Ardennes, which was neither a comparable occasion nor anything like as widespread. Now the one-sided battle of the juggernauts has become by a comfortable margin the biggest traffic jam since the invention of the wheel. In blockaded France there is a strong whiff of 1968 as a helpless government fumes in the face of the greatest national chaos since ten million people downed tools in generalised protest against the state. The original cause of the trouble, an overtime ban by Italian customs men (compounded by an unrelated French customs protest now settled), has long since been buried by a catch-all rebellion on the part of French truck drivers against all the frustrations of their trade.

(*2*)   These are obviously considerable, as the growing list of demands to

Paris demonstrates. They give the lie to the image of the long-distance lorry driver as the muscular king of the road, cheerily lobbing chocolate wrappers out of the windows of his lumbering rig and exchanging gobbledygook with his colleagues on the CB radio. That is the American-based myth, not the reality of the crowded roads of Europe with its plethora of border posts. As anyone who has driven over those borders may have seen, the truckers are an increasingly harassed species, entangled in red tape and subject to the whims of any uniformed jack-in-office with a headache and an infinity of regulations to enforce (or not, as he sees fit). Nor are most of them overpaid. This is not to excuse the outrageously selfish, strong-arm tactics of the French routiers, but it does help to explain the explosion of immobile rage an incredulous world has been witnessing in the comfort of its living room for a week.

(3)   Among many other things, the siege of France and the knock-on effect it has had in neighbouring countries is another reminder of how far the cause of European unity still has to travel, and how little the EEC in particular has achieved in easing communications among its members. Wags may say that Nato has now been shown how it can stop a Warsaw Pact invasion without firing a shot; but against this background of continental crisis, the drearily inevitable British demand for monetary compensation rather than the protection and rescue of British drivers seemed a trudging, unhappy first-step; though one at least briskly rectified yesterday.

(4)   That is not to make light of the financial plight facing foreign drivers and small haulage firms caught up in the French upheaval. In this area the reaction of the Netherlands stands out as a demonstration of how to get your priorities right. The Dutch government was the first to call for an urgent meeting of EEC transport ministers, a practical step in what has become an international imbroglio. Meanwhile, in co-operation with road haulage groups, it set about hiring helicopters to take relief drivers and essential supplies to its beleaguered nationals, footing half the bill. But it is the French Government which must find the way out, no easy task when 10,000 lorries have paralysed the country, a fact which precludes a physical solution. Unless the drivers get fed up and go home, capitulation looks inevitable.

This is typical of the discursive prose that is found in the leader columns of a reputable newspaper day by day. The aim is to present facts and discuss important issues coolly, without the hysteria of more popular newspapers. It is assumed that readers are intelligent people, capable of digesting a paragraph of conventional length, and unlikely to be flummoxed by *plethora*, *imbroglio* or *beleaguered*. A leading article may come to a conclusion, or it may set out conflicting arguments – like a judge summing up for a jury – and leave us to make up our own minds. In either case the tone is generally calm and measured, the language that of serious conversation. Casual expressions are admitted (*juggernauts*, *catch-all*, *gobbledygook*, *strong-arm*, *fed up*, *footing the bill*) without the language becoming sloppy or the manner too informal.

There is a notable absence of the normal semaphore of argument – *on the one hand* / *on the other hand*, *first* / *secondly*, *however*, *whereas*. The main divisions of the argument are marked by the four paragraphs:

(*1*) Here is a statement of the general problem with some reference to historical perspectives – the Battle of the Ardennes, the invention of the wheel, the French troubles of 1968. This intellectual appeal to our sense of history is intended to persuade us both of the importance of the subject and of the need to read on.

(*2*) This paragraph lists the particular frustrations of the drivers. (Note the easy transition between paragraphs.) We are invited to discount the *image* – a reference to a well-known television chocolate advertisement depicting lorry-drivers romantically – in favour of the *reality*. This is a useful reminder of how our perceptions of life (and of the topic under discussion) may be distorted or manipulated by commercial myth-making, so much so that the writer finds it necessary to invite us to clear our minds and concentrate on the facts (*as anyone who has driven over those borders may have seen*). Like all good writers, this one is thinking about his readers and the misconceptions they may have.

His impersonality slips a little in the middle of the paragraph, and personal feeling intrudes. Instead of referring to the orders of policemen and officials with a complicated job to do, he writes of *the whims of any uniformed jack-in-office with a headache*. *Whims* and *headache* imply unpredictable behaviour for petty reasons; *jack-in-office* is derogatory; *uniformed* can only have been put there to bring to mind – if we are so minded – our experience of the officiousness or pomposity that sometimes comes with the mere act of donning a uniform. But the balance of argument is carefully restored by condemnation of the lorry-drivers' *selfish* behaviour. The (unspoken) appeal here is to the enlightened reader's understanding of the nature of justice in a democratic society when innocent people – other travellers, for instance – are inconvenienced by private grievance.

(*3*) Some general conclusions are drawn about the effect (*knock-on* is tautological) of the blockade. We are reminded of important matters such as European unity and the need to harmonise bureaucratic procedures. In comparison with such large issues (not to mention NATO and the Warsaw Pact) the small-mindedness of the British response is neatly put in its place.

(*4*) Finally, particular conclusions are listed. Political considerations – the need for ministerial intervention, and the likely capitulation of the French government – are humanely balanced with consideration of the plight of individual drivers. The writer re-establishes his credentials as one who sees the problem from more than one point of view, the man-in-the-lorry's as well as the international commentator's.

This approach rejects, without referring directly to it, the unsympathetic view taken at the time by some people that blockading lorries should have been bull-dozed off the road, and that their drivers were overpaid anyway. The first view is dismissed as impracticable by the quotation of a single statistic (10,000 lorries involved), and the second is simply denied. The tone contrasts with that of other newspapers published at the same time: some contented themselves with fulminations against anarchy (justified but unconstructive) or jingoistic sneers at the French (unjustified). Another lavishly publicised its own generosity in air-lifting chocolate (see above) and copies of its own newspaper to stranded British drivers (capitalising on misfortune). Our own writer prefers a less emotional reporting of the facts, and a measured argument about their implications. He thus brings us with him to a conclusion which is logical, helpful and humane.

13.4

The next extract illustrates a different sort of journalism, that of the 'feature' writer: whereas the *Guardian* piece was described as 'discursive', this one may be described as 'reflective' because the author's own experience, and his reflections on it, are much more to the fore. The *Guardian* leader-writer kept himself in the background so that his personality would not obtrude distractingly into an argument, which is primarily an intellectual, impersonal process. The next writer is under no such constraint: indeed more subjectivity, less objectivity, is central to his purpose.

George Orwell's documentary *The Road to Wigan Pier* has the dual purpose of describing hardships in the depressed industrial north of England in the late 1930's and of recommending, as the last extract does, a political solution. Orwell's aim, again like the last writer's, is to inform and persuade, but his method and tone are different: for example, his extensive use of the *I* of the author and the *you* of his reader make his writing much more personal and the appeal to the reader more direct. The chapter from which the extract is taken relates Orwell's visit in appalling conditions to the coalface of a mine: these concluding paragraphs describe the work of 'fillers', the men who shovel the coal after it has been dislodged by cutting-machines or explosives.

Even when you watch the process of coal-extraction you probably only watch it for a short time, and it is not until you begin making a few calculations that you realise what a stupendous task the fillers are performing. Normally each man has to clear a space four or five yards wide. The cutter has undermined the coal to the depth of five feet, so that if the seam of coal is three or four feet high, each man has to cut out, break up, and load on to the belt something between seven and twelve cubic yards of coal. This is to say, taking a cubic yard as weighing twenty-seven hundredweight, that each man is shifting coal at a speed approaching two tons an hour. I have just enough experience of pick and shovel work to be able to grasp what this means. When I am digging trenches in my garden, if I shift two tons of earth during the afternoon, I feel that I have earned my tea. But earth is tractable stuff compared with coal, and I don't have to work kneeling down, a thousand feet underground, in suffocating heat and swallowing coal dust with every breath I take; nor do I have to walk a mile bent double before I begin. The miner's job would be just as much beyond my power as it would be to perform on the flying trapeze or to win the Grand National. I am not a manual worker and please God I never shall be one, but there are some kinds of manual work that I could do if I had to. At a pinch I could be a tolerable road-sweeper or an inefficient gardener or even a tenth-rate farm hand. But by no conceivable amount of effort could I become a coal miner; the work would kill me in a few weeks.

Watching coal-miners at work, you realise momentarily what different universes different people inhabit. Down there where coal is dug is a sort of world apart which one can quite easily go through life without ever hearing about. Probably a majority of people would even prefer not to hear about it. Yet it is the absolutely necessary counterpart of the world above. Practically everything we do, from eating an ice to crossing the Atlantic, and from baking a loaf to writing a novel, involves the use of coal directly or indirectly. For all the acts of peace coal is needed; if war breaks out it is needed all the more . . . Whatever may be happening on the surface, the hacking and shovelling have got to continue without a pause . . .

It is not long since conditions in the mines were worse than they are now. There are still living a very few old women who in their youth have worked underground, with a harness round their waists and a chain that passed between their legs, crawling on all fours and dragging tubs of coal. They used to go on doing this even when they were pregnant. And even now, if coal could not be produced without pregnant women dragging it to and fro, I fancy that we should let them do it rather than deprive ourselves of coal. But most of the time, of course, we should prefer to forget that they were doing it. It is so with all types of manual work; it keeps us alive, and we are oblivious of its existence. More than anyone else, perhaps, the miner can stand as the type of the manual worker, not only because his work is so exaggeratedly awful, but also because it is so vitally necessary and yet so remote from our experience, so invisible, as it were, that we are capable of forgetting it as we forget the blood in our veins. In a way it is even humiliating to watch coal-miners working. It raises in you a momentary doubt about your own status as an 'intellectual' and a superior person generally. For it is brought home to you, at least while you are watching, that it is only because miners sweat their guts out that superior persons can remain superior. You and I . . . and the Archbishop of Canterbury and Comrade X, author of *Marxism for Infants*, all of us *really* owe the comparative decency of our lives to poor drudges underground, blackened to the eyes, with their throats full of coal dust, driving their shovels forward with arms and belly muscles of steel.

Orwell presents himself not as an expert but as an observer. In fact he is very diffident – he would make only a *tolerable* or *inefficient* or *tenth-rate* manual worker (even though he can write books). He is a modest commentator, and this helps to put us on his side, as most of us prefer modesty to brow-beating. This notion of the author as an unassuming presence in his own writing is central to the impact of the piece.

At the outset, he is concerned to relate the business of coal-getting to our own personal experience. He does not just tell us that the filler shifts two tons every hour; he takes us through the calculations with the air of a man doing a few sums on the back of an envelope. Then he makes the miner's *stupendous* feat more real and accessible to us by comparing it to the everyday activity of gardening. which he and most of us are familiar with. In this way we are drawn into the subject. Instead of being lectured we are invited to realise for ourselves, by exercise of the imagination, something of the nature of the miner's achievement by relating it to something we ourselves have done. It is important that we should be made to identify in this way, because Orwell knows that he is describing something *remote from our experiences* and *invisible* that he wants to make us aware of. The degree of remoteness too is made more actual by being described in terms we can understand; hence the invitation to imagine the author performing on the flying trapeze or winning the Grand National.

Orwell uses a similar technique when he goes on to argue, in the second paragraph, that we all depend on coal. Alongside the general statement that *all the arts of peace* and *war* need coal he is careful to include homely references to *eating an ice* and *baking a loaf* as familiar examples, drawn from daily life, to illustrate our personal dependence on the miner's labour. The effect is once again to draw us into the subject by this appeal to our own experience. This is the main difference between this piece of writing and the last one. There is the same provision of information and argument, but Orwell is much more concerned with involving the reader, engaging our sympathy by bringing us into the argument – taking us into his confidence, so to speak – within the general context of the special relationship created between the amiable *I* of the author and the directly addressed *you* of the reader. In short, the approach is subjective, whereas the leader writer's was objective.

By the time we reach the end, we understand more clearly where all this has been designed to lead. Orwell is not merely giving us information about historically interesting working conditions, or entertaining us with a description of unfamiliar territory, or diverting us with autobiographical reminiscences about an unusual expedition underground. He is concerned that we should apprehend by feeling, not just know theoretically by being told, that miners work hard and dreadfully, that civilised life depends on them, and that we should be grateful. The reference to *pregnant* women *crawling on all fours* with a chain *between their legs* is clearly intended to touch our feelings. *Poor drudges* is emotive, conveying feeling as well as fact. The word *humiliating* describes the author's feelings while watching miners at work; the reader who has accompanied him throughout the hardships related in the chapter is likely by now to share those feelings.

But Orwell wants us to share too his more important conclusions, and he is confident enough at this stage to use the relationship he has carefully built up with us to adopt a slightly more aggressive and moralising tone. *And even now, if coal could not be produced without pregnant women dragging it to and fro, I fancy that we* (the reader too, that is) *should let them do it rather than deprive ourselves of coal*; this is deliberately provocative, demanding that we assent or disagree. Orwell's argument takes an important step forward when he brings in *all types of manual work* and reminds us again that *we* (the *I* and *you* again united) *are capable of forgetting it as we forget the blood in our veins* – yet another glance at personal experience in order to make a point more immediately. The implication is that we are guilty of ingratitude, even selfishness. Explicitly, our feelings of superiority depend on the literal inferiority of miners underground. *You and I*, author and reader emphatically brought together at the beginning of the clinching last sentence, owe the quality of our lives to the drudgery of others.

It is only later in the book, when Orwell moves on to his advocacy of socialism, that we fully understand the place of these paragraphs, and of the chapter they conclude, in his general thesis, which has to do with justice and freedom, the abolition of tyranny and exploitation, the need for cooperation between different classes in society, the overthrow of capitalism, the elimination of poverty, and the bringing of dignity into the work and lives of those who lack it. Aware of the unpalatable nature of this thesis to some of his readers, he must – as a starting point – persuade them that manual labour is sometimes inhuman, that society depends on it, and that ordinary decency (moral duty?) should compel us to acknowledge the work (and the rights?) of those who make possible *the comparative decency of our lives*. Orwell's problem, that of the propagandist, is to convince his reader. He can attack us by railing against our prejudice, ignorance and insensitivity, but that is more likely to alienate than persuade. The method he chooses is to enlarge our awareness of how others live, to take us by the hand and show us, in our imagination, what he himself has seen. Having thus established his credentials as a sympathetic, straightforward guide – and in language that is always straightforward – he can expect us to agree with the conclusions *he* draws from what *we* have seen together, without our feeling that we are being manipulated, even though we are. The early chapters of *The Road to Wigan Pier* are a good example of descriptive writing engaged in the service of ideas, and ultimately of moral and political conviction.

13.5

The next extract is the first of two examples of descriptive and narrative writing used for more familiar literary purposes. *A Portrait of the Artist as a Young Man* is autobiographical, though the writer, James Joyce, writes of himself not as *I* but as a character in the story, Stephen Dedalus. In this scene, from Stephen's schooldays at a Roman Catholic boarding school, a class is interrupted by the arrival of Father Dolan, who as prefect of studies is responsible for school discipline. The 'pandybat' he carries is for administering corporal punishment.

The door opened quietly and closed. A quick whisper ran through the class: the prefect of studies. There was an instant of dead silence and then the loud crack of a pandybat on the last desk. Stephen's heart leapt up in fear.

'Any boys want flogging here, Father Arnall?' cried the prefect of studies. 'Any lazy idle loafers that want flogging in this class?'

He came to the middle of the class and saw Fleming on his knees.

'Hoho!' he cried. 'Who is this boy? Why is he on his knees? What is your name, boy?'

'Fleming, sir.'

'Hoho, Fleming! An idler of course. I can see it in your eye. Why is he on his knees, Father Arnall?'

'He wrote a bad Latin theme,' Father Arnall said, 'and he missed all the questions in grammar.'

'Of course he did,' cried the prefect of studies, 'of course he did! A born idler! I can see it in the corner of his eye.'

He banged his pandybat down on the desk and cried, 'Up, Fleming! Up, my boy!'

Fleming stood up slowly.

'Hold out!' cried the prefect of studies.

Fleming held out his hand. The pandybat came down on it with a loud smacking sound: one, two, three, four, five, six.

'Other hand!'

The pandybat came down again in six loud quick smacks.

'Kneel down!' cried the prefect of studies.

Fleming knelt down, squeezing his hands under his armpits, his face contorted with pain; but Stephen knew how hard his hands were because Fleming was always rubbing rosin into them. But perhaps he was in great pain for the noise of the pandybat was terrible. Stephen's heart was beating and fluttering.

'At your work, all of you!' shouted the prefect of studies. 'We want no lazy idle loafers here, lazy idle little schemers. At your work, I tell you. Father Dolan will be in to see you every day. Father Dolan will be in tomorrow.'

He poked one of the boys in the side with his pandybat, saying, 'You, boy! When will Father Dolan be in again?'

'Tomorrow, sir,' said Tom Furlong's voice.

'Tomorrow – and tomorrow and tomorrow,' said the prefect of studies. 'Make up your minds for that. Every day Father Dolan. Write away. You, boy, who are you?'

Stephen's heart jumped suddenly.

'Dedalus, sir.'

'Why are you not writing like the others?'

'I . . . my . . .'

He could not speak with fright.

'Why is he not writing, Father Arnall?'

'He broke his glasses,' said Father Arnall, 'and I exempted him from work.'

'Broke? What is this I hear? What is this your name is?' said the prefect of studies.

'Dedalus, sir.'

'Out here, Dedalus. Lazy little schemer. I see schemer in your face. Where did you break your glasses?'

Stephen stumbled into the middle of the class, blinded by fear and haste.

'Where did you break your glasses?' repeated the prefect of studies.

'The cinderpath, sir.'

'Hoho! The cinderpath!' cried the prefect of studies. 'I know that trick.'

Stephen lifted his eyes in wonder and saw for a moment Father Dolan's whitegrey not young face, his baldy whitegrey head with fluff at the sides of it, the steel rims of his spectacles and his no coloured eyes looking through the glasses. Why did he say he knew that trick?

'Lazy idle little loafer!' cried the prefect of studies. 'Broke my glasses! An old schoolboy trick! Out with your hand this moment!'

Stephen closed his eyes and held out in the air his trembling hand with the palm upwards. He felt the prefect of studies touch it for a moment at the fingers to straighten it and then the swish of the sleeve of the soutane as the pandybat was lifted to strike. A hot burning stinging tingling blow like the loud crack of a broken stick made his trembling hand crumple together like a leaf in the fire: and at the sound and the pain scalding tears were driven into his eyes. His whole body was shaking with fright, his arm was shaking and his crumpled burning livid hand shook like a loose leaf in the air. A cry sprang to his lips, a prayer to be let off. But though the tears scalded his eyes and his limbs quivered with pain and fright, he held back the hot tears and the cry that scalded his throat.

'Other hand!' shouted the prefect of studies.

Stephen drew back his maimed and quivering right arm and held out his left hand. The soutane sleeve swished again as the pandybat was lifted and a loud crashing sound and a fierce maddening tingling burning pain made his hand shrink together with the palms and fingers in a livid quivering mass. The scalding water burst forth from his eyes and, burning with shame and agony and fear, he drew back his shaking arm in terror and burst out into a whine of pain. His body shook with a palsy of fright and in shame and rage he felt the scalding cry come from his throat and the scalding tears falling out of his eyes and down his flaming cheeks.

'Kneel down,' cried the prefect of studies.

Stephen knelt down quickly pressing his beaten hands to his sides. To think of them beaten and swollen with pain all in a moment made him feel so sorry for them as if they were not his own but someone else's that he felt sorry for. And as he knelt, calming the last sobs in his throat and feeling the burning tingling pain pressed into his sides, he thought of the hands which he had held out in the air with the palms up and of the firm touch of the prefect of studies when he had steadied the shaking fingers and of the beaten swollen reddened mass of palm and fingers that shook helplessly in the air.

'Get at your work, all of you,' cried the prefect of studies from the door. 'Father Dolan will be in every day to see if any boy, any lazy idle little loafer wants flogging. Every day. Every day.'

There is much that one could comment on, such as the way the scene is dramatised and actualised by the use of the spoken word, and the curious effect of Joyce's occasional invention (*whitegrey*), odd expression (*no colour eyes*), declamatory rhythms (*in shame and rage he felt the scalding cry . . .*) and insistently repetitive vocabulary. The main point that is to be stressed, however, is the way the writer focuses our attention and sympathy not on the narration of an event but on what passes through the mind and feelings of the boy Stephen.

The fourth sentence, *Stephen's heart leapt up in fear*, immediately takes us inside the character. The author is claiming to know how the boy felt. This is not a description of the boy's outward appearance – how he looked, how his expression changed, how he showed fear on his face or in his movement, from which we may deduce for ourselves how he felt. The author claims insight into the boy's feelings, and thus gives it to the reader. In this way the author's viewpoint, and ours, is Stephen's. From then on, throughout the extract, the point is reinforced: *Stephen's heart was beating and fluttering . . . Stephen's heart jumped suddenly . . . He could not speak with fright*. We are given no such insights into the feelings of Fleming, who is described only from the outside, or of the prefect of studies, who is to be understood through what he says and does. By placing us within the boy, so to speak, the author causes us to experience the scene through the eyes, ears, feelings and physical pain of the boy. Ours is the victim's viewpoint. As in the Orwell extract, we are drawn into the subject – which is thus made more actual – instead of being objective observers; but the method of drawing us in is not by any *I* or *you*, by any persuasive *we forget* or *you realise*, nor by any appeal to the reader's feelings, but simply by making us a party to the emotions and viewpoint of one actor, and no other, so that we experience everything as he does. The peculiar force of this passage stems from this device.

The effectiveness of the device may be seen by comparing our response to Fleming's beating with our response to Stephen's. Even though Fleming is struck twelve times, and Stephen only twice, we feel the latter's pain far more intensely. This is partly, of course, because Joyce dwells on it in more detail. But the reason why he can provide the detail is that he has claimed insight into Stephen (he *is* Stephen). Fleming's beating is described by an observer; Stephen's is felt as by a recipient.

The experience is one of physical pain vividly realised. There is deliberately drawn out preparation, the closing of the eyes, the holding out of the palm, the *feel* of the prefect's hand straightening the fingers, the *sound* of his sleeve as he lifts the pandybat – all carefully observed details building the tension. *A hot burning stinging tingling blow* comes immediately, the piled-up adjectives unconventionally unpunctuated so that they run together into a single experience. Words are repeated: *scalding . . . scalded . . . scalded*; *shaking . . . shaking . . . shook*; *like a leaf . . . like a loose leaf*; *pain . . . pain*; *tears . . . tears . . . hot tears*; *crumple . . . crumpled*; *fright . . . fright*; *cry . . . cry*; *burning . . . burning*. The tumbling reiteration gives a sense of blind helplessness; lost in a panic, one does repeat oneself. Carefully varied vocabulary would be too calculated, inappropriate to confused rushing sensations.

Worse is to follow. The second blow is conveyed in a similar style but in stronger words – *fierce, maddening, livid, agony, palsy, rage, flaming*. The tears are no longer checked: *the scalding water burst forth*. Instead of holding back his cry *he burst out into a whine of pain*. The extremity of pain is matched by extremity of language in *livid quivering mass*, *his body shook with a palsy of fright* and *scalding tears falling out of* (not just from) *his eyes*. The shouted short commands at the ends of these two paragraphs intensify, by their sharp contrast, the inhumanity.

Again it is to be noted that this experience of pain is felt by us directly because we share the sufferer's viewpoint. Only the boy/writer/reader knows about the *prayer to be let off*, the *agony and fear*, the feelings and (in the penultimate paragraph) the thoughts that are within the boy. Had the author chosen to describe the scene from the point of view of an invisible observer in the classroom, Stephen's punishment would have had to be described as objectively as Fleming's is. Had the central character in the story been, say, Father Arnall, we would have seen the incident from his point of view, with a statement of his thoughts and feelings which could not have possibly been as immediately and directly painful as Stephen's. By locating the narrative in the boy (*he felt . . . he thought . . .*) Joyce makes us feel as he does the pain, fright, humiliation and rage, and feel it more personally, strongly and unforgettably than we otherwise could have done.

As in a play, the prefect's character is revealed through what he says and how he says it. His opening words show brutal aggression; the repeated *Hoho* suggests a sort of enjoyment. His immediate assumption is that boys are shirkers. Fleming is greeted as *An idler of course* (note the last two words), and the prefect claims special insight: *I can see it in your eye.* The repetition – *A born idler! I can see it in the corner of his eye* – implies a mindless, perhaps gleeful, obsession. His references to himself as Father Dolan (*Father Dolan will be in to see you every day*) may imply pride in his title; it certainly reminds us of his priesthood – for reasons which will soon be apparent – in a way that *I will be in to see you every day* would not.

Stephen is greeted as Fleming was (*Lazy little schemer. I see schemer in your face*) but an important moment is reached when he explains that he lost his glasses on the cinderpath and the prefect cries (he cries or shouts more than he speaks) *Hoho! The cinderpath! I know that trick.* Stephen lifts his eyes *in wonder* and again we are taken inside his mind to hear him ask himself *Why did he* (the prefect) *say he knew that trick?* The moment quickly passes as the prefect goes on immediately to the punishment, but the point is made: the question that crosses Stephen's mind, and is therefore put into ours, is a question about the prefect's mentality. There was no 'trick', as Stephen well knew. The accident with the glasses had been genuine. Why should the prefect say he knew that trick? He didn't *know* it, because there was no trick to know. The priest was lying. He could, one assumes, have beaten the boy just for breaking his glasses and being unable to do his school work. But that was apparently not enough for the priest: he has to invent the accusation of trickery, and claim to know the unknowable. Why? Warped conceit? Self-delusion? To impress the children? To justify what he was about to do? None of these is a priestly attribute, and Father Dolan stands condemned – not explicitly by an all-knowing author, but simply in the priest's own words *I know that trick* and the boy's unspoken *Why did he say he knew that trick?* We are not told that the priest is deluded: we know it, because we hear his words, hear the boy's interior response to them, and reach that knowledge simultaneously with the boy's insight. By lodging our viewpoint in

Stephen, the author causes the reader to apprehend the truth *for himself*, as an actor in the drama.

This truth, it may well strike the reader, may have to do with more than the delusion, or even the madness, of an individual priest. It may have to do not merely with the unjustified viciousness of this particular act of punishment but with the whole nature of an authority – religious, educational or just human – that expresses itself in such a way. Stephen may be uncomprehending – it is we, not he, who answered the question *Why did he say he knew that trick?* – but the adult reader may be stirred to relate this incident to wider issues of crime and punishment, law and order, authority and revolt, and innocence and experience. While Joyce's main intention was to tell a story, describe an act of discipline, and shape the reader's hostile response to it by making him identify with the victim, the writing has another effect, and may have been intended to have it: to make us consider how the exercise of all authority may brutalise, not just in a priest's mind but in life itself. It is one of the great themes of literature. Less explicitly and more discreetly or cunningly than Orwell, Joyce uses descriptive writing to raise important questions of ideas and principles by involving the reader in the imaginative re-living of a fictional event.

13.6

It was a magnificent morning in early spring when I watched among the trees to see the procession come down the hillside. The upper air was woven with the music of the larks, and my whole world thrilled with the conception of summer. The young pale wind-flowers had arisen by the wood-gale, and under the hazels, when perchance the hot sun pushed his way, new little suns dawned, and blazed with real light. There was a certain thrill and quickening everywhere, as a woman must feel when she has conceived. A sallow tree in a favoured spot looked like a pale gold cloud of summer dawn; nearer it had poised a golden, fairy busby on every twig, and was voiced with a hum of bees, like any sacred golden bush, uttering its gladness in the thrilling murmur of bees, and in warm scent. Birds called and flashed on every hand; they made off exultant with streaming strands of grass, or wisps of fleece, plunging into the dark spaces of the wood, and out again into the blue.

A lad moved across the field from the farm below with a dog trotting behind him, – a dog, no, a fussy, black-legged lamb trotting along on its toes, with its tail swinging behind. They were going to the mothers on the common, who moved like little grey clouds among the dark gorse.

I cannot help forgetting, and sharing the spink's triumph, when he flashes past with a fleece from a bramble bush. It will cover the bedded moss, it will weave among the soft red cow-hair beautifully. It is a prize, it is an ecstasy to have captured it at the right moment, and the nest is nearly ready.

Ah, but the thrush is scornful, ringing out his voice from the hedge! He sets his breast against the mud, and models it warm for the turquoise eggs – blue, blue, bluest of eggs, which cluster so close and round against the breast, which round up beneath the breast, nestling content. You should see the bright ecstasy in the eyes of a nesting thrush, because of the rounded caress of the eggs against her breast!

What a hurry the jenny wren makes – hoping I shall not see her dart into the low bush. I have a delight in watching them against their shy little wills. But they have all risen with a rush of wings, and are gone, the birds. The air is brushed with agitation. There is no lark in the sky, not one; the heaven is clear of wings or twinkling dot – .

Despite the sudden emptiness of these closing sentences, which herald the arrival of the procession the narrator has come to see – a funeral procession – what is memorable and striking about this description of a morning in the countryside (from D. H. Lawrence's first novel, *The White Peacock*) is its extraordinary sense of vitality. How is this effect achieved?

As may be inferred from the child-like tone and youthful breath-lessness, including an occasional clumsiness, in some of the ex-pressions, the *I* of the passage is a young man. He clearly takes an unashamed, adolescent delight in his experience of spring's awakening. From the start his senses and sensibilities are fully engaged in the life around him: *my whole world thrilled*, he says comprehensively in the second sentence before going on to illus-trate this central idea in fine detail. *I cannot help . . . sharing the spink's triumph* does not describe what the bird looked like: it attributes emotion (*triumph*) to the bird, and tells us that the young man shared that same feeling. The following two sentences in that third paragraph take us as much into the bird's own being as the narrator's: is it he or the bird who knows that the fleece will fit *beautifully* and has been captured *at the right moment*? It is as if the narrator knew how the bird felt: there is full identification between writer and subject. Similarly he claims to know that the thrush's ecstacy is caused by the feel of *eggs against her breast* and that the wren is *hoping I shall not see her*. Much of the force of the passage stems from such empathy.

Additionally, direct expressions of personal feeling (the *Ah* at the beginning of the last but one paragraph; the *I have a delight . . .* in the final one) and the sense of running commentary in *a dog, no, a fussy, black-legged lamb*, demonstrate the immediacy of his re-sponse to the scene. Excitement is conveyed by the repetitions *It will cover the bedded moss, it will weave* . . . and *It is a prize, it is an ecstasy*. . . . There is vitality in words expressing movement (*flashed, plunging, hurry, dart, rush*) and in the perception of activity where in fact there is none (the air is *woven*; the sun *pushed its way*; the tree is personified as *voiced* and *uttering its gladness*). There is the bold use of strong, emotive vocabulary (*magnificent, thrilled, blazed, exultant, streaming, triumph, beautifully, ecstasy, bright ecstasy*). In these ways the description is made vivid with light, movement and force.

This is no mere photographic record of a scene. There are, it is true, precise visual details which can only come from the observant eyes of the informed countryman (*wind-flowers, woodgale, spink*) who takes careful note of the moss and cowhair of one bird's nest, the mud of another's, with the moss further observed to be *bedded* and the cowhair to be *soft* and *red*. We note not only the sense of sight (e.g. in the frequent reference to colour) but also the senses of hearing (*music, hum, murmur*) and smell (*warm scent*) at work and appealing to the reader's senses. But what gives the passage its special dynamic is the *feeling* that informs the description; this feeling is specially evident in the author's infusion of emotion into what he sees – birds are *exultant*, the lamb is *fussy*, the spink experiences *triumph*, the thrush is *scornful*, the wren *shy*. Such attribution of human emotion to natural life provides a sense of nature palpitating with feeling in terms the non-countryman can understand. *Sacred* adds a religious dimension (and *fairy* perhaps a pagan one) to guide our responses.

Spring is the rebirth of the year, and the theme of birth, firmly announced in *conception* in the second sentence, underlines the whole passage. This is explicit in *a certain thrill and quickening everywhere, as a woman must feel when she has conceived*, and in the allusion to the sheep as *mothers*. Usually it is more subtle: the idea of newness is present in *morning, early* spring, *young* wind-flowers, *new little* suns *dawned*, summer *dawn*, and perhaps too in *lad* and *lamb* – a new season, a new day, new plants, a new animal, a new generation (poignantly contrasting, in the context of the chapter as a whole, with the funeral procession of a friend). The whole idea of birds nesting is closely related to the theme of new birth. This is specially prominent in the description of the thrush in the fourth paragraph, in the overtones of fertility in *eggs against her breast!*, and in the sensuousness of *caress* (and *bedded* earlier) and *round up beneath the breast*. There is almost sexuality here, betrayed in the unconscious shift to *her* breast (it was *his* voice at the beginning of the paragraph). The emotive word *breast* is lingered over in four successive repetitions. The whole paragraph is heightened by the lyricism of the uninhibited introductory *Ah*, the rhapsodic dwelling on *blue, blue, bluest*, the worked-up emphasis of *round . . . round . . . rounded* and *nestling . . . nesting*, the enthusiastic button-holing of the reader in *You should see the bright ecstacy . . .* , and the rhythm and near rhyme of *the rounded caress of the eggs against her breast*! The paragraph needs perhaps to be read aloud to bring out other rhythms and interplaying sounds, such as *cluster so close* and *. . . breast, nestling content*. This is prose which is close to the condition of poetry.

It may be asked whether such a short passage can bear the weight of so much detailed analysis. The reader must decide whether too much has been read into what Lawrence wrote. It may also be asked whether Lawrence himself, during the act of writing, deliberately intended or was even consciously aware that so many of his words could be interpreted as carrying so much meaning. The answer is, probably not – though like all good writers he revised his work three or four times before deciding that it was complete. Much of what has been analysed here is, quite simply, instinctive artistry. The purpose of the analysis has been to demonstrate that, if earlier passages were intended to inform, persuade or convince, this passage is an example of prose in the service of sensation, the author's intention being not merely to provide a picture but to put his reader in touch with life itself.

14

Comprehension: Techniques of Prose Writing

The last chapter showed how words have layers of meaning that can be used to create certain effects ranging from the communication of neutral fact to communication in which emotions and feelings are deeply engaged. The present chapter, while still being fundamentally concerned with words as the raw material of language, illustrates certain techniques that are available to writers, particularly but not exclusively writers of fiction.

With the exception of people who have to compose for examination purposes (a topic dealt with in the next chapter) few users of English may find themselves writing fiction. Many more, however, will read it (and some of these may have to demonstrate in the exam room the quality of their understanding). Now it is perfectly possible to enjoy reading a piece of writing without being conscious of the particular skills that have gone into its making, just as one may enjoy a meal without knowing anything about cookery. But enjoyment is deepened if it additionally involves some awareness and recognition of the skill, care and selectivity exercised by artist or craftsman. The following sections are therefore intended to demonstrate some of the tools at his disposal. A knowledge of what they can do should enrich our reading-experience – and also help to make our own writing more effective.

14.1 Imagery – the making of pictures

(*a*) **Simile** is a comparison of two differing objects with one thing in common – the point of comparison. In the simile *He went as white as a sheet* the two things compared (*He*, *sheet*) are unlike, except in the point of comparison, whiteness. A simile is usually introduced by *as* or *like*.

Its purpose is to clarify or illustrate, often by introducing a visual element:

> Money is like muck, not good unless it be spread.

Similes are found in everyday speech:

> He was as happy as a dog with two tails.
> The news spread like wildfire.

Very often they are clichés, to be avoided like all over-used expressions, though with a little imagination they can make writing vivid:

> She bit into her toast as if it were a personal enemy.

They can also be used to add meaning:

> Although he is already a millionaire, he has much enjoyed acquiring a national newspaper – like a boy with a new train-set.

The simile here neatly summarises a range of attitudes and behaviour.

(*b*) **Metaphor** is more subtle and persuasive. It too works by comparison, but this is implicit rather than stated, and the introductory *as* or *like* is omitted. Metaphor is exemplified in *He towers above his contemporaries*: this implies a comparison between *he* and a *tower*, in that both stand out prominently, and there are other possible implications – towers are usually strong, or make people feel small. But these points of comparison are not spelled out; the reader has to work to supply them for himself. The meaning is therefore more complex and interesting, allusive rather than explicit. Metaphor is also more compressed than simile because of the element of identification between its components (he *is* a tower, not just *like* one).

Metaphor is widely, often unconsciously, used in daily speech, and is seen in the difference between the literal and figurative use of words:

> *literal*:   The escorting ships laid a smoke-screen to hide their position from the enemy.
> *figurative*:   His explanation was a smoke-screen of lies.

The imagery (as the name suggests) creates a picture.

Like simile, metaphor can easily degenerate into cliché: *tip of the iceberg, grind to a halt, food for thought, hit the nail on the head, a dog's life, wild goose chase, old hat, tongue in cheek, bite the dust,* etc. Properly used, however, it is a rich resource for varied and powerful expression.

(c) For instance, metaphor may be used to clarify abstract argument by a pictorial example. John Donne, in a sermon expressing the idea that people in a society are dependent on one another, wrote:

> No man is an island, entire of itself. Every man is a piece of the continent, a part of the main(land). If a clod be washed away by the sea, Europe is the less, as well as if a promontory were, as well as if a manor of thy friend's or of thine own were. Any men's death diminishes me, because I am involved in mankind. And therefore never send to know for whom the bell tolls: it tolls for thee.

As was printed out in **11.1**, the concrete is more memorable than the abstract.

(d) Metaphor often has a brief 'snapshot' effect:

> The conversation lapped on in little wavelets.
> A fountain of sparks shot high into the air.
> They were inundated with offers of help.

In developed prose, metaphor may be extended, as it is in this description of a mouse-like woman:

> . . . she was so small and silk and quick and made no noise at all as she whisked about on padded paws, dusting the china dogs . . . setting the mousetraps that never caught her; and once she sneaked out of the room, to squeak in a nook or nibble in the hayloft, you forgot she had ever been there,
>
> (Dylan Thomas, *A Prospect of the Sea*)

(e) In its most heightened form, when prose comes close to the intensity of poetry, metaphor is not a decoration but a fused-together, organic part of meaning. At the beginning of *The Rainbow*, D. H. Lawrence expresses the interrelation of men and their country environment, a relationship so close, powerful and surging that only very sensual, even sexual imagery can do justice to its intimacy and force:

> They felt the rush of the sap in spring, they knew the wave which cannot halt, but every year throws the seed forward to begetting and, falling back, leaves the young-born on the earth. They knew the intercourse between heaven and earth, sunshine drawn into the breast and bowels, the rain sucked up in the day-time, nakedness that comes under the wind in autumn, showing the birds' nests no longer worth hiding. Their life and interrelation were such; feeling the pulse and body of the soil, that opened to the furrow for the grain, and became smooth and supple after their ploughing, and clung to their feet with a weight that pulled like desire, lying hard and unresponsive when the crops were to be shorn away. The young corn waved and was silken,

and the lustre slid along the limbs of the men who saw it. They took the udders of the cows, the cows yielded milk and pulse against the hands of the men, the pulse of the blood of the teats of the cows beat into the pulse of the hands of the men. They mounted their horses, and held life between the grip of their knees, they harnessed their horses at the wagon, and, with hands on the bridle-rings, drew the heaving of the horses after their will.

(*f*) At the other extreme, insensitivity to the pictorial element in metaphor may produce the incongruity of mixed metaphor:

He has other irons in the fire, but he's playing them close to his chest.
Instead of smelling a rat, the teachers' unions paddled towards their doom with the naïveté of a new bride outside Dracula's castle.
The policy is a hot potato that could leave the Government with egg on its face.

(*g*) **Hyperbole** is exaggeration for the sake of emphasis (*I'm fearfully sorry*), often for comic effect:

I have had occasion, I fancy, to speak before now of these pick-me-ups of Jeeves's and their effect on a fellow who is hanging to life by a thread on the morning after . . .

For perhaps the split part of a second nothing happens. It is as though all Nature waited breathless. Then, suddenly, it is as if the Last Trump had sounded and Judgement Day set in with unusual severity.

Bonfires burst out in all parts of the frame. The abdomen becomes heavily charged with molten lava. A great wind seems to blow through the world, and the subject is aware of something resembling a steam hammer striking the back of the head. During this phase, the ears ring loudly, the eyeballs rotate, and there is a tingling about the brow.

And then, just as you are feeling that you ought to ring up your lawyer and see that your affairs are in order before it is too late, the whole situation seems to clarify. The wind drops. The ears cease to ring. Birds twitter. Brass bands start playing. The sun comes up over the horizon with a jerk.

And a moment later all you are conscious of is a great peace.

(P. G. Wodehouse, *Right Ho, Jeeves*)

But there he was, always, a steaming hulk of an uncle, his braces straining like hawsers, crammed behind the counter of the tiny shop at the front of the house, and breathing like a brass band; or guzzling and blustery in the kitchen over his gutsy supper, too big for everything except the great black boats of his boots. As he ate, the house grew smaller; he billowed out over the furniture, the loud check meadow of his waistcoat littered, as though after a picnic, with cigarette ends, peelings, cabbage-stalks, birds' bones, gravy; and the forest fire of his hair crackled among the hooked hams from the ceiling.

(Dylan Thomas, *A Prospect of the Sea*)

Exaggerated metaphors and similes play their part in both passages, and in the second of them extra emphasis is provided by initial consonants repeated insistently (*breathing like a brass band, black boats of his boots*) – see **alliteration** under **14.9** on page 208.

(*h*) Imagery ought not to draw attention to itself, otherwise writing becomes too contrived and artificial. However, this objection does not apply to writing where a larger-than-life or artificial element is deliberate, as it is for comic purposes in the passages just quoted.

14.2   Other figures of speech which may be used from time to time, preferably sparingly because they do draw attention to themselves, include

(*a*) **euphemism** – the use of an elaborate expression to divert notice away from its disagreeable meaning. The motive may range from politeness to dishonesty:

pass on (*die*)	made redundant (*sacked*)
disadvantaged (*poor*)	capital punishment (*hanging*)
over-weight (*fat*)	take industrial action (*strike*)
Peoples' Democracy (*Marxist state*)	pre-emptive strike (*surprise attack*)

(*b*) **personification** – ascribing human attributes to inanimate things:

All Nature waited breathless.
The shop doors yawned and the windows blinked in the afternoon haze.

(*c*) **paradox** – a statement that appears self-contradictory but contains a truth:

The child is father to the man.
Cowards die many times before their death.

(*d*) **understatement** – the use of a consciously restrained term. The motive may be modesty, humour or good manners:

rather unnerving (*terrifying*); tired and emotional (*drunk*); misunderstanding (*blunder*)

14.3   **Rhythm in prose**   In the passage from *Right Ho, Jeeves* (see page 184) it is noticeable that when Wodehouse comes to describe calm after upheaval – the soothing effect of a pick-me-up on a hangover – he consciously introduces short sentences:

The wind drops. The ears cease to ring. Birds twitter. Brass bands start playing. The sun comes up over the horizon with a jerk.

Wodehouse, a good though inimitable stylist, knows that the more full stops there are, the more pauses or silences there are: these slow down the movement or pace of the writing in a way that reflects or even induces a feeling of relaxation appropriate to the sense of well-being.

This is an example of rhythm in prose. So is the next sentence, which comes after the even greater pause at the beginning of a new paragraph; this sentence is longer, smoothly unpunctuated, leisurely, again reflecting the mood:

> And a moment later all you are conscious of is a great peace.

For most purposes, and certainly in prose that communicates only at a factual level, rhythm is no more than the product of the normal syntax (order of words) of the language. For most purposes, that is, the writer's job is merely to make sense, and the rhythm looks after itself, though an alert writer will check that it does not become monotonous as a result of sameness in sentence or paragraph structure or length. In this respect, rhythm is just part of normal communication, and to say that prose has rhythm is to say no more than that English has a natural rhythm – a pattern of stresses – caused by

(*a*) the way words are pronounced: we automatically accent the first syllable in *blanket*, the second in *today*, the third in *alteration*, the fourth in *examination*, and so on.

(*b*) the way words are grouped into units of sense, separated by pauses (e.g. punctuation) of varying lengths.

(*c*) the way in which we instinctively stress some words but not others in a sentence:

> You don't *really* mean that!
> You don't really *mean* that!
> Do you mean *that* one?

(*d*) the way in which the voice rises and falls, e.g. rises at the end of a question, falls at the end of a sentence.

(*e*) the way in which different speeds suit different contexts.

For certain purposes, however, these natural rhythms can be organised and manipulated. Rhythm is often noticeable, and purposeful, in imaginative prose (like the Wodehouse sentences) or in writing which is aiming at special effects such as dignity, persuasiveness, emotionalism or emphasis. The following examples illustrate some ways in which rhythm can be put to work.

(*a*) Because the natural breathing space is provided by the full stop, long sentences make the reader hold on and on. Provided that they are not heavily interrupted by punctuation, their feel and movement are smooth, relaxed and drawn-out, as if lulling the reader by not letting him go. The unhurried rhythm of long sentences both matches and reinforces the mood of the following descriptions, the first a peaceful rural scene, the second a sentimental (some would say over-done) account of a caged skylark's song heard by miners in Australia, far from home.

> That rich undulating district of Loamshire to which Hayslope belonged lies close to a grim outskirt of Stonyshire, overlooked by its barren hills, as a pretty blooming sister may sometimes be seen linked in the arm of a rugged, tall, swarthy brother; and in two or three hour's ride the traveller might exchange a bleak treeless region, intersected by lines of cold gray stone, for one where his road wound under the shelter of woods or up swelling hills, muffled with hedgerows and long meadow-grass and thick corn; and where at every turn he came upon some fine old country-seat nestled in the valley or crowning the slope, some homestead with its long length of barn and its cluster of golden ricks, some gray steeple looking out from a pretty confusion of trees and thatch and dark-red tiles. It was just such a picture as this last that Hayslope church had made to the traveller as he began to mount the gentle slope leading to its pleasant uplands, and now from his station near the Green he had before him in one view nearly all the other typical features of this pleasant land.
>
> (George Eliot, *Adam Bede*)

The gentle movement is not the product solely of long sentence structures: other unobtrusive devices contribute, such as calm repetition (*some fine old country-seat . . . some homestead . . . some gray steeple*), the preference for leisurely conjunctions (*hedgerows and long meadow-grass and thick corn . . . pretty confusion of trees and thatch and dark-red tiles*) instead of more economical but jerkier commas (*hedgerows, long meadow grass and thick corn*), and the delaying of noun after noun by adjective after adjective. But it is the ample structure of clauses and sentences, with punctuation widely-spaced, that is mainly responsible for the passage's unruffled rhythm.

> And then the same sun that had warmed his little heart at home came glowing down on him here, and he gave music back for it more and more, till at last, amidst breathless silence and glistening eyes of the rough diggers hanging on his voice, out burst in that distant land his English song.
> It swelled his little throat and gushed from him with thrilling force

and plenty, and every time he checked his song to think of its theme, the green meadows, the quiet stealing streams, the clover he first soared from and the Spring he sang so well, a loud sigh from many a rough bosom, many a wild and wicked heart, told how tight the listeners had held their breath to hear him; and when he swelled with song again, and poured with all his soul the green meadows, the quiet brooks, the honey clover, and the English Spring, the rugged mouths opened and so stayed, and the shaggy lips trembled, and more than one drop trickled from fierce unbridled hearts down bronzed and rugged cheeks.

(Charles Reade, *It is Never too Late to Mend*)

(*b*) Short sentences have a special character not only because they are separated from other sentences by the marked silences of full stops but also because their sense is more tightly packed. Long sentences have subordinate clauses, and weak linking words – conjunctions and relative pronouns – that carry no great weight of meaning. Shorter sentences have fewer of these, and simple sentences are cluttered by none.

I ducked down, pushed between two men, and ran for the river, my head down. I tripped at the edge and went in with a splash. The water was very cold and I stayed under as long as I could. I could feel the current swirl me and I stayed under until I thought I could never come up. The minute I came up I took a breath and went down again. It was easy to stay under with so much clothing and my boots. When I came up the second time I saw a piece of timber ahead of me and reached it and held on with one hand. I kept my head behind it and did not even look over it. I did not want to see the bank. There were shots when I ran and shots when I came up the first time. I heard them when I was almost above water. There were no shots now. The piece of timber swung in the current and I held it with one hand. I looked at the bank. It seemed to be going by very fast. There was much wood in the stream. The water was very cold. We passed the brush of an island above the water. I held on to the timber with both hands and let it take me along. The shore was out of sight now.

(Ernest Hemingway, *A Farewell to Arms*)

Because Wodehouse used short sentences to suggest calm, it does not follow that they always have that purpose. Hemingway's short sentences, in fact, have a rather abrupt rhythm, and their purpose is not to match rhythm with sense in the way demonstrated by previous extracts. If that had been Hemingway's aim he could have used a more vigorous movement reflecting the animation of the incident he is narrating. The effect of Hemingway's style (seen extensively in his novel) is taut, matter-of-fact, unadorned, understated, reflecting the style and character of the narrator, not the atmosphere of the scene. However, in the next passage we see short sentences (and short paragraphs) used for a different purpose: the creation of tension and a sense of danger.

> The cries, suddenly nearer, jerked him up. He could see a striped savage moving hastily out of a green tangle, and coming towards the mat where he hid, a savage who carried a spear. Ralph gripped his fingers into the earth. Be ready now, in case.
>
> Ralph fumbled to hold his spear so that it was point foremost; and now he saw that the stick was sharpened at both ends.
>
> The savage stopped fifteen yards away and uttered his cry.
>
> Perhaps he can hear my heart over the noises of the fire. Don't scream. Get ready.
>
> The savage moved forward so that you could only see him from the waist down. That was the butt of his spear. Now you could see him from the knee down. Don't scream.
>
> (William Golding, *Lord of the Flies*)

(*c*) Rhythm is not simply a matter of long or short sentences. Internal punctuation has an important role.

> Mr Casaubon's home was the manor-house. Close by, visible from some parts of the garden, was the little church, with the old parsonage opposite. In the beginning of his career, Mr Casaubon had only held the living, but the death of his brother had put him in possession of the manor also. It had a small park, with a fine old oak here and there and an avenue of limes towards the south-west front, with a sunk fence between park and pleasure-ground, so that from the drawing-room windows the glance swept uninterruptedly along a slope of greensward till the limes ended in a level of corn and pastures, which often seemed to melt into a lake under the setting sun. This was the happy side of the house, for the south and east looked rather melancholy even under the brightest morning. The grounds here were more confined, the flower-beds showed no very careful tendance, and large clumps of trees, chiefly of sombre yews, had risen high, not ten yards from the windows. The building, of greenish stone, was in the old English style, not ugly but small windowed and melancholy-looking: the sort of house that must have children, many flowers, open windows, and little vistas of bright things, to make it seem a joyous home. In this latter end of autumn, with a sparse remnant of yellow leaves falling slowly athwart the dark evergreens in a stillness without sunshine, the house too had an air of autumnal decline, and Mr Casaubon, when he presented himself, had no bloom that could be thrown into relief by the background.
>
> (George Eliot, *Middlemarch*)

The closing sentences, like the opening ones, have a leisurely pace. The intervening ones (beginning 'The grounds here were more confined') are more heavily punctuated; the rhythm is more broken and disturbed, suiting that part of the scene which is more jarring.

(*d*) Punctuation is a form of timing. The success of a joke, for example, depends partly on word-order and partly on timing, especially the use of pause before delivery of the punch-line:

> On an occasion of this kind it becomes more than a moral duty to speak one's mind. It becomes a pleasure.
>
> > (Wilde, *The Importance of Being Ernest*)

The structure of the joke is the antithesis between 'duty' and 'pleasure', between a high-minded statement and its puncturing by a contrasting, down-to-earth pay-off; the pause before the laugh-line is clearly indicated by the full stop. A different phrasing and punctuation would have killed the joke:

> On an occasion of this kind it becomes a pleasure rather than a moral duty to speak one's mind.

Something similar is seen in Stella Gibbons' *Cold Comfort Farm*, where the pause before the new paragraph sets up the joke:

> The spurt and regular ping! of milk against metal came from the reeking interior of the sheds. The bucket was pressed between Adam Lambsbreath's knees, and his head was pressed deep into the flank of Feckless, the big Jersey. His gnarled hands mechanically stroked the teat, while a low crooning, mindless as the Down wind itself, came from his lips.
> He was asleep.

This is an example of deliberate anti-climax, a useful device, but one that needs to be carefully timed with punctuation.

(*e*) Some of these devices are seen again in the next extract – long, spaciously punctuated sentences establishing a rolling rhythm, this time to match the dignity of the theme; a shorter sentence providing contrast and emphasis. However, it is the device of repetition that is specially noteworthy here:

> On this the ninth anniversary of the Armistice which ended the greatest and the most fateful of all wars, the heart of this world-wide Empire turns in a special manner to the memory of those whose lives were the price of our deliverance. As there has been no struggle in our annals so terrible and so exacting, no danger so prolonged and imminent, no cause so great, no sacrifices so cruel, and no victory on which larger and more lasting issues hung, so there is no day in our calendar like to this. For over four years we stood on the edge of the abyss, of ruin as an Empire, as a nation, perhaps of ruin as a race. The

men we commemorate to-day saved us from that ruin by their death. The appeal is universal.

(*The Times*, November 11, 1927)

The repetition is a parallelism of phrases (*of ruin as . . . perhaps of ruin as . . .*). In one carefully structured sentence, such parallelism is framed within a larger parallelism of two balancing sentence-parts:

> *As there has been no* struggle . . . no danger so . . . no cause so . . . no sacrifices so . . . *so there is no* day . . .

Such a conscious balancing establishes a pattern that recalls the repetitiveness of incantation. The effect is solemn, declamatory, perhaps a little mesmerising:

> Though I speak with the tongues of men and of angels, and have not charity, I am become as sounding brass, or a tinkling cymbal.
>
> And though I have the gift of prophecy, and understand all mysteries, and all knowledge; and though I have all faith, so that I could remove mountains, and have not charity, I am nothing.
>
> And though I bestow all my goods to feed the poor, and though I give my body to be burned, and have not charity, it profiteth me nothing.

(*The Bible*, I Corinthians 13)

Orators recognise the emphatic value of repetition:

> Let me give you my vision: a man's right to work as he will, to spend what he earns, to own property, to have the state as servant and not as master: these are the British inheritance. They are the essence of a free country, and on that freedom all our other freedoms depend.

(Margaret Thatcher, speech of October 1975)

The rhythm here is of insistent repetition (*to work . . . to spend . . . to own . . . to have . . .*) brought to a climax, after the anticipatory pause of the colon, by a clinching simple sentence – *these are the British inheritance* – inviting applause.

There is a particular force in three-part emphasis:

> But in larger sense we cannot dedicate, we cannot consecrate, we cannot hallow this ground . . . government of the people, by the people, and for the people, shall not perish from the earth.

(Abraham Lincoln, Gettysburg Address 1863)

though there is no need for the three-fold cadence to be confined to the oratorial or rotund:

> But in their salty, sunburnt eyes, in the twist of their copper lips, and in their silences, one saw what they could not say – a savage past, an inglorious present, a future choked with unmentionable hopes.

(Laurie Lee, *A Rose for Winter*)

(*f*) Repetition has other uses, in impressionistic description for example:

> Fog everywhere. Fog up the river, where it flows among green aits and meadows: fog down the river, where it rolls defiled among the tiers of shipping, and the waterside pollutions of a great (and dirty) city. Fog on the Essex marshes, fog on the Kentish heights. Fog creeping into the cabooses of collier-brigs; fog lying out on the yards, and hovering in the rigging of great ships; fog drooping on the gunwales of barges and small boats. Fog in the eyes and throats of ancient Greenwich pensioners, wheezing by the firesides of their wards; fog in the stem and bowl of the afternoon pipe of the wrathful skipper, down in his close cabin; fog cruelly pinching the toes and fingers of his shivering little 'prentice boy on deck. Chance people on the bridges peeping over the parapets into a nether sky of fog, with fog all around them, as if they were up in a balloon, and hanging in the misty clouds.

> (Dickens, *Bleak House*)

Incidentally, there is not a single grammatical sentence in the whole of that paragraph. Non-sentences are an additional resource for the writer, often having the spontaneous, immediate feel of diary-entries:

> Noon. Empty streets. Silence, except for the distant music from a muffled radio. Broiling sun.

(*g*) Closely related to the device of repetition is that of accumulation:

> The past few months have been a new world, of which the succession of sensations erratically occupies my mind; the bowed heads of working parties and reliefs moving up by 'trenches' framed of sacking and brushwood; the bullets leaping angrily from charred rafters shining in greenish flare-light; an old pump and a tiled floor in the moon; bedsteads and broken mattresses hanging over cracked and scarred walls; Germans seen as momentary shadows along wire hedges; tallowy, blood-dashed, bewildered faces – but put back the blanket; a garden gate, opening into a battlefield; boys, treating the terror and torment with the philosophy of men; cheeky newspaper-sellers passing the gunpits; stretcher-bearers on the same road an hour after; the old labourer at his cottage door, pointing out with awe and circumstance (the guns meanwhile thundering away on the next parish) his eaves chipped by anti-aircraft shrapnel; the cook's mate digging for nose-caps where a dozen shells have just exploded; the 'Mad Major' flying low over the Germans' parapet and scattering out his bombs, leaving us to settle the bill; our own parapet seen in the magnesium's glare as the Germans were seeing it; stretchers or sooty dixies being dumped round trench corners; the post-cards stuck on the corner of Coldstream

Lane; the diction of the incoming and outgoing soldiers squeezing past one another in the pitch-black communication-trench . . .

(Edmund Blunden, Undertones of War)

Though phrases, like sentences, normally follow each other in some sort of order, deliberate discontinuity may suit certain contexts, as it does here. The haphazard piling-up of phrases in a rambling sentence is natural to a writer allowing his memory to wander randomly.

(*h*) It should now be clear that rhythm in prose is not the same as regular metrical rhythm in poetry, though there may be occasions in very heightened prose when a strongly worked-up rhythm becomes indistinguishable from a familiar poetic form. Two such occasions are found in D. H. Lawrence (page 183) and Charles Reade (page 187) which could be set out as metrical poetry:

> The pulse of the blood of the teats of the cows
> Beat into the pulse of the hands of the men.

> From fierce unbridled hearts
> Down bronzed and rugged cheeks.

Dickens deviates into regular metre in a part of *Dombey and Son* that evokes the repeated di-di-DUM rhythm of train-wheels on railway track:

> Away, with a shriek, and a roar, and a rattle, from the town, burrowing among the dwellings of men and making the streets hum, flashing out into the meadows for a moment, mining in through the damp earth, booming on in darkness and heavy air, bursting out again into the sunny day so bright and wide; away, with a shriek, and a roar, and a rattle, through the fields, through the woods, through the corn, through the hay, through the chalk, through the mould, through the clay, through the rock, among objects close at hand and almost in the grasp, ever flying from the traveller, and a deceitful distance ever moving slowly within him: like as in the track of the remorseless monster . . .

Such a rhythm is said to be onomatopoeic – the sound echoing the sense – just as single words may be onomatopoeic – *cuckoo*, *hissing*, *sizzle*, *buzz*.

These are not devices which are frequently encountered, or needed, but they do illustrate the versatility of prose, and the need to read it feelingly.

(*i*) As a final illustration, here are two contrasting passages that highlight extremes of rhythm:

'Well it was once when I was a kid. I was at Junior school, I think, or somewhere like that, and went down to Fowlers Pond, me and this other kid. Reggie Clay they called him, he didn't come to this school; he flitted and went away somewhere. Anyway it was Spring, tadpole time, and it's swarming with tadpoles down there in Spring. Edges of t'pond are all black with 'em, and me and this other kid started to catch 'em. It was easy, all you did, you just put your hands together and scooped a handful of water up and you'd got a handful of tadpoles. Anyway we were mucking about with 'em, picking 'em up and chucking 'em back and things, and we were on about taking some home, but we'd no jam jars. So this kid, Reggie, says, "Take thi wellingtons off and put some in there, they'll be all right 'til tha gets home." So I took 'em off and we put some water in 'em and then we started to put taddies in 'em. We kept ladling 'em in and I says to this kid, "Let's have a competition, thee have one welli' and I'll have t'other, and we'll see who can get most in!" So he started to fill one welli' and I started to fill t'other. We must have been at it hours, and they got thicker and thicker, until at t'end there was no water left in 'em, they were just jam packed wi'taddies.'

(Barry Hines, *A Kestrel for a Knave*)

Prose of its very nature is longer than verse, and the virtues peculiar to it manifest themselves gradually. If the cardinal virtue of poetry is love, the cardinal virtue of prose is justice; and, whereas love makes you act and speak on the spur of the moment, justice needs inquiry, patience, and a control even of the noblest passions . . . By justice here I do not mean justice only to particular people or ideas, but a habit of justice in all the processes of thought, a style tranquillized and a form moulded by that habit. The master of prose is not cold, but he will not let any word or image inflame him with a heat irrelevant to his purpose. Unhasting, unresting, he pursues it, subduing all the riches of his mind to it, rejecting all beauties that are not germane to it; making his own beauty out of the very accomplishment of it, out of the whole work and its proportions, so that you must read to the end before you know that it is beautiful. But he has his reward, for he is trusted and convinces, as those who are at the mercy of their own eloquence do not; and he gives a pleasure all the greater for being hardly noticed. In the best prose, whether narrative or argument, we are so led on as we read, that we do not stop to applaud the writer, nor do we stop to question him.

(A. Clutton-Brock, *Modern Essays*)

The first, of course, has the natural rhythms of speech with its hesitations, loose constructions and heaped-on conjunctions. The second is highly polished, with balancing phrases and clauses (*and whereas love makes . . . justice needs . . . ; we do not stop to . . . nor do we stop to . . .*), gently persuasive repetitions, and the carefully placed signposts of measured argument

> If . . . ; and, whereas . . . ; I do not mean . . . but . . . ; for . . . ; so . . . that . . . ; not . . . nor . . .

The first is spontaneous in its feel; the second has the poised, conscious rhythm of graceful argument. The one has the informality of a slice of life; the other the deliberate formality and complexity of finished craft.

The writer's viewpoint

14.4 In the analysis of the passages by George Orwell (page 168) and James Joyce (page 172), stress was laid on the importance of the writer's viewpoint, in that it affects the whole nature of a piece of writing and shapes the reader's response. For example, the location of that viewpoint within the consciousness of the boy receiving corporal punishment (page 174) gives the scene a power and immediacy which it could not have had if it had been described objectively, just as Orwell's manipulation of *I* and *you* (page 170) persuades the reader personally into the argument in a way which the anonymous *Guardian* leader-writer avoids (page 164) in favour of a more impersonal appeal to the intellect rather than the emotions.

Examples of some of the viewpoints available to writers are given in the following snapshots.

(*a*) The author as a character in the author's fiction:

> I have noticed that when someone asks for you on the telephone and, finding you out, leaves a message begging you to call him up the moment you come in, and it's important, the matter is more often important to him than to you. When it comes to making you a present or doing you a favour most people are able to hold their impatience within reasonable bounds. So when I got back to my lodgings with just enough time to have a drink, a cigarette, and to read my paper before dressing for dinner, and was told by Miss Fellows, my landlady, that Mr Alroy Kear wished me to ring him up at once, I felt that I could safely ignore his request.
>
> (W. Somerset Maugham, *Cakes and Ale*)

(*b*) The author as a character, but conscious also of the reader:

> You may wonder whether I ever thought of marrying Anna. I did think of it. But marriage remains for me an Idea of Reason, a concept which may regulate but not constitute my life. I cannot help, whenever I consider a woman, using the possibility of marriage as an illuminating

hypothesis which is not in any serious sense an instrument of the actual. With Anna, however, I did come near to taking the thing seriously; and that, although I'm sure she would never have said yes, was perhaps why I let myself drift away from her in the end.

(Iris Murdoch, *Under the Net*)

(*c*) The author as objective narrator – the 'film-camera' view:

The car door opened and a man got out and stood beside the car. His companion remained seated. Now all the squatting men looked at the newcomers and the conversation was still. And the women building their fires looked secretly at the shiny car. The children moved closer with elaborate circuitousness, edging inward in long curves.

Floyd put down his wrench. Tom stood up. Al wiped his hands on his trousers. The three strolled towards the Chevrolet. The man who had got out of the car was dressed in khaki trousers and a flannel shirt. He wore a flat-brimmed Stetson hat. A sheaf of papers was held in his shirt pocket by a little fence of fountain pens and yellow pencils; and from his hip pocket protruded a note-book with metal covers. He moved to one of the groups of squatting men, and they looked up at him, suspicious and quiet. They watched him and did not move; the whites of their eyes showed beneath the irises, for they did not raise their heads to look. Tom and Al and Floyd strolled casually near.

(John Steinbeck, *Of Mice and Men*)

(*d*) The author claiming insight into the personality of a character:

Finding somebody she could love had been the main quest of Adela's life until about the time of her fiftieth birthday, when its impracticability had become clear to her. The prospect of receiving love she had abandoned much earlier. She had never been kissed with passion, and not often with even mild and transient affection. This she explained to herself as the result of her extreme ugliness. She was a bulky, top-heavy woman with a red complexion, hair that had always been thin, and broad lips. To love somebody, she had found, was impossible unless something was given in return: not indeed love, nor so much as positive liking, but interest, notice.

(Kingsley Amis, *Ending Up*)

(*e*) Claiming insight into more than one character – the all-knowing author:

It was a fine September day. By noon it would be summer again but now it was true autumn with a touch of chill in the air. As Joseph Howe stood on the porch of the house in which he lodged, ready to leave for his first class of the year, he thought with pleasure of the long indoor days that were coming. It was a moment when he could feel glad of his profession.

On the lawn the peach tree was still in fruit and young Hilda Aiken was taking a picture of it. She held the camera tight against her chest. She wanted the sun behind her but she did not want her own long morning shadow in the foreground. She raised the camera but that did not help, and she lowered it but that made things worse. She twisted her body to the left, then to the right. In the end she had to step out of the direct line of the sun. At last she snapped the shutter and wound the film with intense care.

(Lionel Trilling, *Of this time Of that place*)

(*f*) The author intruding on his story to comment on it, directing the reader's response.

The chief – almost the only – attraction of the young woman's face was its mobility. When she looked down sideways to the girl she became pretty, and even handsome, particularly that in the action her features caught slantwise the rays of the strongly coloured sun, which made transparencies of her eyelids and nostrils, and set fire on her lips. When she plodded on in the shade of the hedge, silently thinking, she had the hard, half-apathetic expression of one who deems anything possible at the hands of Time and Chance, except, perhaps, fair play. The first phase was the work of Nature, the second probably of civilisation.

That the man and woman were husband and wife, and the parents of the girl in arms, there could be little doubt. No other than such relationship would have accounted for the atmosphere of stale familiarity which the trio carried along with them like a nimbus as they moved down the road.

(Thomas Hardy, *Mayor of Casterbridge*)

14.5   Here are two possible approaches to the opening paragraph: the specific to introduce the general, and the general to introduce the specific.

(*a*) The attention-grabbing opening illustration, which is to be followed by discussion of the more general theme it epitomises:

There was a little-regarded news item the other day, about a woman and her fifteen-year-old son being found floating in a collapsible dinghy in the Baltic; her husband and their two daughters, aged twelve and fourteen respectively, had been in a similarly frail vessel, but had drowned.

(Bernard Levin)

The author later reveals that these people had been trying to flee from a repressive government. His article is about the nature of totalitarianism.

(*b*) The generalised observation followed by the specific illustration:

After a lifetime acquaintance with some fairly dotty judges, not a few lunatic lawyers, a smattering of eccentric business men and pop-eyed politicians, it was refreshing this week to take a cup of morning coffee with a chap who is articulate, reasonable and possessed of a robust common sense. The fact that the chap in question appeared to be got up as Madam Butterfly at 11 o'clock in the morning came as no particular surprise to me. After all, I have been used to carrying on conversations across crowded court rooms with elderly men in scarlet, fur trimmed frocks and white curly wigs. As a one-time barrister I know about the irresistible attractions of dressing up.

(John Mortimer)

What follows is an account of an interview with a popular singer well known for his curious dress.

Description

14.6 (*a*) Descriptions gain actuality if the writer uses more than one of his five senses:

So in the ample night and the thickness of her hair I consumed my fattened sleep, drowsed and nuzzling to her warmth of flesh, blessed by her bed and safety. From the width of the house and the separation of the day, we two then lay joined alone. That darkness to me was like the fruit of sloes, heavy and ripe to the touch. It was a darkness of bliss and simple langour, when all edges seemed rounded, apt and fitting; and the presence for whom one had moaned and hungered was found not to have fled after all.

My Mother, freed from her noisy day, would sleep like a happy child, humped in her nightdress, breathing innocently and making soft drinking sounds in the pillow. In her flights of dream she held me close, like a parachute to her back; or rolled and enclosed me with her great tired body so that I was snug as a mouse in a hayrick.

They were deep and jealous, those wordless nights, as we curled and muttered together, like a secret I held through the waking day which set me above all others. It was for me alone that the night came down, for me the prince of her darkness, when only I would know the huge helplessness of her sleep, her dead face, and her blind bare arms. At dawn, when she rose and stumbled back to the kitchen, even then I was not wholly deserted, but rolled into the valley her sleep had left, lay deep in its smell of lavender, deep on my face to sleep again in the nest she had made my own.

(Laurie Lee, *Cider with Rosie*)

In his sporting frenzies, the barber got careless sometimes, and it would feel as if he were pulling my hair out by the roots with his agitated scissors. When he tilted my head or turned it, he would do so as if he wanted to knock it off. He often nicked the back of my neck. He was rough with his hard brush and sharp comb, and his violent exertions used to make my ears sing. I would stagger out of his saloon, plucked, battered and scarred, my hair drenched with cheap oil and plastered down on my skull with a cream that dried as hard as varnish, and the back of my neck and my spine itching with chopped hair.

(James Kirkup, *Sorrows, Passions and Alarms*)

(*b*) Simple details, or an incident clearly related, communicate more vividly than generalisations.

Describing a tour through rural Spain in the 1930s, Laurie Lee writes:

Later I was sitting in the courtyard under the swinging light-bulbs, hungrily watching the supper cooking, when the inn-keeper came out, a towel round his waist, and began to scrub his young son in the horse-trough. The infant screamed, the old crone roared, the father shouted, sang and lathered. Then suddenly, as by a whim, he shoved the child under the water and left him to see what he'd do. The screams were cut off as though by a knife, while the old woman and the father watched him. In a fierce choking silence the child fought the water, kicking and struggling like a small brown frog, eyes open, mouth working, his whole body grappling with the sudden inexplicable threat of death. He was about one year old but for a moment seemed ageless, facing terror alone and dumb. Then just as he was about to give in, the woman picked up a bucket and threw it at the father's head, and at that he snatched up the child, tossed him in the air, smothered him with kisses, and carried him away.

(*As I Walked Out One Midsummer Morning*)

The author does not comment, moralise, show feelings or attempt to draw any conclusions about the nature of Spanish people. The reader is simply allowed to form his own impressions, and add them to others.

(*c*) These two descriptions of places, one real, one imaginary, illustrate different approaches. The first is matter-of-fact.

Several of the houses wear a patently nationalistic look. The Norwegian Ambassador's residence, for example, just around the corner from the Drosselstrasse, is an austere, redbricked farmhouse lifted straight from the stockbroker hinterlands of Oslo. The Egyptian consulate, up the other end, has the forlorn air of an Alexandrian villa fallen on hard times. Mournful Arab music issues from it, and its windows are permanently shuttered against the skirmishing North African heat. The season was mid-May and the day had started glorious, with blossom and new leaves rocking together in the light breeze. The magnolia trees were just finished and their sad white petals, mostly shed, afterwards became a feature of the débris. With so much greenery, the bustle of the commuter traffic from the trunk road barely penetrated. The most audible sound until the explosion was the clamour of birds, including several plump doves that had taken a liking to the Australian Military Attaché's mauve wistaria, his pride. A kilometre southward, unseen Rhine barges provided a throbbing stately hum, but the residents grow deaf to it unless it stops. In short, it was a morning to assure you that whatever calamities you might be reading about in West Germany's earnest, rather panicky newspapers – depression, inflation, insolvency, unemployment, all the usual and apparently incurable ailments of a massively prosperous capitalist economy – Bad Godesberg was a settled, decent place to be alive in, and Bonn was not half so bad as it is painted.

(John Le Carré, *The Little Drummer Girl*)

The second is impressionistic and more obviously contrived:

It was a town of red brick, or of brick that would have been red if the smoke and ashes had allowed it; but as matters stood it was a town of unnatural red and black like the painted face of a savage. It was a town of machinery and tall chimneys, out of which interminable serpents of smoke trailed themselves for ever and ever, and never got uncoiled. It had a black canal in it, and a river that ran purple with ill-smelling dye, and vast piles of building full of windows where there was a rattling and a trembling all day long, and where the piston of the stream-engine worked monotonously up and down like the head of an elephant in a state of melancholy madness. It contained several large streets all very like one another, and many small streets still more like one another, inhabited by people equally like one another, who all went in and out at the same hours, with the same sound upon the same pavements, to do the same work, and to whom every day was the same as yesterday and to-morrow, and every year the counterpart of the last and the next.

(Dickens, *Hard Times*)

In contrast to the direct style and uncomplicated rhythm of the first extract, this one has pointed imagery chosen for its unpleasant, sometimes bizarre associations – simile (*like the head of an elephant in a state of melancholy madness*) and metaphor (*serpents of smoke . . . uncoiled*) – and strongly marked repetition (*very like . . . still more like . . . equally like . . . same . . . same . . . same*) framed in the long unwinding third and fourth sentences which are plainly intended to underline a sense of monotony.

(*d*) However, there is no need to resort to such ostensible literary devices to introduce feeling. In the first of these two descriptions of animals, the viewpoint is that of an observer:

A black kitten was playing in the sun. He was hitting a piece of brown paper with his fore-paws and pushing it along the grass near a circular flower bed. He struck it daintily, with one paw at a time, following it in quick rushes, noiselessly, with his body crouched against the short grass. The sharp sound made by the impact of his paws against the paper amused him.

Suddenly he felt a desire for violent movement. He struck the paper with both paws and held it securely. Then he stood up on his haunches and hurled it into the air. As it came down, he thrust forth his claws and struck at it savagely. There was a tearing sound as the claws pierced it. This excited him. He pretended to be frightened and ran away as fast as he could, with his tail half raised.

(Liam O'Flaherty, *Two Lovely Beasts and other stories*)

The second description has an extra dimension because the author places the viewpoint in a character in the story. We perceive the animal though the eyes and feelings of the boy, Jody, and the effect is one of greater immediacy:

Every morning, after Jody had curried and brushed the pony, he let down the barrier of the stall, and Gabilan thrust past him and raced down the barn and into the corral. Around and around he galloped, and sometimes he jumped forward and landed on stiff legs. He stood quivering, stiff ears forward, eyes rolling so that the whites showed, pretending to be frightened. At last he walked snorting to the water-trough and buried his nose in the water up to the nostrils. Jody was proud then, for he knew that was the way to judge a horse. Poor horses only touched their lips to the water, but a fine spirited beast put his whole nose and mouth under, and only left room to breathe.

Then Jody stood and watched the pony, and he saw things he had never noticed about any other horse, the sleek, sliding flank muscles and the cords of the buttocks, which flexed like a closing fist, and the shine the sun put on the red coat. Having seen horses all his life, Jody had never looked at them very closely before. But now he noticed the moving ears, which gave expression and even inflection of expression to the face. The pony talked with his ears. You could tell exactly how he felt about everything by the way his ears pointed. Sometimes they were still and upright and sometimes lax and sagging. They went back when he was angry or fearful, and forward when he was anxious and curious and pleased; and their exact position indicated which emotion he had.

(John Steinbeck, *The Red Pony*)

(*e*) Description need not be static, though it often has to be. William Golding's *Lord of the Flies* tells what happens when some children survive a crash on a tropical island; his description of one group of them joining up with the main party follows them slowly from indistinct long-shot to clear close-up, ending with the sharp actuality of the spoken word, as if a silent film had suddenly burst into sound:

> Within the diamond haze of the beach something dark was fumbling along. Ralph saw it first, and watched till the intentness of his gaze drew all eyes that way. Then the creature stepped from mirage on to clear sand, and they saw that the darkness was not all shadow but mostly clothing. The creature was a party of boys, marching approximately in step in two parallel lines and dressed in strangely eccentric clothing. Shorts, shirts, and different garments they carried in their hands: but each boy wore a square black cap with a silver badge in it. Their bodies, from throat to ankle, were hidden by black cloaks which bore a long silver cross on the left breast and each neck was finished off with a hambone frill. The heat of the tropics, the descent, the search for food, and now this sweaty march along the blazing beach had given them the complexions of newly washed plums. The boy who controlled them was dressed in the same way though his cap badge was golden. When his party was about ten yards from the platform he shouted an order and they halted, gasping, sweating, swaying in the fierce light. The boy himself came forward, vaulted on to the platform with his cloak flying, and peered into what to him was almost complete darkness.
>
> 'Where's the man with the trumpet?'
>
> Ralph, sensing his sun-blindness, answered him.
>
> 'There's no man with a trumpet. Only me.'

Character

14.7   (*a*) People in stories may be viewed and described externally. Selective detail is more telling than head-to-toe description (which is not usually how we perceive people anyway):

> Gustave von Aschenbach was somewhat below middle height, dark and smooth-shaven, with a head that looked rather too large for his almost delicate figure. He wore his hair brushed back; it was thin at the parting, bushy and grey on the temples, framing a lofty, rugged, knotty brow – if one may so characterize it. The nose-piece of his rimless gold spectacles cut into the base of his thick, aristocratically hooked nose. The mouth was large, often lax, often suddenly narrow and tense; the cheeks lean and furrowed, the pronounced chin slightly cleft. The vicissitudes of fate, it seemed, must have passed over his head, for he held it, plaintively, rather on one side . . .
>
> (Thomas Mann, *Death in Venice*)

An alternative approach is to view a character internally, as in **14.4**(*d*) on page 196. We may learn about a person from the shaping events of his past life, and draw conclusions about him from them:

> He sat at his window, he gazed past his own reflection at the night: he became, as always when he made this journey, a spectator looking upon his own life. Somewhere in that blackness was the railway line which had brought the goods train on its slow journey from the East; somewhere the very siding where it had parked for five nights and six days in dead of winter to make way for the military transports that mattered so much more, while Kurtz and his mother, and the hundred and eighteen other Jews who were crammed into their truck, ate the snow and froze, most of them to death. 'The next camp will be better,' his mother kept assuring him, to keep his spirits up. Somewhere in that blackness his mother had later filed passively to her death; somewhere in its fields the Sudeten boy who was himself had starved and stolen and killed, waiting without illusion for another hostile world to find him. He saw the Allied reception camp, the unfamiliar uniforms, the children's faces as old and hollow as his own. A new coat, new boots and new barbed wire – and a new escape, this time from his rescuers. He saw himself in the fields again, slipping southwards from farm to village for weeks on end as the escape line handed him on, until gradually the nights grew warm and smelled of flowers, and he heard for the first time in his life the rustle of palm trees in a sea wind. 'Listen to us, you frozen little boy,' they whispered to him, 'that's how we sound in Israel. That's how blue the sea is, just like here.' He saw the rotting steamer slumped beside the jetty, the biggest and noblest boat he had set eyes on, so black with Jewish heads that when he boarded it, he stole a stocking cap and wore it till they had cleared harbour. But they needed him, fair hair or none at all. On the deck in small groups, the leaders were giving lessons in how to shoot with stolen Lee-Enfield rifles. Haifa was still two days away, and Kurtz's war had just begun.
>
> (John Le Carré, *The Little Drummer Girl*)

Again, the interpolation of direct speech gives life and immediacy to the passage.

Occasionally, a writer may cast his narrative in the first person and speak directly about his feelings in what is sometimes called a 'stream of consciousness':

> Sometimes I think that I've never been so free as during that couple of hours when I'm trotting up the path out of the gates and turning by that bare-faced, big-bellied oak tree at the lane end. Everything's dead, but good, because it's dead before coming alive, not dead after being alive. That's how I look at it. Mind you, I often feel frozen stiff, at first. I can't feel my hands or feet or flesh at all, like I'm a ghost who wouldn't know the earth was under him if he didn't see it now and again through the mist. But even though some people would call this frost-pain suffering if they wrote about it to their mams in a letter, I don't, because I know

that in half an hour I'm going to be warm, that by the time I get to the main road and am turning on to the wheatfield footpath by the bus stop I'm going to feel as hot as a pot-bellied stove and as happy as a dog with . a tin tail.

(Alan Sillitoe, *The Loneliness of the Long Distance Runner*)

(*b*) Character may be revealed in meetings or through dialogue:

'I expect we'll want to know all their names,' said the fat boy, 'and make a list. We ought to have a meeting.'

Ralph did not take the hint so the fat boy was forced to continue.

'I don't care what they call me,' he said confidentially, 'so long as they don't call me what they used to call me at school.'

Ralph was faintly interested.

'What was that?'

The fat boy glanced over his shoulder, then leaned towards Ralph.

He whispered.

'They used to call me "Piggy".'

Ralph shrieked with laughter. He jumped up.

'Piggy! Piggy!'

'Ralph – please!'

Piggy clasped his hands in apprehension.

'I said I didn't want –'

'Piggy! Piggy!'

Ralph danced out into the hot air of the beach and then returned as a fighter-plane, with wings swept back, and machined-gunned Piggy.

'Sche-aa-ow!'

He dived in the sand at Piggy's feet and lay there laughing.

'Piggy!'

Piggy grinned reluctantly, pleased despite himself at even this much recognition.

'So long as you don't tell the others –'

Ralph giggled into the sand. The expression of pain and concentration returned to Piggy's face.

(Golding, *Lord of the Flies*)

(*c*) Most writers prefer to place their characters in incidents or conversations in this way and allow the reader to draw his own conclusions, rather as he does in the theatre, though his feelings, sympathies and judgements can of course be prompted by the writer just as they can be shaped by the interpretation of an actor or director in the theatre. To work by implication (giving the reader something to do) rather than by explicit statement (telling the reader what to think or feel) is a common approach. Thus, instead of saying that his character is lonely, Ray Bradbury writes:

On this particular evening he began his journey in a westerly direction, toward the hidden sea. There was a good crystal frost in the air; it cut the nose and made the lungs blaze like a Christmas tree inside; you could feel the cold light going on and off, all the branches filled with invisible snow. He listened to the faint push of his soft shoes through autumn leaves with satisfaction, and whistled a cold quiet whistle between his teeth, occasionally picking up a leaf as he passed, examining its skeletal pattern in the infrequent lamplights as he went on, smelling its rusty smell.

'Hello, in there,' he whispered to every house on every side as he moved. 'What's up tonight on Channel 4, Channel 7, Channel 9? Where are the cowboys rushing, and do I see the United States Cavalry over the next hill to the rescue?'

The street was silent and long and empty, with only his shadow moving like the shadow of a hawk in mid-country. If he closed his eyes and stood very still, frozen, he could imagine himself upon the center of a plain, a wintry, windless Arizona desert with no house in a thousand miles, and only dry river beds, the streets, for company.

(*The Golden Apples of the Sun*)

(*d*) Finally, a method akin to that of the cartoonist, who seizes on a single dominant trait and exaggerates it, is seen in the following description, though this technique is unlikely to be much found outside contexts that are humorous or grotesque:

It was Miss Murdstone who was arrived, and a gloomy-looking lady she was; dark, like her brother, whom she greatly resembled in face and voice; and with very heavy eyebrows, nearly meeting over her large nose, as if, being disabled by the wrongs of her sex from wearing whiskers, she had carried them to that account. She brought with her two uncompromising hard black boxes, with her initials on the lid in hard brass nails. When she paid the coachman she took her money out of a hard steel purse, and she kept the purse in a very jail of a bag which hung upon her arm by a heavy chain, and shut up like a bite. I had never, at that time, seen such a metallic lady altogether as Miss Murdstone was.

She begged the favour of being shown to her room, which became to me from that time forth a place of awe and dread, wherein the two black boxes were never seen open or known to be left unlocked, and where (for I peeped in once or twice when she was out) numerous little steel fetters and rivets, with which Miss Murdstone embellished herself, generally hung upon the looking glass in formidable array.

(Charles Dickens, *David Copperfield*)

14.8 Irony is saying the opposite of what you mean while making it clear what you do mean. A person who speaks ironically (for example, saying *That was clever* to someone who has just done something foolish) expresses his real meaning by his ironical tone of voice. A person who writes ironically must signal the fact clearly if his irony is to be detected; if it is not, serious misunderstanding will occur.

Irony derives its richness from having a double meaning, an apparent one and a camouflaged one, sometimes finely balanced. Its usefulness is that it allows a writer to make a judgement on his subject without being direct or heavy-handed (*That was clever* is a judgement, very different in its effect from *That was stupid*). Irony is favoured by satirists who feel that its subtlety, and especially the humour that comes from the incongruity between the apparent and real meanings, are just as effective as explicit judgement, condemnation or ridicule. Indeed irony is often more effective, because the ironist remains detached by his disguise – as if poised and impersonal – and because humour can be more wounding than straightforward statement.

Like several of the devices illustrated in this chapter, irony makes demands on the reader's perceptions: accepting two layers of meaning and appreciating their relationship is more stimulating and absorbing for the reader than the response required by a single level of meaning. Understanding irony, and writing it, are among the most complex of literary activities.

(*a*) As a fairly simple example of irony in action, here is a journalist seeking to discredit a foreign government whose police force was believed to use vicious methods to control the black population and who resorted to deceit to justify such methods:

> The death in captivity in South Africa of John Cheekykaffir, leader of the movement among black South Africans to persuade the government to admit that they mostly have only two legs each, has given rise to a considerable amount of disquiet, controversy, criticism and kicking demonstrators in the head. It will be recalled that Cheekykaffir, who was twenty-two years old at the time of his death, was said by the Minister of Justice, Mr Sjambok-Goering, to have died of old age. Asked at a press conference how a man of twenty-two could die of old age, he said that he was himself a qualified doctor and had examined the body shortly before the murder, and it was quite clear to him that old age was the cause. 'All the signs of old age were present,' he said; 'a broken nose, torn ears, boot marks on his ribs, the lot. Anyway, the inquest decided that it was old age, which settles it.' At this, several reporters pointed out that the inquest had not been held, and the Minister explained that that had nothing to do with it. 'If we

are going to wait for an inquest to be held before we announce its findings,' he said, 'our admirable and overworked police force would never have time to murder anybody at all.'

(Bernard Levin, *Taking Sides*)

The reader needs to be tuned in, so the writer carefully provides early indication that he is writing obliquely. In the very first sentence it is obviously absurd that there needs to be a *movement* to persuade a government that the people *have only two legs each*. From this we know that the writer is not to be taken literally. Or is he? A government which has its eyes closed may well need a *movement* to persuade them that black people *have only two legs*. A government which is prejudiced certainly needs one to persuade them that black people have not got four. The complexity of the ironic mode is at once established.

(*b*) A feature of irony is the tongue-in-the-cheek equation of things that do not in fact equate: *disquiet, controversy, criticism and kicking demonstrators in the head* are listed as if they were comparable activities. There is a similar shift into irony in *all the signs of old age were present; a broken nose, torn ears . . .* , though there is more horror than humour in this preposterous equation of the signs of medically attested old age with those of torture.

Discussing MPs' official visits to foreign parts, Simon Hoggart writes,

> Naturally, fact-finding visits are very important. It is essential that our legislators are acquainted with the latest situation regarding tea prices in Ceylon, aircraft spares in Los Angeles, political unrest in the Caribbean, Common Market support for olive oil producers in Sicily, and the dangers in skiing holidays at St Moritz. Now and again they go somewhere unpleasant too, but this is usually tacked on to an urgent mission to some more agreeable and sunny clime.

(*On the House*)

There is irony in the inclusion of *skiing holidays at St Moritz* alongside aircraft spares, political unrest and Common Market support. The final sentence, however, reveals that the whole list has a certain irony and that all the visits are perhaps not as *very important* as we were originally lead to believe.

(*c*) Irony in fiction is more usually a matter of prevailing tone or viewpoint than of occasional technique, but something of its flavour is seen in this extract from Malcolm Bradbury's *Who Do You Think You Are?*

But it was good to be near the city centre, to see the new sky-scraper blocks rising, the neon flashing, the ambulances roaring, the rattle of terrorist explosions, the pulse and throb of modern urban living. They moved through the new Bull Ring, the new underpasses, the multi-storey car-parks, the concrete complexities of New Street station; Edgar was frequently at New Street station, because he had constantly to travel up to London, on the Inter-City, to sit on committees, see his publisher, advise reform groups, take part in a demo, do a television programme. He was not a narrow academic; and he had arranged his teaching timetable at the university so that he could have one free day a week to keep up in the world.

The straight-faced equation of skyscrapers, neon lights and ambulances with *the rattle of terrorist explosions* as equally authentic parts of *the pulse and throb of modern urban living* is little more than a cynical joke, but the later equation of seeing a publisher or doing a television show with taking part in a demonstration tells us that Edgar viewed these activities as equally important and may suggest that the author regards this view, or all these activities, with amusement, given that *constantly* attending demos suggests habit rather than sincerity. There may also be an implied judgement on the trendy lecturer in social psychology who takes a day off every week to *keep up in the world* when the list of his activities implies *get on in the world* or even *augment his income*. Perhaps he is more *narrow* than we are told (or he himself believes). Irony can be delicate and suggestive.

(*d*) Irony should not be confused with *sarcasm*, though they are close; sarcasm too is a form of words that means one thing but says another. Sarcasm, however, is always bitter or taunting, and its intention is to hurt. Both the nature and the effects of irony are far more subtle and elusive than that.

14.9   A little has already been said about the sound of words (**14.1**(*g*), **14.3**(*h*) and **11.11** refers to the danger of ugliness when sounds are repeated needlessly. In studied prose, repeated sounds can fall pleasantly on the inner ear, just as they can add emphasis to rhetoric.

The two most common devices are **alliteration**, the repetition of initial letters or sounds (*mean, moody and magnificent*) and **assonance**, the repetition or similarity of sounds, especially vowels (A stitch in *time* saves *nine*). Both of these, together with other formal patternings – repetition, strong and occasionally regular rhythms – and the poetic dimension of metaphor and personification, come together in this final extract, from Dickens' description of the death of Little Nell in *The Old Curiosity Shop*:

> Oh! it is hard to take to heart the lesson that such deaths will teach, but let no man reject it, for it is one that all must learn, and is a mighty, universal Truth. When death strikes down the innocent and young, for every fragile form from which he lets the panting spirit free, a hundred virtues rise, in shapes of mercy, charity, and love, to walk the world and bless it. Of every tear that sorrowing mortals shed on such green graves, some good is born, some gentler nature comes. In the Destroyer's steps there spring up bright creations that defy his power, and his dark path becomes a way of light to Heaven.

15

Essay Writing

15.1 The word 'essay' is associated with the classroom and the examination hall. This chapter is intended to help those who have to compose a piece of writing as part of an English course in a school or college. As most of these courses end in a written examination, the chapter places special emphasis on writing against the clock. None the less, many of the following pages should be helpful to those who have to plan and execute pieces of writing for other readers besides teachers or examiners.

The timed exam-essay is much criticised as a test of English. In the normal course of events few people – if any – have to write against such a strict deadline as an exam imposes. Even journalists, who habitually have to deliver their work by a given time, are usually allowed more than a few minutes to gather their material, think about it, organise it into shape and then put it down. Certainly no serious short-story writer or novelist would consider it reasonable or even feasible to be expected to produce, within an hour or so, a competent piece of creative writing with a title not of his choosing. However, these are the circumstances which face an examinee, and he has to prepare himself accordingly.

There are several Examination Boards, and they vary in the way they frame essay titles. Some give plenty of information to help the candidate get started; others provide photographs, drawings, strip-cartoons or maps as a basis for composition. But most typically an exam paper provides six or eight short titles, and the candidate is given an hour in which to deal with one of them. The following, culled from past papers, are typical:

1. A strange and unusual object was bought at an auction sale and brought home. Describe how your family was affected by the purchase.

2. Do you consider superstitions to be silly nonsense, or do you think that some should be taken seriously?

3. Breaking records.

4. Photography and its uses.

5. You have been given a book token. Describe your difficulties in selecting a book, and the reasons for your final choice.

6. Write a story entitled 'The Stowaway'.

7. Droughts and floods. Describe your experiences of one or both.

8. Some people claim that borrowing and lending goods and money are always unwise. Give your opinion, referring to some of your own experiences and others you have heard of.

9. A day on a farm, in a factory or in an office.

10. Losing things.

11. Films and television have been blamed for increases in crimes of violence. Do you think that they really influence people in this way?

12. Noise.

13. Describe a well known contemporary figure whom you admire or dislike.

14. An addition to the family.

15. The family breakfast table.

16. A surprise present.

17. Sympathy.

18. How far is soccer hooliganism an insoluble problem?

19. The amount of public money available for major undertakings is limited. How do you think it should be spent?

20. Spare time.

21. Describe how your family wake up in the morning and prepare for work.

22. Odd habits. Describe any amusing, annoying or particularly strange ones which you yourself have or which you have seen in other people.

23. In what ways would you like your children's upbringing to differ from or be similar to your own?

24. Boys have an easier time than girls.

25. Write an original short story based on one of the following:
   a) a failure to obey someone's instructions

b) a generous gift put to bad use
c) a small fire that got out of control
d) the use of faulty building materials

26. Many people have the urge to travel. Where would you most like to travel, and why?

27. Memories, pleasant and unpleasant.

28. 'Wild Life in Danger'. What do you think we should do to preserve endangered species from extinction?

29. All the fun of the fair.

30. The corner shop.

31. The bomb.

32. Grandad.

33. 'Suddenly the brakes failed'. Write a story including this sentence.

34. Have you learnt from your mistakes? Give examples from your personal experience.

35. The Wedding.

36. The fascination of the sea.

37. Disaster area.

38. Write a short story, using the following sentence as a starting point: 'Sometimes he wondered whether he was safe – danger just seemed to go on travelling with him'.

39. Foxhunters were once described as 'The unspeakable in pursuit of the uneatable'. What are your own views on foxhunting?

40. The Sweet Smell of Success.

41. The pleasures and pains of gardening *or* cooking *or* jogging *or* camping.

42. Give an account of the most important ways in which your outlook on life is different from that of your parents.

43. Explain why professional games-players are among the most highly-paid of people, and say whether they ought to be.

44. 'The first time is the worst'. Describe an occasion or occasions when you have found this to be true.

45. The Intruder.

46. Describe a journey made in bad weather by land, sea or air.

47. Digging up the past.

48. Suddenly the discordant sound of a siren was heard approaching. With headlights blazing and indicators and roof-lights flashing an ambulance tore down the street past the crawling line of traffic. It skidded to a halt, and its doors flew open as the attendants sprang out.
Write a story in which this incident plays an important part.

49. From your own experience, would you say that television exerts a good or a bad influence on people today?

50. Unwelcome visitors.

51. Describe a stop during the course of a long journey of any kind.

52. An unexplained mystery.

53. Sunday afternoon.

54. Clowns.

55. Describe the person who has influenced you most during the course of your life, making clear the effect he or she has had on you.

56. Refugees.

57. Uniforms and uniformity.

58. How has the 'micro-chip' revolution affected you, and what do you foresee as possible effects in the future?

59. Select an area, either town or countryside, that you know well and write a description of it, bringing out its special character.

60. 'Never again!' you said. Describe the circumstances that caused you to make the comment.

15.2 In this list, four main types of composition are discernible:

(*a*) *narrative*: writing a story (e.g. 6, 25, 38);

(*b*) *descriptive*: a word-picture of a person (13, 32, 55), place (29, 30, 59), event (35, 46, 51) or experience (7, 27, 44);

(*c*) *discursive*: facts, opinions and arguments have to be marshalled, in an orderly way, to answer a question or reach conclusions (2, 11, 18, 24, 43, 57). The *Guardian* article quoted at **13.3** exemplifies the characteristic objectivity of such writing;

(*d*) *reflective*: may be similar to (c) but is more personal or speculative (8, 26, 34, 41, 42). The emphasis is more on feelings, less on logical argument. The Orwell passage quoted at **13.4** exemplifies the characteristic subjectivity of such writing.

Some titles contain more than one of these elements. *In what ways would you like your children's upbringing to be different from your own?* is likely to be *descriptive* of your own upbringing and *reflective* or speculative about your children's. *From your own experience, would you say that television exerts a good or bad influence on people's lives?* may be *discursive* in its handling of pro's and con's, but descriptive of *your own experience* or reflective about it. Other titles are so worded that they could be taken as the titles of stories (*An addition to the family*; *A surprise present*; *The Wedding*) or as starting-points for descriptive or reflective pieces. The four categories are helpful, however, in beginning to define different approaches to composition and the different sorts of writing-skill it entails.

Writing-material

15.3   (*a*) If you are preparing for an examination, it is wise to obtain past papers from the Examination Board and study the normal style of its questions.

(*b*) If you practise essay-writing (especially against the clock) you will soon learn that you may be more successful in some types of writing than in others. It would be foolish to go into an exam room determined at all costs to write a discursive essay, say, and avoid writing a story: the discursive titles may, of course, turn out to be on subjects you have few thoughts about. You must be prepared in the full range of skills, but self-confidence is helped if you know in advance what your strengths are.

(*c*) Inescapably, a test of 'English' is a test of what is inside your mind or feelings. It draws on imagination (especially in narrative writing), knowledge, experience, the quality of thought-processes (especially in discursive writing), observation (in descriptions), opinions, emotions, recollections – everything that makes up a person's inner life.

Preparing for an English exam may therefore mean cultivating this inner life: certainly a candidate who fears he may have nothing to say – in which case he cannot possibly pass an English exam – cannot avoid this cultivation. It requires learning by listening, thinking, talking and above all by reading short stories, novels, plays, poetry, fact and fiction, autobiographies and essays, newspapers and magazines, and reflecting on both the content and the techniques that writers use to make their effects. The previous two chapters provide some guide-lines for this.

(*d*) The raw material of writing is the perceptions, feelings, thoughts, opinions, beliefs, ideas, aspirations, memories and impressions that we all have, however disorganised or incoherent they may normally be.

The craft of writing is the organisation of these into a coherent form and shape, using the principles and techniques outlined in this chapter.

(*e*) What makes this raw material unique is that it bears the individual stamp of our own lives and personalities. It may not be the stuff with which great literature can be made, but being unique it can be turned into an original and satisfying piece of prose, certainly good enough to please us or an examiner even if it is not successful enough to deserve publication or be the first step on the way to fame as an artist.

(*f*) It follows that the golden rule is to write from personal experience or observation whenever possible. That will guarantee originality and probably freshness and interest in writing. Even a discursive essay on blood-sports, censorship, vivisection or capital punishment, about which your knowledge, arguments and opinions may not be much different from those of hundreds of other people, will be distinctly personal and valuable if it reflects *your* feelings or uses illustrations or incidents drawn from *your* personal store of experience and observation.

(*g*) Many writers amass raw material by keeping a diary or commonplace book in which they jot down miscellaneous observations as they go about their daily lives, just as painters often make quick sketches of scenes, people, buildings or happenings on the spot and later work them into more carefully finished pieces of work in the studio, improving and refining, selecting and discarding as they do so. The writer's sketch-book may include a random thought; a snatch of recorded conversation; something striking, peculiar or memorable in an incident, event or news item; a quick description or impression of a person, real or imagined; a feeling aroused by something seen, heard or read; a dream or recollection; an idea for a story; a note about a distinctive mannerism or gesture, or a reflection provoked by an experience or conversation. Such material may never find its way into a finished piece of writing; whether it does or not, the collection of it is a useful discipline, a regular exercise in precise, immediate writing, and an invaluable training in sharp, original observation.

The writer's audience

15.4   A fundamental question to be asked every time you sit down to write is, who are you writing for? Probably a teacher or an examiner in most cases, an imagined reader in others, but what does that mean? If you write a story or a description, you have pictures in your mind, and thoughts and feelings you want to express. The reader is like a blank canvas waiting to be filled with shapes, colour and feeling. Your aim must be to transmit to him exactly what is inside you, using only words. If you spare him a thought from time to time, as if he were a listener to your story, you are more likely to remember the need to interest him; to imagine him as an uninterested listener may help you to adopt the sort of manner that will make him sit up and take notice. When writing discursively, picture him as a tolerably intelligent listener; in that way you are unlikely to make the mistake of stating the obvious or treating him like an idiot. Better still, if you think of him as unconvinced or questioning or opposed to your views you will be stimulated to anticipate his objections and deal with them, so that your treatment of the subject will be more comprehensive, and your style sharper or more persuasive. You will be helped and your style will be more natural if you remember that you are writing for a person, not committing words into a void.

If you are writing for an examiner you should remember that his assessment will be based on four main criteria:

(*a*)   The quality of the material: is it interesting, original, fresh, personal, sincere, relevant?

(*b*)   the quality of the expression: is it lively or dull? is there width of vocabulary? is the style fitting?

(*c*)   the quality of the organisation: is there order or logic? is there a sense of controlled flow? are sentences and paragraphs related to each other? does the piece hang together with a bright beginning, a helpful development and a satisfying conclusion?

(*d*)   accuracy: spelling, punctuation and grammar.

Exercise
Write three short articles proposing the enforced repatriation of immigrants for
(*a*)   a popular national newspaper
(*b*)   a newspaper for ethnic minorities
(*c*)   your local newspaper

Write three more, for the same newspapers, opposing repatriation. Finally, write one article, containing arguments both for and against, and arriving at a conclusion, for a serious newspaper.

Writing-practice

15.5 Exam practice, which means writing within a prescribed time-span, can be left until a few weeks before an exam. Before then, writing-practice should range from single paragraphs to more ambitious pieces which are as long as they need to be. During this training period, limbering-up exercises need to be worked through, with an emphasis on short but intensive 'warm-ups', in the way professional athletes, musicians and other performers keep themselves in trim.

The following pages provide suggestions for practice in some of the more important writing-skills one is likely to need for essays: scene-setting, character-portrayal, narrative technique, and ways of handling reflective or discursive topics. Some of these should already be familiar from the previous chapter.

(*a*) Sense impressions are part and parcel of daily life. To make a word-picture, a writer needs the sharp observation of precise visual detail (**14.6(*b*)**). Less obviously, perhaps, sounds, smell, taste and touch are also important to create a feeling of reality. Re-read the passages quoted in **14.6(*a*)** on page 198 as examples. The writer needs to sharpen not only his eye but all five senses if his descriptions are to have actuality and make the reader see, feel, hear and believe as if he were physically present and involved. The importance of specific detail cannot be stressed too much.

Exercise

Write a paragraph describing the room you are in, the place where you work, the garden, the street, part of your route to work – any place that is very familiar. Pay attention to all five senses. Focus on significant detail.

Recall an experience of happiness or pain as precisely as you can, and set it down with all the particularity and honesty you can muster.

Think of a scene with a cacophony of sounds and a number of smells (e.g. a covered market, a fairground or a zoo). Write a descriptive paragraph, making the sounds and smells stronger than the sights.

(*b*) The characteristic fault of the inexperienced writer when setting a scene or describing a place is either to be so unspecific that the reader's mind's eye is not sufficiently focused, or to cram in too much because of a mistaken feeling that a description has to include everything. If we think of a place we know – a friend's house, the school we used to go to, a place where we spent some time on holiday – we remember salient features which are etched on our mind, probably because they are specially interesting or typical or associated with particular memories. Other features are forgotten or were never observed in the first place because the mind or memory rejected them as unimportant.

In descriptions of places, therefore, selected significant detail is all-important. There is no point in a clutter of distracting or irrelevant description, as if we were afraid of short-changing the reader. Re-read the first passage in **14.6**(*c*) on page 199.

Exercise
Write a paragraph beginning
>   The street where I live is . . .
>   The school I used to go to was . . .
>   The sort of house I like best is . . .
>   My grandparents live(d) in . . .
>   The best place for holidays is . . .
>   A place I shall never forget is . . .

(*c*) Many places have an atmosphere as well as an appearance. A piece of description will be more firmly based if it tells not merely what somewhere looks like but also how it feels. This presupposes that the writer himself is sensitive to atmosphere and has tried to develop a sense of relationship with places. He looks at them carefully, thinks about them, considers how they affect him or how he feels towards them, so that his response is personal and his vision unique.

Re-read the second passage in **14.6**(*c*), again noting how telling detail can suggest atmosphere better than comprehensive description that may remain undifferentiated.

Exercise
Think of a place you know that has atmosphere (a church, a hospital, a piece of countryside, for example), and try to define it as accurately as you can.

Imagine a place or event with a frightening atmosphere (e.g. a building, an underground passage, a crowd) and describe it precisely.

(*d*) When interviewing someone who has had a specially harrowing or joyful experience, television reporters have a favourite question: how did it feel? The inadequacy of most replies shows how difficult it is to describe emotions. Re-read the section on imagery (**14.1**) and note how comparisons may help.

Look again at the description of the inn-keeper washing his child (**14.6(**b**)**). It is simply set down with no statement of the writer's emotions. If the reader feels fear, anger, revulsion or bafflement, or a mixture of them, it is because the incident itself provokes them, not because the author has ostensibly directed them. To set down a carefully chosen and observed incident – a concentration of life in a brief moment – and to allow it to speak for itself is often more effective than to gloss it with vague emotive adjectives like *shocking*, *frightening*, *exciting* or *sad*. The reader should be shown, not told. The more he has to work, the more he will respond. He may well object if the writer jumps out and tells him how he ought to feel (**14.4(**f**)**).

Exercise
Recall two strong but contrasting experiences from your life (e.g. one happy, one sad; one frightening, one pleasing) and describe them in the form of two successive paragraphs from your autobiography.

(*e*) The advice about describing places and scenes by selected detail (**15.5(**b**)**) applies equally to persons, whether real ones in a piece of reflective or descriptive writing or imagined ones in a piece of fiction. People make an impression by their looks, dress, gesture, speech, movement, mannerisms and behaviour. Their outward appearance is seldom important unless it reveals something of the sort of people they are – which is far more interesting – or unless it is strikingly memorable as a display of human beauty or ugliness, somehow interesting in itself.

If we think for a moment about people we know – someone we like, or dislike, or know well, or know only in passing (a person we meet regularly but briefly when we buy something from him, for example) – we think of revealing detail, specific memories and striking features. That is how it should be in writing. There is usually no need for the sort of blow-by-blow description that would be appropriate to a police photo-fit.

As was shown in **14.7**, people may be described by aspects of their external appearance, or we may infer what sort of people they are from what they say and do, or we may learn about them from the way they react to events or each other. An author may set them down and allow us to make up our own minds about them from our own observations, or he may direct our feelings towards them by commenting on his own story (**14.8(**c**)**), or being a character in it himself, or making us identify with one of the characters as James

Joyce does (**13.5**). All these devices are available to the essay-writer composing a short story or a descriptive passage.

The best approach is to ask the sort of questions we normally ask about someone. What kind of person is he? How do we know? Do we take to him or against him? Why? Is our judgement based on something he has said, or done, or alleged to have said or done? Is it based on physical attraction, or because he is kind and helpful, dominant or submissive, successful, self-important, thick-skinned, elusive . . . ? Does he startle, frighten, rouse pity or hatred, amuse? How? By asking such questions, a writer shapes up a character in his mind.

Having created him, the writer then lets him loose in incidents, conversations, relations and reactions so that the reader comes to know him from what he says and does, from how he responds to other characters or events, and from his manner and development. To sustain artistic consistency, however, the writer must always exercise his imagination to put himself in the position of the characters, envisaging how they would feel and act as the story unfolds, so that they remain alive, credible and convincing.

Exercise
Write paragraphs describing
  (i) A person you have seen but never met. Do not be afraid to make him or her more unusual or interesting than he appears to be.
 (ii) A fictitious character. Write a snapshot in the style of caricature (**14.7**(*d*)) or using extended metaphor (**14.1**(*d*))
(iii) A fictitious character whose nature is revealed by his past (**14.4**(*d*) and the second quotation in **14.7**(*a*)) or by a 'running commentary' of private thoughts (third quotation in **14.7**(*a*)).
 (iv) A meeting between two strangers travelling on a train at night.
  (v) A quarrel between two contrasting members of a family, (e.g. an adult and a teenager) which brings out not only their points of view but also their personalities.
 (vi) You are in a room at a party, on your own, when a stranger enters. Describe the first impression he makes on you.
(vii) The stranger comes up to you so that you see him more clearly. Show whether events bear out or contradict your first impressions.
(viii) Two people are walking along a cliff path, saying nothing to each other. Describe them, and say how they behave, to bring out their nature and relationship. Do not say what you imagine to be their relationship: present them so that the reader will come to the same conclusion about them that you have already reached.
 (ix) Read **14.7**(*b*). Write a dialogue to bring out the personality and relationship of the speakers.

(*f*) When setting about a short story, some people make the mistake of assuming that they have to write a compressed novel and stuff in as many incidents and characters as a circumspect novelist would use in a full-length work. A short story which takes an hour or so to write will be read in about ten minutes: within that span there is no room for world-shattering events or large-scale human dramas. Unless the writer achieves a suitable balance between length and content, the reader will be confronted with a succession of un-formulated characters, unrealised scene-settings, and an artificial and improbable sequence of happenings.

The novelist can follow his characters through a long period, range over continents and evoke more excitements, crises or shaping experiences than most of us can expect to meet in a lifetime. The short story writer has a restricted span: he can deal only with a limited idea or set of incidents – perhaps only a single surprise, decision or turn of events – with a small-scale cast to match. He must seize the reader's attention immediately and make his effects decisively while ensuring that people, places and events are pictured with sufficient clarity for the reader's mind's eye. The subject matter may not be of any great moment compared with that of a novel, but that does not matter as long as the reader is left with the sense that he has been confronted with something special enough to have engaged his attention, stirred his feelings or provoked some thoughts.

Just as characters and scene-settings have to be made recognis-ably real, narrative must be firmly rooted in place and time: action must be set up and unfolded at a pace consonant with the reader's need to be able to visualise, absorb and be convinced. The rhythm, that is, should be natural. Events may be unexpected or even startling, but they must be reasonably true to life, which means that they must be credible in their circumstantial detail and pay some attention to the normal rules of cause and effect. Above all, the reader must be taken along with them.

A narrative is more likely to command assent if it is drawn from a background the writer knows. Spies, mad scientists, cowboys and cops-and-robbers are best left to writers who know those milieus: to ape them is to risk hackneyed plot, second-hand dialogue and merely sensational incident. A story placed in the distant past or the sci-fi future is on slightly safer ground, as long as the writer is confident of his powers of imagination. But most stories take shape from places, people or incidents in personal experience, even though the imagination may modify them, selecting, rejecting and changing, so that they develop into something different, just as the landscape painter changes the shape of a tree, the position of a house or the colour of a stream to make a more harmonious picture.

Before a story is begun, the ending must be decided. The writer must know where he is heading, otherwise he is unlikely to achieve the sense of momentum and direction which makes for unity and coherence in his story. The ending need not be a shattering climax: many a serviceable story has been ruined because the writer, mistakenly believing that he had to deliver a final knock-out, overloaded his story with a disproportionately weighty conclusion. In fact, no climax is needed at all: an inconclusive or enigmatic ending may well be appropriate for a mystery story, for example. But there must be a satisfying and fitting end which grows naturally from the story itself, brings it to a point, and makes the reader feel that he has experienced something planned, thought through and neatly finished. Two endings to avoid are the lame tailing-off like a joke that misfires, and the trite let-down like 'Then he woke up. It had all been a dream'.

Within many stories there are minor climaxes, scaled-down equivalents of those that novelists often put at the end of chapters to put readers in suspense and make us want to read on. These ensure that the story does not proceed at the same level throughout – though there may be cases when a story does because it has to. Peaks of interest reflect the fact that in most stories, whether told or written down, some moments are more important than others. They are often placed at the ends of paragraphs. But there ought not to be too many of them, perhaps no more than a couple, in case the weight of emphasis, tension or surprise becomes too heavy for the story's slender form.

The importance of coherence and unity has already been mentioned. Re-read **14.4** on page 195 on narrative viewpoint. A viewpoint has to be selected and maintained by the short-story writer, otherwise what he writes will be imaginatively unfocused, puzzling the reader.

Finally, a common error is to concentrate on story to the detriment of setting, atmosphere and character. A bald succession of events will not grip or involve the reader, who needs the human scale provided by people, scenes and relationships. Without them a short story will be as unreal as a speeded-up film. A study of any collection of published short stories will prove the point.

Exercise
Select titles from the list in **15.1**, or select titles of your own, and write short stories in accordance with the above guide-lines.

(*g*) In all the types of writing referred to in this chapter, it is important that the opening should at once take hold of the reader and claim his attention. First impressions matter. If the initial paragraph is dull, predictable or low-key, the reader's attention will immediately drain and his sympathy will be hard to recover. There is a temptation, particularly in discursive writing, to ease oneself into a topic by making a general statement, often telling the reader something he knows ('Everyone has unwelcome visitors at some time or other') or worse still telling him he already knows it ('It is a well known fact that . . .'). The opening paragraph is not a warm-up for the writer but a shop-window to tempt the reader inside.

Re-read **14.5** on two types of opening. Other quoted extracts that happen to be opening paragraphs include **14.4**(*a*), **14.4**(*e*) and **14.8**(*a*), and the first quotations in **14.3**(*e*) and **14.6**(*d*).

Exercise
Choose half a dozen of the titles in **15.1** (including a mix of types) and compose attention-seeking opening paragraphs.

(*h*) Reflective writing usually has two components: a statement of an experience, memory, personal taste or interest, and some reflections or feelings about it. Personal writing of this kind can easily become too private, gossipy or self-indulgent, so it is more than usually important to remember the reader, who has to be given a very precise definition of the subject so that he can understand its nature and recognise (and preferably share) the feelings that stem from it. If the reader is imagined as a stranger, he is more likely to be given a full picture, with nothing taken for granted. If he is imagined as an interested questioner, his questions can be anticipated and answered, so that the subject is treated thoroughly.

In this kind of writing much depends on liveliness of observation and the writer's sense of involvement. The stronger the involvement the more compulsive will be the style, sweeping the reader along with it. There is no point in self-consciously holding back in writing that is personal: if one has to write about an enjoyment, one should do so boldly, enthusiastically and confidently; if that enjoyment involves the senses, one should indulge them without embarrassment. The aim is to engage the reader: with reflective writing one starts with the advantages that few things are more contagious than enthusiasm and that most people enjoy hearing about other people's interests.

The dangers of being too introspective, with over-use of the intrusive or button-holing *I*, may be avoided by
- occasional deviation into the impersonal (*Many people say that . . .*) or address to the reader (*You may think that . . .*)
- the use of illustrative detail to particularise a general point
- the deliberate use of contrast, clarifying something personal by contrasting it with the different or opposing experience of someone else.

As always, a strong ending has to be planned in advance. If the subject is a personal reminiscence, something emphatic should be saved for the end so that the piece ends on a high note. If the aim is to influence the reader (as Orwell tries to do in the reflective piece quoted in **13.4**) a clinching argument should be held back to provide a firm conclusion.

Exercise
Select one of the reflective titles from **15.1**, or use one of the following for a piece of your own:

A place of one's own	Joining the queue
Winning a prize	Being late
Alone at night	Embarrassment

(*i*) In discursive writing the precise example is often worth a paragraph of argument, just as parables are more memorable than preaching. The visual usually makes a stronger statement than the abstract: see **14.1**(*c*) on page 183. A passage of reasoning can often be brought to an effective conclusion with a brief clinching illustration drawn from personal experience.

There is little value in arguments beginning *I think that . . .* or *I believe that . . .* (and such expressions are usually spurious) unless evidence and reasons are brought forward to support them and give them more validity and authority than unaided thoughts or beliefs (or prejudices) can have.

It is a mistake, then, to assume that an invitation to write a piece of discursive prose (on, say, *Is television responsible for some of the violence in our society?*) is an invitation to pour out one's own opinions. There are usually at least two sides to every argument, certainly to those chosen for examination purposes. Alternative or contradictory views should be raised. One's own stand out more clearly against a background of dissent, demonstrating that conclusions are not being drawn from unthinking bias but from an evaluation of other standpoints. A sense of debate or conflict – a sense, that is, of a mind at work – will provide more variety and interest than an unrelieved expression of personal opinions. Honest persuasion works both by supporting one set of propositions and by discrediting others.

Discursive writing needs a particularly clear structure of argument. The planning arrangements recommended in **15.6** are crucial. So is paragraphing: see **11.20** on page 146. Re-read the analysis of the discursive passage in **13.3** on page 164.

Exercise
In the light of these principles, write about one of the discursive topics in **15.1**.

Examination technique

15.6 (*a*) In a sixty-minute exam, with one essay to write, allow about ten minutes for preliminary planning.

Select the title you think you can perform best with. Scrutinise it closely: it has been carefully worded. A surprisingly large number of candidates give it a cursory glance, miss an important point or even misinterpret it altogether, incurring heavy penalities for irrelevance. An examiner cannot easily be generous to someone who ignores the topic he has been specifically asked to write about. *The Leak*, for instance, is not an invitation to write about a prize vegetable.

If the title asks you to 'discuss' a topic, that means dealing with several aspects of it, not just one. 'Compare the contrast' means 'point out the similarities *and* differences', not one *or* the other.

If the title is so worded that it can be approached in various ways (e.g. *The Interview* could be handled narratively, descriptively, or reflectively), decide which one you prefer.

(*b*) Jot down in note form all the ideas that come to mind about the title. At this stage, remember the importance of relevance. For instance, take the title *Wild life in danger: what do you think we should do to preserve endangered species from extinction?* This title does not ask *which* species are endangered, or *why*, *how* or *by whom* they are threatened, or what the consequences of extinction might be. One could legitimately devote just the introductory paragraph to such questions to establish the breadth and seriousness of the topic. Similarly the concluding paragraph could be given power by dealing with, say, the consequences of extinction. But the main body of the essay must be confined to the main thrust of the title – what *we should do* – by presenting a set of practical steps ('practical' because of *do*) to deal with the problem.

Remember too at this stage some of the cardinal rules: jottings should be fresh, lively and personal; illustrations and examples clarify abstract argument; descriptions and narrative should be rooted in personal experience; sharply perceived detail is essential; the reader is to be remembered.

This planning stage is essential. It does not matter if other candidates are already writing away: quality matters more than sheer quantity. There is no point in starting until you know where you are going and what your route is going to be. If you are not satisfied that you have enough material to keep you going, make jottings on one or two other titles: that will usually settle the matter.

(*c*) Organise the material into a shape. In a fifty-minute essay, aim at five paragraphs, certainly not more than six or seven. Two of these will be the introductory and concluding paragraphs; the other three or so will be the main body of the essay. In a reflective or discursive essay, justice probably cannot be done to more than three or four major aspects of the subject in the time available.

A survey of the jotted notes will show that some are more important than others, and some naturally belong together as aspects of the same topic. Regroup the notes under the main headings that are now emerging, rejecting those that do not fit into the pattern: two-sentence paragraphs may be weak and diversionary. Fit these headings into an essay plan: further elimination of subordinate material may be necessary at this stage:

1. Introduction   2. Topic 1   3. Topic 2   4. Topic 3   5. Conclusion

(The paragraphing of a story will probably need to be more flexible than this, but planning of shape is still essential.)

Bear in mind the need for an arresting opening and strong conclusion, the requirement that a paragraph should have a clearly defined topic, and the need for paragraphs to be related. In a narrative essay, this relationship will be determined by the chronology of events, and the paragraphing by the events themselves. In other kinds of essays, the relationship may be governed by the logic of an argument or the order of a description.

(*d*) Once a plan is established. It should be adhered to. Resist the temptation to admit ideas that arise in the course of writing. One great advantage of making a plan is that it is drawn up with the title fresh in mind. Half an hour later, a new inspiration could well lead you away into serious irrelevance. Failure to stick to the point is penalised.

(*e*) Some people are afraid of drying up in an exam. This is unlikely to happen to a well prepared candidate who has practised writing against the clock. Nor is it likely to happen because of examiners' choice of titles: their purpose is to provide opportunities for expression, not to prevent it. A glance at the titles in **15.1** will show how much emphasis there is on titles about candidates' personal experience and about prominent questions of the day that most people will already have thought about.

Nevertheless there may be temporary paralysis under the pressure of an exam. It can only be overcome by looking methodically at the subject of the essay and trying to achieve a new perspective. In a narrative or description, this may involve putting oneself into a scene or a character and imagining how it feels from the inside instead of from the viewpoint of the puppeteer. In a discursive or reflective essay it is always helpful to think of other people's points of view – real people, that is, who can normally be relied on to disagree with you. The imagined reader comes in helpful too. Reminding oneself of the need for detail, sharp definition or helpful illustration may help to restart the flow.

(*f*) Finally, a few minutes should be left at the end for correction. Some inaccuracies, especially of spelling and punctuation, occur because the mind has run ahead to the next few words. Such slips of the pen can quickly be put right while reading over one's work. So can ambiguities, errors in grammar, and clumsy repetition of the same word or idea. Overlong sentences can be clarified by inserting full stops and capital letters.

Revision of this kind is not always easy. It requires the writer to suddenly stand outside his own work and become a reader seeing it for the first time. The writer who cultivates the habit of scrutinising his own work critically will find the process easier.

16

Letter Writing

Because of the telephone, letters are less common than they used to be. Even so, everyone is likely to have to write one from time to time – an application for a job, a reply to a formal invitation, a note of thanks or condolence, or an enquiry to a school or tax office.

Nowadays only a few simple conventions have to be remembered. All of them are exemplified in the following illustration, whether a letter is hand-written or typed.

Standard format
16.1

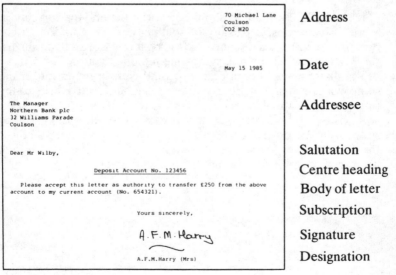

70 Michael Lane Coulson CO2 H20	**Address**
May 15 1985	**Date**
The Manager Northern Bank plc 32 Williams Parade Coulson	**Addressee**
Dear Mr Wilby,	**Salutation**
Deposit Account No. 123456	**Centre heading**
Please accept this letter as authority to transfer £250 from the above account to my current account (No. 654321).	**Body of letter**
Yours sincerely,	**Subscription**
A.F.M.Harry	**Signature**
A.F.M.Harry (Mrs)	**Designation**

(*a*) The address may be written or typed with a straight left-hand margin, as here, or may be staggered:

70 Michael Lane
Coulson
CO2 H2O

The straight margin is more usual. (This is not to imply that there is anything wrong with notepaper with a printed heading that includes an address differently placed e.g. along the top.)

The practice of including punctuation (e.g. a comma after the house number and at the end of each line, with a full stop at the end of the final line) is no longer followed. Punctuation is superfluous.

It is not correct to place the writer's name at the head of the address.

If a telephone number is to be included, the best place for it is on the left hand side of the paper, level with the top line of the address, and against the same margin as that used for the addressee.

(*b*) Leave a space before the date, which should begin against the same margin as that used for the address.

There are various ways of writing the date: the one illustrated has the merit of simplicity. Do not abbreviate (e.g. Sept. 25; 15/5/85) in a way that suggests that the writer cannot be bothered to be complete.

Again, no punctuation is necessary.

(*c*) The name and address of the person to whom the letter is directed is needed only in business letters. A large organisation is likely to receive a large number of letters, and probably they will all be opened in a central office. Inclusion of the addressee's name and address will help the sorter to get the letter to the right desk.

Sometimes the addressee's details are placed at the bottom of a letter, but the most logical – and prominent – position is above the salutation (as illustrated), beginning below the level of the date.

No punctuation is needed at the ends of lines.

(*d*) All the words in the salutation begin with a capital letter; there must always be a comma at the end. The salutation should be placed, as illustrated, against the left-hand margin. Leave a space above it.

The modern custom is to address a person by name, whenever possible, even though you may never have met. If the name is not known, or a degree of distancing seems appropriate, use *Dear Sir* (note the capital letters), *Dear Madam* (note the spelling) or *Dear*

Sirs (for a firm or company). Semi-formality is sometimes possible: *Dear Headmaster*, *Dear Editor*, *Dear Town Clerk*. The secretary of a society may resort to *Dear Member* or *Dear Colleague* when sending a circular letter.

Books of etiquette contain elaborate rules for saluting dignatories, but only the stuffiest will object to uncomplicated courtesies such as *Dear Mr Mayor*, *Dear Bishop* or *Dear Lord Rankworthy* instead of *Your Worship*, *Most Reverend Sir* or *My Lord*. It is correct, however, to include full styles and titles on the envelope and when naming the addressee above the salutation.

(*e*) The centre heading is needed only in business correspondence. It enables the recipient, or someone in his office, to locate the appropriate file without first having to read the whole letter to determine its subject. Alternatively, it enables the letter to be passed, without more ado, to the person best placed to deal with it.

(*f*) The body of the letter usually begins level with the comma that ends the salutation, with subsequent paragraphs conventionally indented (i.e. beginning a little way from the margin). However, different business firms have different 'house styles': for example, the opening paragraph may be conventionally indented instead of being level with the end of the salutation or it may not be indented at all, so that the body of the letter begins against the margin. It is a modern fashion in printing or typing to begin paragraphs without indentation and to signal the beginning of a new paragraph by leaving a clear space. This is not customary when writing by hand.

When replying to a letter that contains a reference number, you are well advised to quote it in the first sentence of your letter or better still to include it in or as the centre heading. This will quickly enable the recipient to locate the relevant correspondence.

(*g*) The subscription is normally placed right of centre, though it is sometimes placed dead centre or, in typed letters, against the left-hand margin. Only two forms are now used: *Yours sincerely* at the end of a letter in which the salutation contains a name, and the more formal *Yours faithfully* if the letter begins *Dear Sir/Madam/ Sirs*. More informal, affectionate or jocular ways of signing off are, of course, used in intimate letters where conventions are unimportant, e.g. *Best wishes*, *Love*, etc.

Note that only the first word of the subscription needs a capital letter (and that *Yours* never has an apostrophe). It is a common error to give capital letters to *faithfully* and *sincerely*. A comma concludes the subscription.

(*h*) The signature consists of initials and surname (formal), or forename and surname (less formal). Letters to relatives and friends end with the writer's forename only, or with a family name (*Grandma, Uncle Jack and Auntie Jill*) as appropriate.

Ladies normally write *Mrs* (no full stop) or *Miss* in brackets after their signature so that a reply may be properly addressed. Ladies who resent this distinction prefer *Ms*, though neither its meaning nor its pronunciation is much known.

(*i*) If a signature is indistinct (it should not be) it is as well to print or type one's name (and title, if need be) underneath the signature, level with the subscription.

This is common in business letters, the signatory's position (e.g. *Personnel Manager, Hon Treasurer*) being typed under the signature or the signatory's typed name. Other common forms are

A. C. Bracegirdle	*P. J. Makepeace*	*John Fisher*
for Managing Director	for R. I. Peace	Hon Secretary
	Managing Director	Burkwood Angling Society

Points to bear in mind

16.2 (*a*) The appearance of a letter is important. There should be good balance between the size and shape of paper and what is written on it. If a letter is short, do not crowd it all into the top third of the writing-paper; spread the components carefully, with generous margins top and bottom and to right and left, so that the total effect is well ordered. If it is long, avoid a crowded appearance with the subscription crammed into a corner or with a second page containing only the signature. A letter should be a pleasure to look at as well as to read.

(*b*) In this regard – as with many other types of composition – a rough draft is advisable, so that the fair copy can be adjusted to suit the size of paper. No letter should contain crossings-out or last-minute insertions.

(*c*) There is a curiously English prejudice against lined writing-paper, ink that is not blue or black, and writing on both sides of the page.

(*d*) Apart from chatty letters to friends, most letters are transactional, making arrangements, giving or requesting information, stating a case, lodging a protest or responding to an enquiry. Points should therefore be made clearly, accurately, relevantly, and as briefly as possible. Any deficiency in these respects will merely protract a correspondence: questions cannot be accurately answered unless they are accurately framed; information cannot be acted upon unless it is complete and specific. The recipient of a letter is unlikely to feel cooperative if he has to spend time puzzling out what the writer means.

Clear paragraphing is essential, so that points are made separately. A lengthy paragraph containing a number of jumbled points, some perhaps less important than others, is less likely to provoke a point-by-point response, and may enable an evasive or careless reader not to make a clear reply. Make it easy for the reader to understand what you say, and difficult for him to avoid replying as you would wish. Imagine yourself in his position.

(*e*) Courtesy costs nothing. Strong feelings may be effectively expressed in dispassionate language, with rational argument or an unemotional statement of facts (as you see them; there may be others you do not know). Indeed, such an approach may be more effective than tones of outrage, larded with accusation or speculation, especially if there is a possibility that your reader has personally committed no offence, though his colleagues or subordinates may have. Bullying letters, or complaints dashed off thoughtlessly in the heat of the moment, are unlikely to inspire a constructive reply; if the recipient is innocent, he may devote his reply to defending himself, neatly leaving the complaint unanswered.

16.3 Informal letters to relations and friends are written in a tone of friendly conversation, though there are times (e.g. when writing a letter of condolence or apology) when special care needs to be taken: a remark intended in a certain spirit may be interpreted in a different one. The impact of a spoken remark is made not only by the words used but also by gesture, tone of voice, and the fact that you can develop or change what you are saying while actually saying it, depending on the effect you can see yourself making. Once set down, the written word is fixed, however, and liable to be taken in different or unexpected ways; you cannot anticipate all the possible moods of your reader, but you can try to imagine his feelings, and examine your writing to make sure it can only be taken in the way intended.

Many people have a typewriter at home, and may be tempted to use it for all correspondence, but a typed letter has a formal air, unsuitable for personal letters, which should always be hand-written. Commercially produced and illustrated cards are available for all contingencies between birth and death, but there is no substitute for the personal touch of a private letter.

16.4 Formal invitations are often worded impersonally:

> Mr and Mrs R. D. Whittaker
> request the pleasure of the company of
> . . . .
> at the marriage of their daughter, Jane,
> to Mr Andrew Gray
> at St Christopher's Church, Coulson
> on Saturday, October 3, 1985, at 3 p.m.
> and afterwards at the Swan Hotel, Wigley.
> R.S.V.P.

The conventional reply is similarly impersonal, and sent without salutation or signature:

> 15 Simons Way
> Brackley
>
> September 4 1985

> Mr and Mrs H. F. Threlkeld thank Mr and Mrs R. D. Whittaker for their kind invitation to Jane's wedding, and will be very happy to attend.

A more informal reply, in standard letter format, would not be out of place if the invitation comes from friends, but the conventional form is better if replying to *The Mayor and Corporation of Hamlin* or *The Chairman and Directors of Shipps Biscuits*.

16.5 Job applications may have to be in a form prescribed by an advertisement. If no form is laid down, the best method is to send

(*a*) a curriculum vitae (a potted biography), usually typed and in note-form, setting out the applicant's personal details under various side-headings. These should include Full Name, Date of Birth, Address, Telephone Number, Marital Status, Nationality, Education and Qualifications, Previous Experience, and Referees, by which is meant the names and addresses of people, usually two, who have agreed to submit their opinions of the candidate's suitability if requested to do so. Other headings may have to be included if a job advertisement asks for them, e.g. one's personal interests.

Open testimonials, written by a friend, acquaintance or previous employer and handed by him to the subject to be used in future applications, generally carry little weight and should not be included with an application unless they are specifically asked for. Nearly all employers prefer confidential references supplied by an applicant's nominees but not seen by him.

(*b*) a letter of application, formally set out and preferably hand-written. This should include relevant information not contained in the curriculum vitae, such as the reasons for one's interest in the particular post, and should be succinct without being terse.

16.6   Official or business letters. If it is part of your job to write letters on behalf of your employers, you are likely to have access to secretaries who are expert at setting out letters in a correct and neat format, usually in a 'house-style' devised by the employer to ensure uniformity. Most large organisations issue guide-lines to establish the general style and tone they wish their staff to use when formulating letters; many companies are sensitive to the opinion that the reader of a letter will form about their efficiency, sympathy, courtesy or flexibility. Typical guide-lines include the following do's and dont's.

(*a*)   Make up your mind what needs to be said before you start, not as you go along. This gives direction and coherence to a letter.

(*b*)   Always try to anticipate the reader's reactions to a letter.

(*c*)   Be accurate. Written communication may be legally binding.

(*d*)   Be logical. Jot down notes, and re-order them if necessary, before beginning.

(*e*)   Be clear, and do not confuse issues with irrelevant material. Keep paragraphs short, and the whole letter as short as it can be without sounding peremptory or unsympathetic.

(*f*)   Use comprehensible words, as simple and as few as possible, avoiding over-long expressions or indigestible sentences that may make the reader feel that wool is being pulled over his eyes.

(*g*)   Cultivate a natural and direct tone while avoiding colloquialism or slang. If in doubt, read out loud what you have written.

(*h*) Be polite and helpful, even if writing to someone who has been neither. There is usually a tactful way of expressing an unpalatable truth. Show sympathy and understanding.

(*i*) Avoid technical language or the jargon of one's trade unless writing to someone who understands it, and always avoid the inert jargon of the traditional business letter. Jargon's second-hand formulae imply second-hand thinking.

Jargon	*Objection*	*Preferred Form*
Enclosed please find herewith	If it is enclosed it must be herewith.	I enclose
We are in receipt of	It is obvious that a letter has been received if a reply is being sent.	Thank you for
I would advise you . . . For your information . . .	Condescending. Also it is obvious, without saying so, that the writer's purpose is to offer advice or information.	Omit
We would respectfully request that you	Over-elaborate and slightly obsequious.	Would you please
The goods were forwarded per post	Archaic	We posted the goods
I beg to inform you that	Unnecessary and servile.	Omit
Reference your letter	Illiterate	Thank you for your letter.
It is much regretted that	The passive rather than the active. Also unnecessarily impersonal.	I am sorry that
At your earliest convenience	Peremptory and seldom necessary.	Omit

(*j*) Cover all the points that need to be covered, otherwise further correspondence will ensue.

(*k*) Check through the finished letter to make sure it meets the above criteria. Edit. Put yourself again in the recipient's shoes. Is the letter calculated to make him respond in the way you want?

(*l*) Re-write if you are not completely happy.

17

Report Writing

Many people have to write reports as part of their jobs. The subjects of reports and the circumstances in which they have to be written are so numerous that little useful guidance can be given about the handling of specific topics, but certain guiding principles may be set out.

17.1 In many cases a report is written to provide information for someone who needs it. Therefore, the person who writes the report knows more about the subject than the person for whom it is written. The writer must bear this fact in mind. Clarity and simplicity are the hallmarks of effective report writing.

Often a report is written for someone in a senior position by a more junior person who has more time to explore a subject. In these circumstances one must strike a careful balance between the brevity a busy reader will expect and the need for sufficient detail so that he can understand, form an opinion and, if necessary, make decisions. Knowing one's reader, or at least making an honest attempt to put oneself in his position and imagine his needs and responses, is a skill that needs to be studied.

17.2 As with all writing, an essential first step in preparing a report is to have a clear idea of its purpose. Is it to state facts, to persuade, to present options, to set out pro's and con's, with or without recommendations, to criticise an existing report, to evaluate a state of affairs, to set out a line of action to be followed? Is the report to be read by one man, discussed by a committee, circulated for the guidance of others, published to attract comment? The answers to these questions will determine the manner in which the report is written and set out.

17.3 A standard report is likely to contain some or all of the following components in the order given:

(*a*) **Title**   This should be short and to the point.

(*b*) **Purpose**   A statement of what the report is intended to achieve. Terms of reference may, of course, have been dictated to the writer, or invented by him. Whichever is the case, it is useful to state them at the outset, to enable both reader and writer to keep them in mind while working through what follows.

(*c*) **Method**   A description of the procedure the writer has followed while compiling the report. If the writer merely wishes to list some facts and draw conclusions from them, there will probably be no need for this section. If he has done some research, carried out interviews, or circulated a questionnaire, for example, these sources and working methods have to be defined, because they are the basis of the report's authority or lack of it. A reader is unlikely to be persuaded that a report's conclusions are sound unless he is able to evaluate for himself how the underlying information has been established and handled.

(*d*) **Body of the report**   The main information or argument to be transmitted. The order in which this is set out will depend very much on the content. If a series of events is to be described, a chronological order is likely to recommend itself; if an argument is to be deployed, a logical order is necessary; if a collection of facts has to be presented, there is likely to be an order that is methodical and helpful rather than random or jumbled.

(*e*) **Conclusions**   The most important feature of a report, and perhaps the only section that will be read by a busy reader. At this stage, the writer must re-read his terms of reference, and ensure that his conclusions or recommendations cover all the issues he was required to deal with.

A report normally ends with the writer's name and the date.

17.4 A longer report, the body of which may run to several chapters, is likely to include some additional features:

(*a*) **Table of contents**   With page numbers, similar to that found at the front of a book.

(*b*) **Summary**   For the benefit of the reader who may be interested in only part of a report, or who does not wish to concern himself with detail, or who wishes to know what a report's findings are before he decides whether or not to spend time reading it, a summary of findings, conclusions or recommendations (with cross-references to the main body of the text) may be placed as a separate chapter at the beginning of a report.

(*c*) **Appendices**   Often, reports have to contain supporting material such as statistical tables, graphs, or quotations from other documents. These may need placing in the body of the text to develop a particular point. Sometimes, however, they are not integral, and may be placed as separate appendices at the end of a report, so that the flow of the main text is not interrupted. Appendices thus contain evidence which validates the main text but may not need to be consulted by all readers.

Many writers (and readers) object to footnotes because they distract the attention, especially if they run from the foot of one page to the foot of the next. They may be gathered into a section at the end of each chapter or assembled into a single appendix. In this way the reader who does not need to consult them can conveniently ignore them.

A bibliography of useful reference material may also be included as an appendix.

17.5   A report is often written to be discussed, perhaps by a committee, or to be sent to someone for his written comments. Ease of reference is therefore essential. This means not only a clear system of numbering but also a cultivation of short paragraphs – one paragraph, one point. If several points are put into a long paragraph, anybody who wishes to refer to just one of them will have to spend time counting lines in order to locate it for the benefit of whoever he is talking or writing to.

17.6   Centre-headings and side-headings are useful sign-posts for the reader, especially in a lengthy report. Differences of emphasis or prominence may be added by using block capitals or underlining. There should be consistency in the use of these devices: matters of comparable importance should be given headings of identical style. A centre-heading is more prominent than a side-heading, and a heading that is underlined stands out more than one that is not. Block capitals are more assertive than lower-case letters.

17.7 The system of numbering used in this book is a useful one for reports, where a single number denotes a main section and a double number a sub-section. A third number can also be added as a further sub-division.

> 9   <u>The causes of flooding</u>
> 9.1. In addition to exceptionally high rainfall during July and August, and the reduction in industrial demand for water during these holiday months, two contributory factors have been identified, although neither of them . . . etc.
> 9.1.1 One such factor was . . . etc.
> 9.1.2 The other factor was . . . etc.
> 9.2   Other suggested causes have been investigated but . . . etc.
> 10.   <u>The results of flooding</u>

Another method, rather more cumbersome, is to use a mixture of numbers and letters to identify paragraphs, sub-paragraphs and sub-sub-paragraphs which are progressively indented:

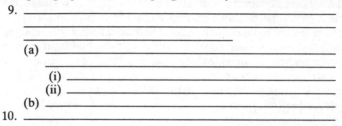

17.8 A report, or parts of it, may have to be based on notes made at a meeting, an interview or a visit of inspection, for example. It is not difficult to develop a technique, including a set of abbreviations, for note-taking if the following points are borne in mind.

Notes should be too full rather than too sketchy. Something that may seem not worth recording at one time may be important at a later stage of research, investigation or discussion. A four-word note that means something at the time it is made may mean nothing a few hours later.

When taking notes at a meeting, do not hesitate to interrupt if you are not clear about what is being said or agreed. A good chairman will ensure that every item under discussion is brought to a firm conclusion; a bad chairman will have to be prompted. In formal meetings, it is necessary for propositions, amendments and resolutions to be recorded verbatim.

Notes should be written up as continuous prose as soon as possible. Whatever is irrelevant, unimportant or digressive has to be pruned, and the residue reorganised into a coherent pattern. This first draft should be systematically reworked by applying the normal criteria for transactional writing: clarity, accuracy, conciseness and simplicity.

If notes are to be retained for future reference without being written up into continuous prose, they should be revised soon after they are made. By then it should be possible to pare them down by eliminating the irrelevant or incidental. A set of brief notes in the form of numbered and well spaced key points will be more useful, more easily remembered and more convenient to refer to than a continuous jumble of miscellaneous jottings made under the pressure of a meeting, a telephone call or whatever.

17.9   The style of a report is normally expected to be impersonal and formal, on the grounds that anything else (e.g. frequent use of *I* and *we*, or an idiosyncratic style that draws attention away from the subject to the personality of the writer) is inappropriate to statements intended to be objective and authoritative. Formulae such as *I think* and *we conclude* may be omitted (it goes without saying that a report embodies the thinking and conclusions of whoever wrote it); a statement such as *Four thousand employees are likely to be affected* is more persuasive than *We estimate that four thousand employees will be affected*, yet just as accurate. Personal judgements (e.g. in forecasting a trend) or opinions may have to be offered if the terms of reference of a report demand them, but normal convention requires an impersonal style. Earlier chapters have made it clear that such writing does not have to be as flat, circumlocutory or cliché-ridden as official or commercial writing sometimes is.

17.10   If someone else's words, written or spoken are to be quoted in a report, they should be placed in quotation marks. A long quotation from a printed document should be set out as a separate paragraph, with an indented margin to make a distinction from the rest of the text. Every quotation should be followed by an acknowledgement, in brackets or as a footnote, of its precise source in such a form that a reader may check the original if he wishes. The usual style is to give author, title, publication detail, and page or chapter number thus: H. B. Spatchcock and R. Tweed, *Flood Prevention* (HMSO, 1950) pp. 171–3. Subsequent references to the same work may be abbreviated: Spatchcock and Tweed, p. 94.

17.11 Even though you may never have to write a report for business purposes, you may be made secretary of a local society or group and have to deal with the conventional formalities of agendas and minutes.

An agenda is a list of business to be transacted, and is usually sent out with the notice or letter which announces when and where a meeting is to take place. The agenda is normally drawn up in consultation with the chairman; its purpose is to warn committee-members about what is to be discussed so that they can prepare themselves.

The normal elements include

    Apologies for absence
    Confirmation of the minutes of the previous meeting (see below)
    Matters arising from these minutes
    Correspondence
    Secretary's report
    Treasurer's report
    Named items of business
    Any other business (i.e. non-agenda items that members wish to raise)
    Date of next meeting

Minutes are the formal record of the proceedings of an organisation. In the case of a local society or amenity group, whose affairs are usually conducted by an executive committee elected by members to carry out business on their behalf, properly maintained minutes are the committee's evidence that business has been conducted in accordance with the constitution of the society, that is, in accordance with its aims and rules. Minutes are important; in some cases they may have legal or financial significance.

Minutes usually summarise proceedings in the order determined by the agenda. They conventionally include

(*a*) **Title**, saying when and where the meeting took place.

(*b*) **Attendance**, including apologies for absence. (This is important: most committees are not allowed to make decisions unless a stated number of members are present.)

(*c*) **Minutes of the last meeting** Corrections should be recorded, as should the fact that a copy of these minutes was signed by the Chairman as a correct record, and filed.

(*d*) **Matters arising** – notes of any discussions, decisions or actions on any matter raised at the previous meeting.

(*e*) **Correspondence** – summaries of correspondence received and replies sent or to be sent.

(*f*) **Reports**, briefly summarised. (Minutes should always record a committee's approval of financial transactions; an auditor may well wish to check that all expenditure has been properly authorised.)

(*g*) **Other items**   Not every twist and turn, digression or irrelevance needs to be recorded, only the salient features and decisions. If a discussion is inconclusive or deferred, this must be recorded to remind members to take it up at a later meeting.

18

Précis and Summary

18.1 These two words have similar meanings in that they have to do with abstracting the most important ideas from a piece of writing and expressing them clearly and concisely in a polished restatement. By précis, however, is normally meant the reduction of the *whole* content of a passage; in an exam there is a stated number of words, usually about a third of the total, to which a passage must be abbreviated. By summary is meant the selection of material related to a *particular* aspect of a given passage: for example, the selection and reformulation of one line of argument from a passage presenting more than one.

These are not merely examination exercises. Précis and summary are important features of communication in official or commercial transaction. It is common for someone in a senior position to want salient matters presented to him in their briefest form, uncluttered by supporting evidence or reasoning. More importantly, the practice of précis and summary is the practice of reading carefully, distinguishing and understanding a central thread, and recognising the less important, the incidental or the irrelevant, in order to grasp and then arrange essential material precisely and coherently. In other words, précis and summary sharpen comprehension and help to cultivate a clear and pointed style of expression.

Précis

18.2 The normal ground-rules may be simply stated:
(*a*) One's own words must be used, though the occasional use of a word or phrase from the original is permitted if it is unavoidable or the most economical. A précis is not a string of quotations of key bits in the original. It is a reformulation.

(*b*) Nothing should be said more than once.

(*c*) Not only the sense but also the balance and emphasis of the given passage must be retained. The précis-writer's own views or emphases are immaterial.

(*d*) The aim is to present the essence of the original, omitting illustrative detail or examples and anything that is irrelevant or subordinate to the main statement.

If important points are made solely by the use of examples, those points should be made in general terms. For instance:

Original

> At a typical football match we are likely to see players committing deliberate fouls, often behind the referee's back, trying to take a throw-in or a free kick from incorrect but more advantageous positions in defiance of the clearly stated laws of the game, and challenging the rulings of the referee or linesmen in an offensive way which often deserves exemplary punishment or even sending-off. No wonder spectators fight among themselves, damage stadiums, or take the law into their own hands by invading the pitch in the hope of affecting the outcome of the match.
>
> (95 words)

Précis

> Unsportsmanlike behaviour by footballers may cause hooliganism among spectators.
>
> (9 words)

(*e*) Metaphorical language should be replaced by literal statement. The finished précis should be in plain English and not ape the style of the original. Simplicity, conciseness and directness are the watchwords.

(*f*) Passages for précis normally have a discernible structure, which is likely to shape or determine the structure of the précis. However, the final précis has to be a well formed statement in its own right. To achieve this may necessitate altering the original structure – without distorting the original emphasis.

18.3 Recommended method for précis-writing:

(*a*) Read through the given passage to catch its general drift.

(*b*) Re-read it, more slowly and carefully, to establish its exact meaning.

(c) During a third reading, underline essential points: these are likely to be found in the topic-sentences of paragraphs, and in main clauses rather than subordinate ones. Cross out clearly irrelevant material such as illustrations: look out for *in other words, for example* etc. Underline linking words that mark stages in an argument, change in direction or logical steps: *however, but, additionally, firstly . . . secondly . . ., consequently, moreover, as a result*, etc.

(d) Note down the central points, together with important linking words. Take this opportunity to condense as much as possible, abridging clauses into phrases and phrases into single words, and making sure that no distinctive words or expressions are 'lifted'.

(e) A rough count is now helpful. If the number of words is well above target, further pruning is necessary. If the number is well below, something important may have been left out. The finished précis will be in complete sentences, longer than these notes, and so the word-count should ideally be 15—20 below the desired number at this stage.

(f) Write out a draft incorporating these notes in connected prose and in one's own words. If this can be done without looking at the notes, there will be a better chance of achieving flow and original wording.

(g) Check the draft for length, and especially for smoothness of expression. Make sure that sentences are properly linked, and that the précis reads well as a piece of continuous writing, not as an assembly of jerky or disconnected sentences.

(h) Copy out the finished version, stating the number of words used.

18.4 *Exercise*: Make a précis of the following in not more than 140 words:

> In the search for good grazing for his beasts, and later when the first corn was planted, primitive man came to realise the importance of rain and sun. In more temperate regions, sun was always more important than rain. So, with eyes on the mysterious sky, where anything could be going on, his first religious instinct was to pray towards the sun.
>
> The moment of the sun's annual rebirth, in late December, was one of the vital religious times of the year. How did people judge this subtle moment, since one does not usually notice any perceptible lengthening of the days until some time later? Living a life close to the elements,

tied to one slow place and pace and one set of shadows, it would have been more easily apparent; and priesthoods, whose powers depended on accurate predictions, were vitally interested.

This time of year was also the least laborious on the land. There was time for festivity. Early northern peoples with no exact astronomical findings began their winter festival earlier, in November, when signs of the sun's recession and the scarcity of fodder made necessary the slaughter of a proportion of their cattle. Later, the rites moved to mid-December, either to satisfy whatever more sophisticated organisations built such temples as the sun-orientated Stonehenge, or in sympathy with the imported festivities of a richer Roman period. For the legions brought with them the Saturnalia – a seven-day period of riot and feasting celebrating the birth of Saturn, a legendary King of Italy and farmer of an earlier golden age. His festival was followed without much respite by another, the Kalendae. This was concerned with the date of the new year and the two-faced deity, Janus, god of doorways and spirit of deviousness, who gave his name to the first month. The Persian god, Mithras, who accompanied the Roman soldiery, also celebrated his birth at this time.

A pre-Christian message of peace and goodwill was a part of these festivities; it was a practical message based on the probability that the usual farmers' battles, which are often disputes about water supply or cattle destroying crops, were in wintry abeyance, and the snow-bound countryside and wintry blizzards kept the warriors round their own fires. So the time of year was one of lighting fires, praising the new sun, relaxation and feasting.

Not until the middle of the fourth century was the birth of Christ officially celebrated at this time. It was a wise, if obvious, decision, for the early Christians were not puritans, and wine and rejoicing were the natural ingredients of the season. If other people were worshipping their gods at this time it was only naturally competitive for the Christians to worship theirs also; the general atmosphere of rebirth would suggest personal birth.

William Sansom, *Christmas* (adapted)

Summary

18.5 It is less easy to give advice about summary because its nature and purpose vary so much. An exam candidate may be asked to pick out and summarise evidence or arguments that support or disprove one of several conclusions reached in a passage; for example, given a passage dealing with the changing and the unchanging aspects of modern society and the way in which it may develop in the future, the candidate may be asked to summarise the evidence illustrating the changing or the unchanging, or the arguments for or against one future development rather than another. Nowadays, it is common to find a comprehension question (usually the one carrying most marks) asking for aspects of a passage to be summarised and expressed *in a certain way*. For instance, some of the events in a story about a sea-captain or a policeman may have to be described from the point of view of another character in the story or summarised as the captain or policeman might write them in a log, official report, letter or article for publication, i.e. in a style, for a purpose and from a viewpoint different from that of the original.

18.6 None the less, key processes may be identified:

(*a*) an initial reading, to grasp the general outline;

(*b*) a second reading to pay careful attention to the detail of the piece;

(*c*) the extraction of the required material in note form as concisely as possible, in one's own words, in conformity with the rubric. The greatest care is needed at this stage, both in studying the passage and in interpreting the rubric accurately;

(*d*) a word-count to ensure reasonable closeness to the target (see **18.3**(*e*));

(*e*) a rough draft, final check for accuracy and relevance, final word-count and revision if necessary;

(*f*) the fair copy.

18.7 As an example of summary, here is a passage and summary question recently set by an Examination Board:

(The scene is a harvest field in the 1930's. The tractor and reaping-machine are going round a diminishing area of standing wheat. Out-of-work coal-miners are helping with the harvesting, gathering the sheaves into stooks, with tethered dogs bounding near them, hoping to be released to catch the rabbits, or perhaps a hare, when the field is nearly finished. Mr Grooby, a middle-aged holiday visitor, has already shot two rabbits with his double-barrelled gun. But it is a very hot day, and Grooby is feeling unwell. He sits down to recover.)

Opening his eyes, Grooby found the tractor's Ford headplate, as it climbed towards him, centering his vision, and like a drunken man he anchored his attention to it. Slowly his head cleared. He changed his position.

As the world reassembled, he became aware that the farmer was now standing erect in the tractor, pointing with his free arm and shouting. Grooby looked round for some explanation. The stookers had stopped work and were looking towards him, straining towards him almost like leashed dogs, while the dogs themselves craned round, quivering with anxiety, tucking their tails in for shame at seeing nothing where they knew there was something, eager to see something and be off. Grooby took all this in remotely. Then his eyes focused.

A yard out from the wall of wheat, ten yards from Grooby and directly in the path of the tractor, a large hare sat erect.

It stared fixedly, as if it had noted some suspicious detail in the far distance. Actually it was stupefied by this sudden revelation of surrounding enemies. Driven all morning from one side of the shrinking wheat to the other, terrified and exhausted by the repeated roaring charge and nearer and nearer miss of the tractor in its revolutions, the hare's nerves had finally cracked and here it was in the open, trying to recognise the strangely shorn hillside, confronted by the shapes of men and dogs, with the tractor coming up again to the left and a man scrambling to his feet on the skyline above to the right.

Grooby aimed mercilessly. But then he perceived that the farmer's shouts had redoubled and altered in tone, and the farmhand on the cutter had joined in the shouting, flourishing his arms, with violent pushing movements away to his left, as if Grooby's gun muzzles were advancing on his very chest. Accordingly, Grooby realised that the tractor, too, lay above his gun barrels. He held his aim for a moment, not wanting to forgo his prior claim on the hare, and glanced over towards the dogs, flustered and angry. But for those dogs the hare would surely have run straight out, giving a clean, handsome shot. Now, any moment, the dogs would come clowning across the field, turn the hare back into the wheat and hunt it right through and away out at the bottom into the uncut field of rye down there, or round the back of the hill into the other fields.

To anticipate the dogs, Grooby started to run to the left, down the other side of the wheat, thinking to sight the hare against open background. But before he had gone three strides, the hare was off, an uncertain, high-eared, lolloping gait, still unable to decide the safe course or the right speed, till the dogs came ripping long tracks up the field and Grooby fired.

He was off balance, distracted by the speeding dogs. But his target loomed huge, close, and moving slowly. The gun jarred back on his shoulder. The hare somersaulted, as if tossed into the air by the hind legs, came down in a flash of dust and streaked back into the wheat.

For a second, Grooby thought he must have fainted. He could hear the farmer yelling to the miners to call their dogs off, threatening to shoot the bloody lot, but the voice came weirdly magnified and distorted as if his hearing had lost its muting defences. His head spun in darkness. He knew he had fallen. He could hear the tractor protesting on the gradient and it seemed so near, the engine drove so cruelly into his ears, he wondered if he had fallen in front of it. The ground trembled beneath him. Surely they would see him lying there. His sense cleared a little and, as at the moment of waking from nightmare to the pillow and the familiar room, Grooby realised he was lying face downward in the wheat.

He must have fainted and staggered into the wheat and fallen there. But why hadn't they noticed him? Twisting his head, he saw what he could scarcely believe, the red paddling flails of the reaper coming up over him. Within seconds those terrible hidden ground-shaving blades would melt the stalks and touch him – he would be sawn clean in two. He had seen them slice rabbits like bacon.

He uttered a cry, to whoever might hear, and rolled sideways, dragging himself on his elbows, tearing up the wheat in his hands as he clawed his way out of the path of the mutilator, and cried again, this time in surprise, as a broad wrench of pain seemed to twist off the lower half of his body, so that for a moment he thought the blades had caught him. With a final convulsion he threw himself forward and sprawled parallel to the course of the tractor.

The special grinding clatter of the cutter seemed to come up out of the raw soil. The tractor's outline rose black against the blue sky and Grooby saw the farmer standing at the wheel, looking down. Then the flails came over, and he heard the blades wuthering in the air. For a second everything disintegrated in din, chaffy fragments and dust; then they had gone past, and Grooby lay panting. The end of the cutter bar had gone by inches from his face, and now he could see through the thin veil of stalks and out over the naked stubble slope. Why hadn't they stopped and got down to help him? He gathered himself and once more tried to get to his feet, but the baked clods of soil and the bright metallic stalks of wheat fled into a remote silent picture as the pain swept up his back again and engulfed him.

But only for a moment. He jerked up his head. Hands held his shoulders, and someone splashed his face with water that ran down his neck and over his chest. He shook himself free and stood. As if he had tripped only accidentally, he began to beat the dust from his trousers and elbows, ignoring the ring of men who had come up and stood in a circle watching. All the time he was trying to recall exactly what happened. He remembered, as if touching a forgotten dream, that he had been lying in the wheat. Had they carried him out then? He flexed his back cautiously, but that felt easy, with no trace of discomfort. The farmer handed him his trilby.

'All right now?'

He nodded. 'Gun must have caught me off balance. Only explanation. Held it too loose. Knocked me clean out.'

He adopted his brusquest managerial air, putting the farmer and this gang of impudent, anonymous miners' faces back into place. What had they seen, he wondered. They could tell him. But how could he possibly ask?

'One of those flukes,' he added.

The farmer was watching him thoughtfully, as if expecting him to fall again.

'Well, what happened to the hare?' Grooby demanded.

His continued gusty assurance took effect. Whatever they had seen or were suspecting, they had to take account of his voice. The farmer nodded, in his ancient, withered-up way. 'You're all right, then.' He turned on the stookers in surprising fury. 'What the hell am I paying you for?'

As they all trooped off down the field with their sullen dogs, the farmer started the tractor up and the cutter blade blurred into life.

(Ted Hughes – adapted)

Question: Take the place of the farmer in the story, and imagine that you are called upon to explain what has happened in the harvest field. You are to prepare a short, clear statement of what took place, i.e. only your own actions and those events that you saw and heard for yourself. You should include the substance (but not the exact words used) of the conversation at the end of the passage. The total number of words used for this statement, including the opening and closing sentences given below, must not exceed 170 words.

The beginning and end of this statement are written for you: copy them out at the beginning and end of your answer, as follows:

'On one of my last rounds I was surprised to see that Mr Grooby was sitting down.' (opening sentence).

'I sent the men back to work, and started up the tractor again.' (closing sentence).

For the rest of your answer, remember to use your own words, not the phrasing of this passage.

Exercise: Prepare rough notes for this summary before going on to the next section.

18.8 Such rough notes of the *actions* and *events* would include:

Saw a hare, stood up, pointed, shouted.
Grooby got up and aimed.
Gun pointing at tractor – shouted.
Grooby ran. So did hare. Miners loosed dogs.
Grooby fired. Hare ran into wheat.
Shouted to stookers to call dogs off.
Saw Grooby in wheat after I'd gone past him.
Stookers attended to him – splashed water.
Grooby stood up. Gave him his trilby.

Said he'd been knocked off balance.
Expected him to fall again.
Said he was all right.

18.9 Here now are three summaries actually written during the exam for which this question was set. The three candidates were probably aged 16, and their answers are printed exactly as they wrote them. The official examiners described one summary as average, one as weak and one as good. Which is which?

(*a*) On one of my last rounds I was surprised to see that Mr Grooby was sitting down and as I closed in on him sitting there I imformed him that there was a hare sitting in the open field, Mr Grooby got up and took aim at the hare, I then told him to change his position, which he did, I then heard the gun fire and Mr Grooby disappeared out of sight.

    I continued on up the field when I then saw Mr Grooby appear length ways infront of the tractor. I stopped the tractor and stood down over Mr Grooby. Mr Grooby claimed the force of the blast caught him off balance and that it was the only explanation.

    I then ask if he was alright, to which he did not answer. I sent the men back to work and started up the tractor again.

(*b*) On one of my last rounds I was surprised to see that Mr Grooby was sitting down obviously resting, when I saw a hare infront of the tractor. I got Mr Grooby's attention and he aimed but not well so we signalled again and the hare began to move to his left and the hare ran away but he shoot the hare which then somersaulted. I then called off the dogs and started up the tractor again with spluttered a little. Mr Grooby had disappeared so I started work. I was just cutting well when I heard a very faint cry and to my surprise I saw that man Mr Grooby lying by the side of the tractor just inches from the blade. Someone threw some water on him and got up unhurt. He brushed himself down and asked about the hare he shoot after he had explained about his gun knocking him out, and I asked if he was alright and I sent the men back to work, and started up the tractor again.

(*c*) On one of my last rounds, I was surprised to see that Mr Grooby was sitting down in the path of my tractor. I stood up and tried to attract his attention to a hare which had appeared between us. Mr Grooby stood up uncertainly and aimed at the hare and, therefore, at me. I shouted at him and he began to get a clear aim at the hare, which also set off. The stookers' dogs were let loose and, in the subsequent commotion, Grooby fired. I shouted to the stookers to recall their dogs and drove my tractor forwards. I hadn't seen Grooby fall but found him lying in the wheat. I stopped the tractor, jumped down and splashed him with water. He got up slowly, I gave him his hat and he said he was all right.

He still did not look too good to me, but I sent the men back to work and started up the tractor again.

The first summary is the weak one: the mark given for its content was low, and the standard of expression is so weak (e.g. only one full stop instead of four in the first paragraph) that no marks were earned under this heading. The second summary gained half marks. There is some incomprehension (there is nothing in the original about the tractor being started up and spluttering, for instance) and *he aimed but not well* is not an accurate version of what happened. Expression is of a better standard, though sentences ramble. The third summary was adjudged best, the material being carefully chosen and the English economical.

The examiners also reported that the main weaknesses in candidates' answers were, firstly, failure to grasp the exact sequence and geography of the accident and, secondly, lack of balance in spending too much time on the preliminaries to the shooting (in which the farmer himself was not concerned) so that insufficient time was left for describing what happened after the near-fatal passage of the tractor. The main failure of comprehension was that only the better candidates made it clear that the farmer does not see Mr Grooby fall, and that Grooby is only spotted after the tractor and cutter have passed him. Missing these points, many candidates wrote that the farmer saw Grooby collapse and then drove the tractor up to him, missing him only by good fortune. In the absence of any information that the farmer saw Grooby fall, it is a fair inference that the farmer was too busy calling on the stookers to get their dogs out of the standing crop, and did not pay any attention to Grooby after he fired.

19

Pronunciation

All English words of two or more syllables have a stress in one of them, sometimes on more than one, and sometimes with subsidiary stresses. Uncertainty about which syllable should be stressed is the most common cause of mispronunciation.

In the following list of words that are sometimes mispronounced, the stressed syllable is given in block capitals, thus:

HARass   CONtroversy   suPERfluous   EXquisite

ABsent:	adjective
abSENT:	verb
ABstract:	noun, adjective
abSTRACT:	verb
ACCent:	noun
accENT:	verb
ADult:	adjective, noun
ADversary	
adVERtisement	
aged:	pronounced as two syllables when meaning *very old*;
	pronounced *ag'd* when meaning *having the age of*.
ALly:	noun
alLY:	verb
ALternate:	verb. Final syllable rhymes with *mate*.
alTERnate:	adjective. Final syllable as in *pirate*.
anALogous:	the *g* is as in *get*, not *gin*.
apparATus:	the third syllable sounds like *rate*, not *rat*.
anti-:	pronounced with the *i* as in *bit*, not *bite*.
apARTheid:	final syllable pronounced *hate* or *ate*.
appARent:	the normal pronunciation now has the second syllable as in *pat*, not *pair*.

APPlicable	
APposite:	final syllable *zit*, not *zite*.
ARbitrarily	
Argentine:	final syllable rhymes with *mine*, not *mean*.
ARistocrat	
ATTribute:	noun
attRIBute:	verb
banAL:	may rhyme with *canal*, or the second syllable may rhyme with *snarl*.
bouquet:	first syllable *boo* or *book*, not rhyming with *low*.
BROchure	
CHAGrin:	pronounced *SHAG-rin*, not *sha-GREEN*.
COMbat:	noun and verb
COMMunal	
COMMune:	noun
commUNE:	verb
COMpact:	noun
comPACT:	adjective and verb
COMparable	
comparabILity	
COMposite:	final syllable *zit*, not *zite*.
COMpound:	noun, adjective
comPOUND:	verb
COMpress:	noun
comPRESS:	verb
CONcert:	noun
conCERted:	adjective
conduit:	correctly *KUND-it*, normally *KOND-wit* or the more American *KOND-yoo-it*.
CONduct:	noun
conDUCT:	verb
conDUCTion	
CONfine(s):	noun
conFINE:	verb
CONflict:	noun
conFLICT:	verb
CONscript:	noun
conSCRIPT:	verb
CONsort:	noun
conSORT:	verb
CONsummate:	verb. Final syllable rhymes with *mate*.
conSUMMate:	adjective. Final syllable as in *alTERnate*.
CONtact:	noun and verb
CONtents:	noun, meaning *what is contained*.

conTENT:	noun, meaning *contented state*, as in *to his heart's content*. Also verb and adjective.
CONtest:	noun
conTEST:	verb
CONtract:	noun
conTRACT:	verb
CONtrast:	noun
conTRAST:	verb
conTRIBute	
CONtrite	
CONtroversy	
CONverse:	noun, adjective
conVERSEly	
conVERSE:	verb
CONvert:	noun
conVERT:	verb
CONvict:	noun
conVICT:	verb
DAta:	first syllable pronounced *date*.
DECade	
deCORum	
DECorous	
DEfect:	noun
deFECT:	verb
DEity:	first syllable rhymes with *me*, not *may*.
delIBerate:	(verb) final syllable rhymes with *mate*; (adjective) final syllable as in *pirate*.
DEMonstrable	
DESert:	noun, meaning *barren region*.
desERT(s):	noun, meaning *what is deserved*.
desERT:	verb
DESpicable	
DESultory:	final syllable *tri*.
detERiorate:	pronounce with five syllables, not *detererate*.
DICtate	noun
dicTATE:	verb
DIgest:	noun
diGEST:	verb
dilEMma:	first syllabe *di*, not *die*.
discipLINary:	*LIN* rhymes with *sin*, not *sign*. Accent on the first syllable is not incorrect.
DIScount:	noun
disCOUNT:	verb
DISparate	
disPARity	

disPUTE:	noun and verb
disTRIBute	
dogged:	pronounced as one syllable, *dog'd*, when meaning *followed closely*, and as two syllables when meaning *tenacious*.
duel:	pronounce the *d*. Not *jew-el*.
either:	the first syllable may rhyme with *bee* or *by*. The latter is more common.
ENtrance:	noun
enTRANCE:	verb
ENvelope:	the first syllable should be pronounced as written, not as *on*.
enVELop:	verb
EScort:	noun
esCORT:	verb
et cetera:	say *et*, not *ek*.
EXport:	noun
exPORT:	verb
EXquisite	
EXtract:	noun
exTRACT:	verb
FEBruary:	pronounce the first *r* – *FEB-roo-ri*.
FERment:	noun
ferMENT:	verb
FORMidable	
foyer:	say *FOY-ay* or *FWA-yay*.
fracas:	say *FRAK-a*.
FRAGment:	noun
fragMENT:	verb
FREquent:	adjective
freQUENT:	verb
FRONTier	
furore:	*few-ROAR-i*, but the American *FEW-roar* is gaining ground.
GARage:	final syllable has *a* pronounced *ar* (as in *art*) and *g* pronounced like *s* in *vision*. Or rhyme with *barge*.
GLACial:	rhymes with *facial*.
GLACier:	the first syllable rhymes with *gas*; the last sound is as in nast*ier*.
government:	the *n* is to be pronounced.
grievous:	not grie*vi*ous.

half-past:	pronounce the *f*: not *har-*.
habITual:	the *h* is pronounced.
HARass:	not *harASS*.
HARassment	
HECtare:	final syllable *tar*.
heinous:	first syllable *hay*.
herEDitary:	the *h* is pronounced. Final syllable *-tri*.
histORic:	the *h* is pronounced.
homo-:	first syllable rhymes with *bomb*.
HONorary:	the *h* is silent. Pronounce as four syllables, not as *hon-ory*.
HOSPitable	
HOSPitably	
hotel:	the *h* is pronounced.
IMport:	noun
imPORT:	verb
IMpress:	noun
imPRESS:	verb
IMprint:	noun
imPRINT:	verb
INcense:	noun
inCENSE:	verb
INcline	noun
inCLINE:	verb
inCOMparable	
inCOMparably	
INcrease:	noun
inCREASE:	verb
inhERent:	second syllable is pronounced *hear*.
INsult:	noun
inSULT:	verb
INtegral:	not *inTEGral*.
INtricacy	
INvalid:	noun and adjective, meaning *sick* (*person*).
inVALid:	means *not valid*.
INventory:	pronounce *IN-ven-tri*.
irREFutable	
irrelevant:	not *irrevalent*.
irREParable	
irREVocable	
itINerary:	pronounce all five syllables, not as *it-in-ary*.
jewellery:	*jewel-ry*, not *jool-ery*.
JUbilee	

KILometre

LAMentable

learned: pronounced as two syllables it means *erudite*; pronounced as one (*learn'd* or *learnt*) it is the past tense of *learn*.

library: all three syllables should be pronounced, including the first *r*. Not *libry*.

lieutENant: the first syllable is *left* or – in the Navy – *let*. Do not say *loot*.

longEvity: the *g* is soft as in *imagine*.

machinAtion: the *ch* is now pronounced as in *machine*, but purists prefer a *k* sound as in *mechanic*.

MANdatory: final syllable *tri*.

MASSage

MAcho, machismo: the first syllable sounds like *match*.

MIgraine: the first syllable is *me*, not *my*.

MINute: as a noun it rhymes with *win it* and means sixty seconds.

minUTE: as an adjective it is pronounced *mine-YOOT* and means *very small*.

MISchievous: there is no *i* after the *v*.

MISprint: noun

misPRINT: verb

missile: rhymes with *this isle*, not *thistle*.

MOMentarily: *MOM-ent-ril-i*, not with the (American) stress on the third syllable

MOmentary
munICipal

NECessarily: though pronunciation stressing the third syllable is common and unobjectionable.

neither: see either

niche: pronounced *nitch* (or *neesh*)

OBdurate

OBject: noun

obJECT: verb

obscenity: second syllable *sen*, not *seen*.

ORdinarily

oVERT: the first syllable is pronounced *oh*.

OVERthrow: noun

overTHROW: verb

partICularly: pronounce all five syllables, avoiding the slovenly *part-ic-uly*.

PAtron:	first syllable *pay*.
PAtronage:	first syllable *pat*.
pee:	as an abbreviation for *penny* (or plural *pence*) this 'word' is to be avoided in favour of the full *penny* or *pence*.
perhaps:	pronounce as two syllables, including the *h*. The common *praps* is informal.
PERmit:	noun
perMIT:	verb
PERvert:	noun
perVERT:	verb
plastic:	the *a* is pronounced as in *bat*, not as in *farm*.
PRECedence	
PREferable	
PRESent:	noun, adjective
presENT:	verb
PRImarily	
probably:	three syllables: *probly* is informal.
PROceeds:	noun
proCEED:	verb
PROduce:	noun
proDUCE:	verb
PROgress:	noun
proGRESS:	verb
PROject:	noun
proJECT:	verb
PROSpect:	noun
proSPECT:	verb
PROtest:	noun
proTEST:	verb
questionnaire:	the first two syllables are pronounced as in *question*.
RAMpage:	noun
ramPAGE:	verb
rapPORT:	second syllable pronounced *pore*.
really:	rhymes with *dearly*, not *freely*.
reCESS:	noun and verb
recognize:	the *g* is to be pronounced. Not *reconize*.
REcord:	noun, adjective
reCORD:	verb
REfill:	noun
reFILL:	verb
REfit:	noun
reFIT:	verb

REfund:	noun
reFUND:	verb
REFuse:	noun (rhymes with *loose*) meaning *waste*.
reFUSE:	verb (rhymes with *lose*).
REject:	noun
reJECT:	verb
REPutable	
reSEARCH:	noun and verb
RESpite:	second syllable pronounced *spite* (or *spit*)
RIbald:	first syllable pronounced *rib*.
roMANCE:	noun and verb
schedule:	first syllable is *shed* not *sked*.
SECretary:	pronounce the first *r*: *SEK-ret-ri*, not *seketri* or *seketeri*.
simultANeous:	first syllable pronounced to rhyme with *him*, not *time*.
sixth:	pronounce the *x* as *ks*. Not *sikth*.
SONorous	
status:	first syllable pronounced *stay*.
SUBject:	noun
subJECT:	verb
SUBsidence:	second syllable rhymes with *did*, not *died*.
suPERfluous	
SURvey:	noun
surVEY:	verb
SUSpect:	noun, adjective
susPECT:	verb
TEMPorarily	
TEMPorary:	pronounce with four syllables, not *tempary*.
tonne:	pronounced *tun*.
TORment:	noun
torMENT:	verb
trait:	pronounced *tray*.
TRANSfer:	noun
transFER:	verb
TRANSferable	
transpARent:	the second *a* is now usually as in *pat*, not *pair*.
TRANSplant:	noun
transPLANT:	verb
TRANSport:	noun
transPORT:	verb
trauma:	first syllable rhymes with *draw*.
Tuesday:	pronounce the *T*; not *choose-day*.
twenty:	the second *t* should be pronounced; *twenny* is

informal, *twendy* is tv commentators' mid-Atlantic.

unPRECedented:	second syllable like *press*.
unused:	when meaning is *unaccustomed*, the *s* is as in *loose*; when meaning is *out of use*, the *s* is as in *lose*.
UPset:	noun
upSET:	verb
usual, usually:	pronounce the second *u*.
VETerinary:	usually pronounced *VET-rin-ri*.
VITamin:	first syllable rhymes with *bit*, not *bite*.
VOLuntarily	

Appendix: Irregular Verbs

Most verbs form the past tense and past participle by adding -ed to the infinitive (*fill, filled*), or -d if it already ends in -e (*smoke, smoked*). The principal irregular verbs that do not conform to this rule are listed below.

There are three important rules governing the addition of the -ed. ending.

(*a*) Verbs ending in *single vowel + single consonant* double the final consonant before -ed (*fit, fitted*) unless
 (i) the verb has more than one syllable and the accent does not fall on the final one (*falter, faltered; benefit, benefited*). Exceptions: *worship, worshipped; kidnap, kidnapped*. If the final syllable is stressed, the final consonant is doubled (*commit, committed; defer, deferred*). But words ending in *single vowel + l or g* double the final *l* or *g* before -ed wherever the accent falls (*compel, compelled; panel, panelled*). Exception: *parallel, (un)-paralleled*.
(ii) the final consonant is *w, x* or *y*, which are never doubled.

(*b*) Verbs ending in *consonant + y* change the *y* to *i* before -ed (*copy copied*).

(*c*) Verbs ending in *c* add *k* before -ed (*panic, panicked; traffic, trafficked; picnic, picnicked*).

Table of Irregular Verbs
(* = less common form)

Infinitive	Past	Past Participle
arise	arose	arisen
awake	awoke (awaked)*	awoken (awaked)*

bear	bore	born (= given birth)
		borne (= carried, endured;
		also *borne in mind*,
		borne out etc.)
beat	beat	beaten
become	became	become
begin	began	begun
bend	bent	bent
beseech	beseeched (besought)*	beseeched (besought)*
bet	bet	bet
bid	bade, bid	bid, bidden
bind	bound	bound
bite	bit	bitten (bit)*
bleed	bled	bled
blow	blew	blown
break	broke	broken
breed	bred	bred
bring	brought	brought
build	built	built
burn	burnt, burned	burnt, burned
burst	burst	burst
buy	bought	bought
cast	cast	cast
catch	caught	caught
choose	chose	chosen
cling	clung	clung
cost	cost (= required	cost
	payment of)	
	costed (= estimated	costed
	the price)	
creep	crept	crept
cut	cut	cut
deal	dealt	dealt
dig	dug	dug
do	did	done
draw	drew	drawn
dream	dreamt, dreamed	dreamt, dreamed
drink	drank	drunk
drive	drove	driven
eat	ate	eaten
fall	fell	fallen
feed	fed	fed
feel	felt	felt

fight	fought	fought
find	found	found
flee	fled	fled
fling	flung	flung
fly	flew	flown
forbear	forbore	forborne
forget	forgot	forgotten
forsake	forsook	forsaken
freeze	froze	frozen
give	gave	given
go	went	gone
grind	ground	ground
grow	grew	grown
hang	hung	hung
	hanged (= killed by hanging)	hanged
hear	heard	heard
hide	hid	hidden
hold	held	held
hurt	hurt	hurt
keep	kept	kept
kneel	knelt, kneeled	knelt
know	knew	known
lay	laid	laid
lead	led	led
lean	leant, leaned	leant, leaned
leave	left	left
lend	lent	lent
lie	lay	lain
light	lit (lighted)*	lit (lighted)*
lose	lost	lost
mean	meant	meant
meet	met	met
mow	mowed	mown
pay	paid	paid
quit	quit, quitted	quit
rid	rid	rid
ride	rode	ridden

rise	rose	risen
ring	rang	rung
run	ran	run
saw	sawed	sawn
say	said	said
see	saw	seen
seek	sought	sought
sell	sold	sold
send	sent	sent
set	set	set
sew	sewed	sewn, sewed
shake	shook	shaken
shine	shone	shone
shoot	shot	shot
show	showed	shown, showed
shrink	shrank	shrunk
sing	sang	sung
sink	sank	sunk
sit	sat	sat
sleep	slept	slept
sling	slung	slung
slide	slid	slid
slink	slunk	slunk
slit	slit	slit
smell	smelt, smelled	smelt, smelled
sow	sowed	sown
speak	spoke	spoken
speed	sped	sped
	speeded up	speeded up
spell	spelt, spelled	spelt, spelled
spend	spent	spent
spin	spun	spun
spit	spat, spit	spat, spit
split	split	split
spread	spread	spread
spring	sprang	sprung
stand	stood	stood
steal	stole	stolen
stick	stuck	stuck
sting	stung	stung
stink	stank	stunk
stride	strode	stridden
strike	struck	struck
string	strung	strung
strive	strove	striven

swear	swore	sworn
sweep	swept	swept
swim	swam	swum
swing	swung	swung
take	took	taken
teach	taught	taught
tear	tore	torn
tell	told	told
think	thought	thought
throw	threw	thrown
thrive	thrived (throve)*	thrived (thriven)*
tread	trod	trodden, trod
wake	woke (waked)*	woke(n) (waked)*
wear	wore	worn
weave	wove	woven
win	won	won
wind	wound	wound
wring	wrung	wrung
write	wrote	written

Acknowledgements

The author and publishers are grateful to the following for permission to reproduce copyright material in this book:

Kingsley Amis: one extract (p. 196) from *Ending Up*, reproduced by permission of the author and Jonathan Cape Ltd, London, and also © 1974 by Kingsley Amis, reprinted by permission of Harcourt Brace Jovanovitch, Inc, Orlando; *Edmund Blunden*: one extract (p. 192) from *Undertones of War*, reprinted by permission of A. D. Peters & Co Ltd, London; *Malcolm Bradbury*: one extract (p. 208) from *Who Do You Think You Are?* reproduced by permission of the author and Martin Secker and Warburg Ltd; *Ray Bradbury*: one extract (p. 205) from *Golden Apples of the Sun* reproduced by permission of A. D. Peters & Co Ltd; *Anthony Burgess*: one extract (p. 147) from *Language Made Plain* reproduced by permission of Hodder and Stoughton Ltd; *Philip Llewellin* for one extract (p. 163) from *Citroen Magazine*; *Stella Gibbons*: one extract (p. 190) from *Cold Comfort Farm* reproduced by permission of Curtis Brown Ltd, London, on behalf of the author; *William Golding*: three extracts (pp. 189, 202, 204) from *Lord of the Flies* reprinted by permission of Faber and Faber Ltd, London, and also reprinted by permission of the Putnam Publishing Group, New York. Copyright © 1954 by William Gerald Golding, renewed 1982; *Ernest Gowers*: one extract (p. 146) from *Complete Plain Words* reproduced by permission of Her Majesty's Stationery Office; the *Guardian* for one extract (p. 165) from the Leading Article of 24 February 1984; *Ernest Hemingway*: one extract (p. 188) from *A Farewell to Arms*, copyright 1929 Charles Scribner's Sons; copyright renewed © 1957, reprinted with permission of Charles Scribner's Sons, New York, and also reprinted with permission of Jonathan Cape Ltd, London, and the Executors of the Ernest Hemingway Estate; *Barry Hines*: one extract (p. 194) from *A Kestrel for a Knave* reproduced by permission of the author and Michael Joseph Ltd; *Simon Hoggart*: one extract (p. 207) from *On the House* reproduced by permission of the author and Robson Books Ltd; *Ted Hughes*: one extract

(p. 250), slightly adapted, from 'The Harvesting' from *Wodwo*, reprinted by permission of Faber and Faber Ltd; *James Joyce*: one extract (p. 172) from *A Portrait of the Artist As A Young Man* reproduced by permission of the Executors of the James Joyce Estate and Jonathan Cape Ltd, London, and also reprinted by permission of Viking Penguin, Inc, New York, copyright 1916 by B. W. Huebsch; copyright 1944 by Nora Joyce; copyright © 1964 by the Estate of James Joyce; *James Kirkup*: one extract (p. 198) from *Sorrows, Passions and Alarms* reproduced by permission of the author; *John Le Carré*: two extracts (pp. 199, 203) from *The Little Drummer Girl* reproduced by permission of the author and Hodder and Stoughton Ltd, Sevenoaks, and also reprinted by permission of Alfred A. Knopf, Inc, New York, copyright © 1983 by Author's Workshop AG; *Laurie Lee*: one extract (p. 191) from *A Rose for Winter* and one extract (p. 198) from *Cider with Rosie* reproduced by permission of the author and The Hogarth Press, one extract (p. 199) from *As I Walked Out One Midsummer Morning* reproduced by permission of the author and Andre Deutsch Ltd; *Bernard Levin*: three extracts (pp. 142, 197, 206) from *Taking Sides* reproduced by permission of the author and Jonathan Cape Ltd, London, and also reproduced by permission of Curtis Brown Ltd, London; *Thomas Mann*: one extract (p. 202) from *Death in Venice* reproduced by permission of the author and Martin Secker and Warburg Ltd, London, and also reprinted by permission of Alfred A. Knopf, Inc, New York, from *Death In Venice and Seven Other Stories*, translated by H. T. Lowe-Porter; *W Somerset Maugham*: one extract (p. 195) from *Cakes and Ale* reproduced by permission of the Executors of the Estate of W Somerset Maugham, and also copyright 1930 by Doubleday & Company, Inc, New York. Reprinted by permission of the publisher; *John Mortimer*: one extract (p. 198) copyright Advan Press Ltd, reprinted by permission of the author and A. D. Peters & Co Ltd; *Iris Murdoch*: one extract (p. 195) from *Under the Net* reproduced by permission of the author and Chatto and Windus; *Liam O'Flaherty*: one extract (p. 201) from *Two Lovely Beasts and Other Stories* reproduced by permission of the author; *George Orwell*: one extract (p. 168) from *The Road to Wigan Pier* reproduced by permission of the Estate of the late Sonia Brownell Orwell and Martin Secker and Warburg Ltd, London, and also reprinted by permission of Harcourt Brace Jovanovitch, Inc, Orlando; *Simeon Potter*: one extract (p. 146) from *Our Language* (Pelican Books, revised edition 1976) copyright © Simeon Potter, 1950, 1961, 1966, 1976. Reprinted by permission of Penguin Books Ltd; *William Sansom*: one extract (p. 245) from *Christmas* © 1968 by William Sansom; *Alan Sillitoe*: one extract (p. 203) from *The Loneliness of the Long Distance Runner*, copyright © Alan Sillitoe 1959; *John Steinbeck*: one extract (p. 196) from *Of Mice and Men* reprinted by permission of William Heinemann Ltd, London, and also reproduced by permission of Viking Penguin, Inc, New York, copyright 1937, renewed © 1965 by John Steinbeck and one extract (p. 201) from *The Red Pony* reproduced by permission of William Heinemann Ltd, London, and also reproduced by permission of Viking

Penguin Inc, New York, copyright 1933, 1937, 1938 by John Steinbeck, renewed copyright © 1961, 1965, 1966 by John Steinbeck; *Dylan Thomas*: two extracts (pp. 183, 184) from *A Prospect of the Sea* reproduced by permission of the author and Dent; *The Times* for the extract (p. 190) from their Leading Article of 11 November 1927; *Lionel Trilling*: one extract (p. 196) from 'Of this time, of that place' from Smith and Mason, *Short Story Study* reproduced by permission of the author; *John Vaizey*: one extract (p. 147) from *Education for Tomorrow* (Pelican Books 1966) copyright © John Vaizey, 1962, 1966, 1970, reproduced by permission of Penguin Books Ltd; *P G Wodehouse*: one extract (p. 184) from *Right Ho, Jeeves* reproduced by permission of The Executors of the Estate of Lady Wodehouse, and also reprinted by permission of the author and the author's agents, Scott Meredith Literary Agency, Inc, 845 Third Avenue, New York, NY 10022.

Extracts from examination papers and examiners' reports in Chapters 15 and 18 are reproduced by kind permission of the University of Cambridge Local Examinations Syndicate.

Index

ENGLISH GRAMMAR

B. A. PHYTHIAN

This book is intended for the general reader who wishes to familiarise himself with the basic elements of English grammar.

There are chapters on the nature and function of all the principal parts of speech and detailed consideration is given to sentence structure through a study of clauses and phrases. A particular feature of the book is that exercises to test and reinforce comprehension of every stage are built in after each section, with further revision exercises at the end of each chapter.

The student who successfully completes this work will have a sound grasp of correct grammar, and an appreciation of the subtlety and variety of English expression.

TEACH YOURSELF BOOKS

LETTER WRITING

DAVID JAMES

This book is a complete guide to writing letters which say exactly what you want to say — and bring the desired response.

Letter Writing explains how to write effective letters. David James offers practical advice on the choice of layout, style and 'tone', and then examines different kinds of letters ranging from the simple thank-you note to the more involved job application or sales letter to a potential customer.

Numerous sample letters illustrate correct forms and common errors, and highlight the various conventions and courtesies observed in different parts of the world. Forms of address and a list of common abbreviations are also included for easy reference, making this a book for every home or office.

TEACH YOURSELF BOOKS

OTHER TITLES AVAILABLE
IN TEACH YOURSELF

☐ 0 340 35873 4   **English Grammar**   £4.99
                   B. A. Phythian

☐ 0 340 32441 4   **Letter Writing**   £5.99
                   David James

☐ 0 340 28765 9   **Creative Writing**   £4.99
                   Dianne Doubtfire

All these books are available at your local bookshop or newsagent, or can be ordered direct from the publisher. Just tick the titles you want and fill in the form below.

Prices and availability subject to change without notice.

HODDER & STOUGHTON PAPERBACKS, PO Box 11, Falmouth, Cornwall.

Please send cheque or postal order for the value of the book, and add the following for postage and packing:

UK including BFPO – £1.00 for one book, plus 50p for the second book, and 30p for each additional book ordered up to a £3.00 maximum.

OVERSEAS INCLUDING EIRE – £2.00 for the first book, plus £1.00 for the second book, and 50p for each additional book ordered.
OR please debit this amount from my Access/Visa card (delete as appropriate).

Card number ☐☐☐☐☐☐☐☐☐☐☐☐☐☐☐☐

AMOUNT £...

EXPIRY DATE...

SIGNED ....

NAME..

ADDRESS..